FRONTIER MILITARY SERIES
XXVII

Powder River Odyssey

Nelson Cole's Western Campaign of 1865

The Journals of Lyman G. Bennett
and Other Eyewitness Accounts

by
David E. Wagner

THE ARTHUR H. CLARK COMPANY
An imprint of the University of Oklahoma Press
Norman, Oklahoma
2009

Library of Congress Cataloging-in-Publication Data
Wagner, David E., 1939–2008
  Powder River odyssey : Nelson Cole's western campaign of 1865 : the journals
of Lyman G. Bennett and other eyewitness accounts / by David E. Wagner.
    p. cm. — (Frontier military series ; 27)
  Includes bibliographical references and index.
  ISBN 978-0-87062-359-2 (hardcover : alk. paper) — ISBN 978-0-87062-370-7
(leather limited ed. : alk. paper) 1. Powder River Expedition, 1865. 2. Powder
River Expedition, 1865—Personal narratives. 3. Cole, Nelson, d. 1899. 4. Ben-
nett, L. G. (Lyman G.)—Diaries. I. Bennett, L. G. (Lyman G.) II. Title.
  E83.86.W34 2009
  973.8'1--dc22

                          2008029774

Powder River Odyssey: Nelson Cole's Western Campaign of 1865
is Volume 27 in the Frontier Military Series.

The paper in this book meets the guidelines for permanence and durability
of the Committee on Production Guidelines for Book Longevity
of the Council on Library Resources, Inc. ∞

To my parents, Dale and Hannah Marie Wagner
I wish they were here to enjoy the moment.

TABLE OF CONTENTS

Illustrations

MAPS

PREFACE

Lyman G. Bennett ended his diary entry for 8 September 1865 with a simple sentence: "We marched and fought over 15 miles today." Bennett, a civilian employee, worked for the U.S. Army on the Eastern Division of the Powder River Indian Expedition, led by Col. Nelson D. Cole. This single sentence summed up this military command's experiences over the previous eight days: marching and fighting. The rest of the three-month odyssey through virtually unexplored country could best be described as a march with adversity.

The Eastern Division of the Powder River Expedition of 1865 is possibly the least-known major campaign of the western Indian wars. When questioned about it, many history enthusiasts will return a blank stare and say they are not familiar with it. Only when Brig. Gen. Patrick E. Connor is mentioned is there any name recognition, as he was the overall commander of the widespread military operation. Colonel Cole's portion of the action seems to have fallen through the cracks of history.

The campaign is significant because it marked the transition from the Civil War to the Indian war period. The planners of the military expedition envisioned it as the end of the "Indian problems," when in fact it was essentially the opening round of what became known as the Indian wars, leading eventually to the Great Sioux War of 1876 and 1877. The campaign would be the last for the Civil War Volunteer Army, as these units were then mustered out and replaced by a down-sized regular army. Yet the foe, the northern Plains Indians (primarily Sioux, Cheyenne, and Arapaho), remained the same for another twelve years. The Custer disaster in 1876 and the eventual subjugation of the northern Plains tribes in 1877 were milestones of the Indian wars—the wars that began with Brig. Gen. Patrick E. Connor and Col. Nelson D. Cole in the Powder River Expedition of 1865.

This is not just the story of American soldiers fighting Indian warriors, but of going to the plains and returning. The logistics of supplying the expedition and the terrain that it would travel presented immense obstacles to any measure of success. Heretofore, little has been written of this expedition, with much of what is out there incomplete or inaccurate. *Powder River Odyssey* will clear up many of the misconceptions and add to the understanding of this campaign. The injustices to the Plains Indians have been well documented by other authors and are not the focus of this story.

Much of the terrain traveled by Cole's command in 1865 was, at best, a semi-mapped wilderness. The topography of this military expedition has long been a fascination and something of a mystery to me. The goal in starting this research was to make the story work with the landscape. Having traveled most of the route from Omaha to Powder River and then to Fort Laramie, I have been able to make sense of it and tie it to the daily descriptions from the journals and reports of the expedition. Even today, portions of the route are in remote or almost inaccessible areas.

The story of Nelson Cole's Eastern Division of the Powder River Expedition is told here through the eyes and ears of three active participants and faithful recorders by blending their journals and reports into a day-by-day chronology of events. The centerpiece of the story is a remarkable diary kept by Lyman G. Bennett, the civilian chief engineer of Cole's expedition. His previously unpublished journal—discovered in an old desk by descendants in 1988—is a treasure chest of new information and insight into the 1865 campaign.[1] The entire Bennett diary, from 3 July to 4 October 1865, appears here. Having personally transcribed the handwritten journal into typescript, I corrected the spelling of some names so as to not cause confusion with the other accounts. Where periods or commas were occasionally omitted in the original

---

[1]The original handwritten diary resides in the archives of the Western Historical Manuscript Collection at the University of Missouri–Rolla. Lyman G. Bennett Diary, 5 August 1865 entry. Hereafter cited as Bennett diary.

diary, I added punctuation to make it more readable. Paragraph breaks were added to some of the longer narratives when a subject change warranted it. In the case of misspelled or omitted words, bracketed corrections were used to make sure the reader could follow the correct context of the narrative. Otherwise I worked to maintain the integrity of Bennett's original writing and thought process.

Bennett, with an engineering and mapmaking background, kept a detailed daily account, with emphasis on the landscape. His writing is rich in painting word-pictures of the country that he traveled through and of the events of the expedition.

The Bennett diary is supplemented by written accounts from two other members of the expedition: Col. Nelson Cole, through his two official reports of the campaign; and a cavalry officer, 1st Lt. Charles H. Springer, whose journal complements the Bennett diary in bringing to life the daily routine of the adventure.

Colonel Cole wrote two official reports, one at the completion of the expedition at Fort Connor on 25 September 1865, to Brig. Gen. Patrick E. Connor.[2] It is a relatively short report lacking detail of events. On 10 February 1867 he submitted a second longer, more detailed report to Gen. Ulysses S. Grant.[3] I have used excerpts from Cole's official reports as well as summarized some of his lengthy passages.

First Lt. Charles H. Springer of the Twelfth Missouri Volunteer Cavalry kept a diary while on the expedition. His journal was published in 1971 as *Soldiering in Sioux Country: 1865*, edited by Benjamin Cooling III. It is an excellent presentation and a mandatory reference for researching this campaign. Springer wrote in a rambling style rather than a precise day-by-day journal, with some confusion of dates, but all in all, it presents an excellent window to the 1865 adventure. I have generally summarized Springer's daily activity and used selected quotes.

✳   ✳   ✳

Lyman G. Bennett, the eldest of eleven children, was born 1 August 1832 to Charles M. and Louisa Bennett in Schuyler County, New

---

[2]Nelson Cole's official report of 25 September 1856, *The War of Rebellion*.

[3]Cole's official report of 10 February 1867, LeRoy R. Hafen and Ann W. Hafen, *Powder River Campaigns and Sawyers Expedition*, 60–91.

York. Raised and educated there, he moved with his family to Oswego in Kendall County, Illinois, in 1849. Bennett taught school for five years and trained as a civil engineer, working as a railroad and county surveyor in 1856. He went to Minnesota in 1857 and tried his luck at homesteading but had no success. Bennett returned to Illinois later that year to resume teaching school and surveying. He married Melissa E. Lyon of New York State in 1859.[4]

When the Civil War broke out, Bennett quickly responded to his country's call. The Rev. E. W. Hicks, in his *History of Kendall County*, wrote the following description of a patriotic moment:

> Fort Sumpter [*sic*] fell at noon on the 13th of April, and in the evening of the same day, a crowded and excited mass meeting was held in the Court House in Oswego. Speeches were made by Judge Helm, Judge Ricketson, A. B. Smith, and others. At last Lyman G. Bennett was called out. He remarked that this was a time when men were needed; and he asked how many would then and there volunteer for their country. He held in his hand a paper with one name on it—his own. Who would go, if need be? The spark of patriotism caught like fire in dry tinder, and in a few minutes eighty names were enrolled.[5]

Bennett enlisted as a corporal in Company E of the Thirty-sixth Illinois Infantry.[6] Assigned to the engineering staff at Rolla and St. Louis, Missouri, his duties included mapmaking and work on fortifications. He rejoined his regiment, returning from detached service in time for the Battle of Pea Ridge in March 1862. After the battle, Bennett worked on the engineering staff of Brig. Gen. Samuel R. Curtis as mapmaker for the Army of the Southwest, then operating in Missouri and Arkansas. In 1863 Bennett accepted a commission as major in the Fourth Arkansas Volunteer Cavalry (U.S.), which he helped to raise and organize. He resigned his commission and was discharged from the army in August 1864.

Bennett joined the engineering staff of General Curtis—then commanding the Department of Kansas—as a civilian employee. He mapped the battlefields of Confederate general Sterling Price's 1864

---

[4]John F. Bradbury, Jr., "Biographical Sketch of L. G. Bennett."
[5]Ibid.; Rev. E.W. Hicks, *History of Kendall County*, 302.
[6]*American Civil War Research Database.*

Missouri raid. In the spring of 1865, he inspected the army's installations along the overland trail and the route to Denver. Later that year Bennett accepted a position as the engineering officer with the Eastern Division of the Powder River Expedition under the command of Col. Nelson D. Cole.[7]

✳   ✳   ✳

Nelson D. Cole was born 18 November 1833 in Rhinebeck, New York, to Jacob and Hannah Cole. He received his academic education in Rhinebeck and then moved to New York City, where he worked in a planing mill and lumberyard. After a brief stint in Cuba overseeing the building of a sugar refinery, he went to St. Louis in 1854 and worked in the lumber business there until the outbreak of the Civil War. Cole married Annie Scott of St. Louis in June 1856.[8]

With civil war imminent, Cole recruited a volunteer company and enlisted on 21 April 1861, entering the service as captain of Company A, Fifth Missouri Volunteer Infantry (U.S.). He participated in the capture of Jefferson City, Missouri, on 15 June, which resulted in the Southern-sympathizing governor fleeing the city. The flag that had been presented to Cole's company was the first raised at the state capitol after the retreat of the governor.[9] After his original ninety-day enlistment expired, Cole was assigned, at the same rank, to Company E of the First Missouri Volunteer Infantry, which was subsequently transformed into the First Missouri Light Artillery. He participated in an engagement at Booneville and at the battle of Dug Springs near Springfield, Missouri.[10] Cole suffered a wound at the battle of Wilson's Creek on 10 August 1861. His commanding officer, Lt. Col. George L. Andrews wrote in his official report, "Upon arriving to the left of Dubois battery and approaching Co. E, I met Captain Cole of that company being taken to the rear in consequence of a wound in the lower jaw, and, although unable to speak, still by every action encouraging his men."[11]

---

[7]Bradbury, "Biographical Sketch of L. G. Bennett."
[8]Walter B. Stevens, *St. Louis: The Fourth City*, 230–33.
[9]"In Memoriam: Nelson Cole, Brigadier General U.S.V."
[10]William Hyde and Howard L. Conrad, eds., *Encyclopedia of the History of St. Louis*, 420–21.
[11]"In Memoriam: Nelson Cole, Brigadier General U.S.V."

For reasons unknown Cole declined a promotion to major in May 1862. He was later assigned as chief of artillery and ordinance on the staff of Maj. Gen. John M. Schofield of the Department of Missouri and acted in that capacity until spring of 1863. He requested and was granted a return to his regiment in order to participate in the siege of Vicksburg in June 1863, after which he returned to the Department of Missouri as chief of artillery under Schofield. Accepting a commission as major of the First Missouri Light Artillery in August 1863 was Cole's next move. Later he became chief of staff to Maj. Gen. Alfred Pleasanton, who commanded the cavalry in the Department of Missouri. In October 1863 Cole received a commission as lieutenant colonel of the Second Missouri Light Artillery. A promotion to colonel and command of the same regiment followed in February 1864.[12]

In the spring of 1865 Colonel Cole received orders to lead the Eastern Division of the Powder River Expedition under the overall command of Brig. Gen. Patrick E. Connor. His regiment, ordered to St. Louis on 1 June to be equipped as cavalry, then moved to Omaha, Nebraska Territory, in late June, in preparation for the expedition.[13]

✳   ✳   ✳

In his 15 August 1865 journal entry Charles H. Springer wrote, "That is the way I spent my 25th birth-day," which would put his date of birth at 15 August 1840. Born in Germany, Springer immigrated to the United States at some point and settled in St. Joseph, Missouri. He enlisted in the U.S. Army on 1 May 1860, listing his trade as a carpenter. He was assigned to Company F, First U.S. Cavalry. For reasons unknown, Springer deserted the First Cavalry on 8 August 1861 and returned to St. Joseph. In April 1862 Springer enlisted and received a commission as a second lieutenant in Company E of the Fifth Missouri State Militia Cavalry, a unit that operated against Southern-sympathizing "bushwhackers" in that state. He resigned his commission and left the service in January 1863. Eight months later, Springer enlisted again, this time as a private in Company B, Twelfth Missouri Volunteer Cavalry. In November 1863 a promotion to second lieu-

---

[12]Stevens, *St. Louis*, 230–33; Civil War Scrapbook, 2:14–15.
[13]"In Memoriam: Nelson Cole, Brigadier General U.S.V."

tenant in the company due to his previous military experience followed. Springer's unit campaigned in Tennessee, Alabama, and Mississippi in 1864.[14] He proudly recalled those experiences in his 4 July
1865 journal entry:

> [A] year ago we spent the 4th [of July] in Memphis, Tenn., and had some
> hard times to go through yet; the different fights in Mississippi, on the
> Tallahatchie river, at Oxford, and Hurricane Creek, the pursuit of rebel
> General [Nathan Bedford] Forest [sic] through Middle Tennessee, the
> time General [John Bell] Hood with an army of human men tore himself
> loose of his adversary General [William T.] Sherman. It was our Division,
> commanded by the brave and undaunted General [Edward] Hatch who
> lay in front of the Rebel army, from the time they crossed the Tennessee
> river at Florence, Ala. until we arrived at Nashville. It was our Division of
> cavalry who turned the left wing of the Rebels on the memorable 15–16 and
> 17th of December 1864, at the battle of Nashville and pursued the enemy
> down to the banks of the Tennessee again.[15]

His promotion to first lieutenant took place on 1 March 1865. Two
months later his regiment, the Twelfth Missouri Cavalry, moved to
St. Louis and then to Fort Leavenworth, Kansas. Springer and his
company were then transported by riverboat to Omaha in June, in
preparation for their participation in the Eastern Division of the Powder River Indian Expedition. During this period First Lieutenant
Springer was court-martialed for leaving his command without per-
mission, and he was sentenced to loss of his pay for June 1865.[16]

The three men gave us a view of several different perspectives of the
expedition. From Colonel Cole we have a competent military commander trying to give a complete and accurate report, but also
attempting to put everything in the best possible light—which would
become more difficult as the campaign progressed. From Lyman Bennett we have a civilian employee writing in his personal journal, without the restrictions of a military report. He gave an objective account
of the day-to-day details of the journey. As an insider with Cole, it
appears that the colonel put much trust in him, giving Bennett crucial

---

[14]Charles H. Springer, *Soldiering in Sioux Country, 1865*, 3, 4.
[15]Ibid., 5, 6.
[16]Ibid., 3, 4.

assignments along the route that one would expect to be given to officers or scouts.

Springer was promoted from the ranks in his own company, and his
close friends still seemed to be enlisted men, not uncommon in the
Civil War–era Volunteer Army. At times he complained about orders
and command decisions, as a private soldier might. Springer wrote
from the viewpoint from the lower level of the command, as well as
that of the enlisted men, while Bennett socialized primarily with the
officers. Where Bennett concerned himself with logistics and landscape, Springer's main interest seemed to be hunting, fishing, and the
adventure of it all.

✳   ✳   ✳

In the early summer of 1865, Col. Nelson Cole's expedition embarked
on an ill-defined mission into a vast semi-explored wilderness. The
story told here will make readers feel as though they are a part of the
adventure that ensued, with the three voices blending together to give
a clear picture of the Eastern Division of the Powder River Expedition. Although I have included quotes from other officers and soldiers,
I leave it to Bennett, Cole, and Springer to tell the story.

ACKNOWLEDGMENTS

After deciding to research the Powder River Expedition of 1865, I first visited the Fort Laramie National Historic Site Research Library in 2003. Librarian Sandra Lowry was extremely helpful and supportive in getting me started in the right direction. I owe her a debt of gratitude for this.

Individuals at other research facilities who went out their way to assist me in my quest for information include: John F. Bradbury of the Western Historical Manuscript Collection at the University of Missouri–Rolla, for his work with the Lyman Bennett papers; Dennis Northcott at the Missouri Historical Society, for his help in collecting personal data on Nelson Cole; Sharon Avery with the State Historical Society of Iowa, for her assistance with the Grenville Dodge papers; Lory Morrow of the Montana Historical Society, for "discovering" Dan Bowman's photo and manuscript collections for me; Russ Taylor of the L. Tom Perry Special Collections at the Harold B. Lee Library, Brigham Young University, for helping me access the Walter M. Camp papers; Ron Tillotson of Hardin, Illinois, for providing me with information on his great-great-grandfather, Charles L. Thomas; Lee Diebel Hubbard of the Powder River Historical Museum, for sharing files and introducing me to key local people who were helpful in my research. My thanks to all of these individuals, and to all the people at other research facilities who have assisted me over the past few years.

John Billow of Chicago, Illinois; David C. Evans of Centerville, Virginia; Andi Hummel of Hulett, Wyoming; and Fr. Vincent A. Heier of St. Louis, Missouri, were critical readers of my manuscript at various stages of its development and gave sound objective feedback and advice to improve the narrative. My fellow explorers and sounding boards for the story were John Billow; Mike Charnota of Chicago, Illinois; and Phil Parthamer of Vancouver, Washington. Special thanks to Bob McCurdy, Ron Talcott, and Francis Edwards, all of Broadus, Montana, for helping me make sense of the terrain where the action took place on Powder River on 8–10 September 1865.

Last, but certainly not least, I want to express my gratitude to the Bearlodge Writers, without whose positive critique and reinforcement this book probably would not be published. This is an assemblage of very gifted authors and poets who meet bi-monthly in Sundance, Wyoming, to read and review each other's work. I joined in 2005 at the suggestion of local writer Andi Hummel. This exceptional collection of talented people has improved my writing skills and the text of this manuscript immeasurably.

CHAPTER ONE

POINTS OF VIEW

THE MILITARY PERSPECTIVE

After four years of bloody conflict the American Civil War came to a close in early April 1865 with the surrender of Gen. Robert E. Lee and the Army of Northern Virginia at Appomattox Courthouse. On 14 April John Wilkes Booth assassinated President Abraham Lincoln at Ford's Theatre in Washington, D.C. While these monumental events were taking place in the East, an almost unnoticed war between Indian tribesmen and the military entered its second year in the West.

In the early 1850s an uneasy coexistence had developed on the central plains between its native inhabitants, primarily the Cheyenne, Sioux, and Arapaho tribes, and the white travelers of the overland road system following the Platte River west to Oregon, California, and Utah.[1] The Pike's Peak gold rush of the late 1850s increased that traffic, and settlements such as Denver, Colorado City, Blackhawk, and Cañon City cropped up on traditional Indian lands along the front range of the Rocky Mountains. White civilization also pushed westward into eastern Kansas and Nebraska territories, pressuring the nomadic tribes and the buffalo herds that their lifestyle so depended on.

With the outbreak of the Civil War in 1861, the nation focused on the clashes between Union and Confederate armies in the East. Sol-

---

[1]Gregory M. Franzwa, *Maps of the Oregon Trail,* 2–6. The terms "overland road" or "overland trail" will be used throughout this manuscript to define the major east–west route across the plains at that time. In fact there were several trails that made up this route, such as the Oregon Trail, the Mormon Trail, and the Pony Express Trail. The starting points were Independence, Missouri; Fort Leavenworth, Kansas; St. Joseph, Missouri; and Omaha, Nebraska/Council Bluffs, Iowa. The destinations included Denver, Colorado; Salt Lake City, Utah; California; Oregon; and the military posts along the route, such as Fort Kearny and Fort Laramie.

diers in the West manned the military posts and stations along the
overland road, protecting travelers and commerce while keeping communication lines such as the U.S. Mail and the Pacific Telegraph
open. In 1862 the discovery of gold in present-day southwestern Montana increased the westward traffic with another wave of gold seekers
rushing toward the new El Dorado.

Although minor incidents occurred in 1860 and 1861, Indians and
whites remained at relative peace. In August 1862 shock waves rocked
both racial communities when the Santee Sioux of Minnesota staged a
bloody uprising against the white settlers of the area.[2] Although the
army brought the situation under control later that year, punitive campaigns were commenced against the Sioux in the northern sector of
Dakota Territory over the next two years. On 12 April 1864 the First
Colorado Cavalry clashed with Cheyenne warriors at Fremont
Orchards in Colorado Territory while attempting to recover stolen
stock.[3] On 16 May troopers of the same regiment approached a
Cheyenne village near the Smokey Hill River in western Kansas. Chief
Lean Bear, a peace advocate, rode out with several other men to meet
the soldiers. Approaching the troopers, he was shot and killed. Facing
possible annihilation, the badly outnumbered soldiers were saved probably by the actions of Chief Black Kettle, also a peace advocate, as he
rode among the warriors frantically urging them to stop the fighting.[4]

In June Arapaho warriors killed four members of the Hungate family near Denver.[5] The mutilated bodies were displayed in Denver by
local officials, nearly causing a panic and prompting an outcry for
revenge. The Indian depredations reached their height in August
when the Little Blue River raid and the Plum Creek massacre in
Nebraska Territory virtually shut down the overland trail. These raids,
by Cheyenne and Sioux warriors, left over fifty white civilians dead,
and several women and children were taken captive.[6]

Later in the year the Sand Creek massacre in Colorado Territory
increased the intensity of this growing conflict. On 29 November 1864

---

[2]Gregory F. Michno, *Encyclopedia of Indian Wars*, 96–100.
[3]Ibid., 134–35.
[4]Ibid., 137–38.
[5]Ibid., 141–42.
[6]Ibid., 147, 148; Ronald Becher, *Massacre along the Medicine Road*, 148–210, 251–68.

Col. John M. Chivington led 550 men of the First and Third Colorado Volunteer Cavalry in a dawn attack on the Cheyenne village of peace advocate Black Kettle. The Indian casualties of around 150 included women and children.[7] White Americans had a mixed reaction to the news of the Sand Creek massacre. Generally, those in the East reacted with outrage over the inhumanity and savagery of the Colorado Volunteers, while in the West, especially in Colorado Territory, citizens looked upon Chivington as a hero.[8] Justification for the attack, in the eyes of many westerners, came from previous Indian misdeeds.

Maj. Gen. Grenville Dodge, who would play an important role in coming events, described the Indian reaction to Sand Creek:[9] "I found that the Indians, after the Chivington affair, had combined and moved north; had struck the Platte Valley and held the Overland route from Julesburg to Junction Station; had captured trains, demolished ranches, murdered men, women and children; destroyed fifty miles of Telegraph lines etc., etc."[10]

The Indians sought revenge in the aftermath of Sand Creek. About one thousand Cheyenne and Sioux warriors attacked Julesburg, Colorado Territory, on 7 January 1865, and striking there a second time on 2 February. The Sand Creek–avenging warriors, while moving their village north, fought a small garrison at the Mud Springs telegraph station in southwestern Nebraska Territory on 4 February. Troops from Forts Mitchell and Laramie arrived over the next two days, and after some long-range fighting, the warriors moved north.

The relief troops from Mud Springs had an engagement several days later with these same warriors near the mouth of Rush Creek, where it enters the North Platte River. The large village had crossed the river at this point. After fighting on 9 February and the morning of 10 February, the tribesmen withdrew and followed their village north toward

---

[7] Michno, *Encyclopedia of Indian Wars*, 157–59.

[8] *The Nebraska Republican* (Omaha), 30 June 1865, sarcastically reported, "Col. J. M. Chivington was in Omaha a few days since. He was in command of a Colorado regiment at the time a number of hostile Cheyennes were killed last winter. His great mistake was in supposing that fighting was his mission. It is now clear that he should have held a council, made a speech and delivered presents. He didn't see it, hence his persecution."

[9] Major General Dodge later became the chief construction engineer for the Union Pacific Railroad. Stephen E. Ambrose, *Nothing Like It in the World*, 31–41.

[10] Dodge to Bell, operations report, 18 July 1865, Grenville M. Dodge Manuscript Collection.

the Powder River country of eastern Wyoming (Dakota Territory in 1865).[11] Attacks on outposts along the overland road and emigrant trains from South Pass to Fort Kearny continued sporadically in the coming months.

The army reacted predictably: the depredations along the overland route must be stopped and the Indians responsible punished. Plans for action began to formulate early in 1865 with a restructuring of the command in the West. In December 1864, Major General Dodge assumed command of the Department of the Missouri, whose area of responsibility included the region affected by the Indian raids.[12] Maj. Gen. John Pope was appointed commander of the Military Division of the Missouri (all of the Great Plains region except the Department of New Mexico) in January 1865. In the military chain of command, Pope would be Dodge's immediate superior. Dodge created the District of the Plains (including today's Nebraska, Colorado, Wyoming, and Utah) and assigned its command to Brig. Gen. Patrick Edward Connor on 28 March 1865.[13]

Brigadier General Connor came to his new assignment from the District of Utah, headquartered in Salt Lake City. He had gained a reputation as an Indian fighter after a successful attack on a Shoshone village at Bear River in southern Idaho Territory in January 1863.[14] General Dodge's initial instructions to Connor were: "The District of the Plains was formed so as to put under your control the entire northern overland route and to render effective the troops along it. With the force at your disposal you can make vigorous war upon the Indians and punish them so that they will be forced to keep the peace. They should be kept away from our line of travel and made to stand on the defensive."[15]

With the Civil War in the East virtually over and the huge Union Volunteer Army still intact, the time was right to take advantage of this large force and mount a major campaign to once and for all settle the "Indian question" on the northern plains. Early in 1865 Generals

---

[11]Becher, *Massacre along the Medicine Road*, 148–210, 251–68; Michno, *Encyclopedia of Indian Wars*, 147, 148, 161, 164–65; John D. McDermott, *Circle of Fire*, 15–34.

[12]Dodge to Bell, operations report, 18 July 1865, Dodge Collection.

[13]General orders No. 80, 28 March 1865, Hafen and Hafen, *Powder River Campaigns*, 27.

[14]Brigham D. Madsen, *Glory Hunter*, 65–87; Michno, *Encyclopedia of Indian Wars*, 110–11.

[15]Dodge letter of instructions to Connor, 29 March 1865, Hafen and Hafen, *Powder River Campaigns*, 28–30.

Maj. Gen. Grenville Dodge,
commander of the Military
Department of the Missouri.
Courtesy of the National Archives.

Pope and Dodge planned a punitive expedition against the Cheyenne, Sioux, and Arapaho tribes.

These tribes were believed to be located near Bear Butte, north of the Black Hills of Dakota Territory and in Powder River country. Initially the plan called for a two-column converging campaign with experienced Indian fighter Brig. Gen. Alfred Sully leading an eastern column out of Fort Pierre, Dakota Territory, about 1 May, moving west to Powder River and building a fort.[16] Brigadier General Connor would be responsible for the western column departing from Fort Laramie, to move north, with both columns meeting in the Powder River country of eastern Montana Territory. The purpose of the expedition was simple: attack the Indians where they found them and punish and put the hostiles on the defensive, thus keeping the warriors away from the transportation routes to the south.[17]

---

[16]Sully letter to Dept. of the Northwest, 15 March 1865, *The War of Rebellion*; Dodge short letter to Connor, 29 March 1865, Hafen and Hafen, *Powder River Campaigns*, 28.
[17]Dodge letter to Connor, 29 March 1865, Hafen and Hafen, *Powder River Campaigns*, 28–30.

Maj. Gen. John Pope,
commander of the Military
Division of the Missouri.
Courtesy of the National Archives.

The plan changed in late May when General Sully's troops were
sent to Devils Lake in northern Dakota Territory to deal with a
potential Indian problem there. On 31 May General Dodge in Fort
Leavenworth notified Connor of this change: "You will see by General Pope's and General Sully's dispatches that we will have no movement toward the Black Hills by General Sully. We have got to take
care of the Indians there. Establish the post on Powder River, supply
it, & c. I shall send all the cavalry going from here well supplied with
transportation. . . . I think we should strike those Indians as soon as
possible, even if we have to make two campaigns."[18]

Brigadier General Connor would now lead the western, or left, column of the Powder River Indian Expedition (as it was officially called)
and build the fort on Powder River. He added a third column to his
plan: Lt. Col. Samuel Walker and his Sixteenth Kansas Volunteer Cav-

[18]Dodge letter to Connor, 31 May 1865, *The War of Rebellion.*

alry, designated as the center column out of Fort Laramie, would move north along the western slopes of the Black Hills. The eastern, or right, column would now be commanded by Col. Nelson D. Cole, with his Second Missouri Volunteer Light Artillery (equipped as cavalry), and the Twelfth Missouri Volunteer Cavalry. The plan called for the eastern command to march out of Omaha City, Nebraska Territory.[19]

THE POWDER RIVER INDIANS' PERSPECTIVE

Two large groups of Indians occupied Powder River country in the summer of 1865. The first group that Cole's command would eventually encounter was a northern Sioux coalition of Hunkpapa, Blackfoot Sioux, Miniconjou, and Sans Arc warriors from a large Sioux village that had been located in the vicinity of Fort Rice, on the Missouri River in what is today North Dakota. These were not the warriors who had been raiding on the overland road along the North Platte River, but they had been harassing Fort Rice all spring, and then launched an attack of about three hundred warriors on the fort and its stock herds on 28 July. The fort's defenders successfully repulsed this attack with steady infantry fire and effective use of artillery, after which the big Sioux village moved west toward Powder River country.[20] They were probably camped on the Little Missouri River in late summer.

The other group of Indians that Cole would encounter on Powder River was a mixed village of Northern Cheyenne, Southern Cheyenne, Oglala and Brule Sioux, and probably a few Arapaho. They had been disrupting travel and communications to the south and were the group targeted for retribution by Dodge and Connor's orders. In August and early September these Indians could be found in a large village near the mouth of the Little Powder River, close to today's Broadus, Montana. On 10 September 1865 Cole, with his command, passed through the abandoned village site and described "1500 to 2000 lodges had recently

[19]Robert M. Utley, *Frontiersmen in Blue*, 324–25.
[20]Robert M. Utley, *The Lance and the Shield*, 67–68. The previous year, these same northern tribesmen had suffered a defeat at Killdeer Mountain, in present western North Dakota, by Brig. Gen. Alfred Sully. The northern Sioux warrior force included many names that would become famous in the coming years, including Sitting Bull, Gall, White Bull, and Bull Head. Ibid., 55–57. Coincidently this battle was fought on 28 July 1864, one year to the day before the Fort Rice fight.

moved."[21] Lyman Bennett was a bit more conservative in his estimate of the size of the village of "at least 1000 lodges,"[22] but it was still a sizable encampment. Even using Bennett's conservative estimate, there was a potential warrior force of at least 2,000 to 3,000 men.

In the aftermath of Sand Creek, the Southern Cheyenne joined with their allies—the Oglala Sioux, Brule Sioux, and Arapaho—and intensified raiding on the overland trail. In the spring of 1865 the warring tribes moved north into Powder River country and were joined by the Northern Cheyenne. George Bent, the mixed-blood son of William Bent of Bent's Fort in Colorado, was in the village at that time and estimated that as many as three thousand warriors headed south in late July for an attack on the Platte Bridge Station, guarding the crossing of the North Platte River near today's Casper, Wyoming.[23] This fight took place on 26 July and was viewed as a success by the tribesmen, as they killed six men who defended the bridge and another twenty who were escorting a government train.[24]

Cole's command would eventually encounter these Indians in early September. The list of prominent warriors reads like a who's who from the Indian wars period: from the Southern Cheyenne, George Bent and his younger brother, Charlie Bent; from the Northern Cheyenne, Roman Nose, Dull Knife, and Little Wolf; from the Oglala Sioux, Red Cloud, Old Man Afraid of His Horses, Young Man Afraid of His Horses, and a warrior soon to become a legend, Crazy Horse.[25] In the late summer of 1865, Brigadier General Connor's western column would have contact with a large village of Arapaho camped on the headwaters of the Tongue River, near today's Ranchester, Wyoming, under Chief Black Bear.[26]

[21]Cole's official report, 10 February 1865, Hafen and Hafen, *Powder River Campaigns*, 81.
[22]Bennett diary, 10 September 1865 entry.
[23]Hyde, *Red Cloud's Folk*, 126.
[24]Michno, *Encyclopedia of Indian Wars*, 178–81.
[25]McDermott, *Circle of Fire*, 86; Utley, *The Lance and the Shield*, 69; David Fridtjof Halaas and Andrew E. Masich, *Halfbreed: The True Story of George Bent*, 196; Mari Sandoz, *Crazy Horse: The Strange Man of the Oglalas*, 174–76.
[26]Hafen and Hafen, *Powder River Campaigns*, 46–48.

CHAPTER TWO

20–30 *June*

PROCEED WITHOUT DELAY TO OMAHA

As a late appointment to lead the eastern column of the Powder River Expedition, Col. Nelson D. Cole replaced seasoned Indian fighter Gen. Alfred Sully, who had been moved with his command to northern Dakota Territory in anticipation of Indian problems at Devils Lake. With Sully out of their plans, Generals Pope, Dodge, and Connor all felt pressure to get the expedition underway immediately, before the summer campaigning season on the northern plains had passed. Events began to move quickly for Cole as the army hurried to put this military expedition together. On 21 May 1865 Gov. Thomas C. Fletcher of Missouri made a recommendation to General Dodge: "The Second Missouri Artillery, Col. N. Cole commanding, has 1,400 men and 800 horses. Average unexpired term of enlistment nearly two years. I suggest that it be converted into a cavalry regiment."[1] This suggestion was followed, and on 1 June the various batteries of Colonel Cole's Second Missouri Light Artillery were ordered to St. Louis to be equipped as cavalry.[2] On 10 June General Dodge ordered Colonel Cole and eight batteries of his regiment to "proceed without delay to Omaha, Nebr., reporting through the sub-district

---

[1]Fletcher letter to Dodge, 21 May 1865, *The War of Rebellion*.
[2]Dean S. Thomas, *Cannons: An Introduction to Civil War Artillery*, 3. During the Civil War, artillery companies were known as batteries. A battery, at full strength, consisted of over one hundred soldiers and was armed with six cannon. Second Missouri Artillery Regimental History, *The War of Rebellion*.

commander to Brig. Gen. P. E. Connor, commanding District of the Plains."[3] Eight Companies of the Twelfth Missouri Volunteer Cavalry commanded by Col. Oliver Wells were also ordered to Omaha to be a part of the pending expedition to places unknown.[4]

Colonel Cole arrived at Omaha City, Nebraska Territory, on 20 June and began to hastily organize the expedition, although he had only a general idea of its purpose and destination at this time. Confusion surfaced as to who would have overall command of the eastern column. Brigadier General Connor, from Fort Laramie, had ordered Col. Herman H. Heath, Seventh Iowa Cavalry, to Omaha with the intent of having him in charge of the expedition. Although Cole felt that he should be in command, because of his seniority in rank over both Colonels Heath and Wells, he did report to Colonel Heath, sub-district commander of the District of the Plains, as directed by General Dodge.

Omaha in 1865 was a busy place. In 1863 it had been named by President Lincoln as the eastern terminus of the soon-to-be constructed transcontinental railroad. Now that the war had ended, preparations advanced at a rapid pace to get construction under way. In fact, on 10 July, soon after Cole's expedition left Omaha, the first rails were laid.[5] Omaha's weekly newspaper, the *Nebraska Republican*, reported the excitement generated by the pending expedition: "The city is all astir with the active preparations for the great military expedition now organizing to move up the north side of the Platte against the Indians. Two boatloads of soldiers and a large quantity of government transportation arrived from Leavenworth today."[6]

Douglas County, of which Omaha was the major center, reported a population of 4,328 people in the 1860 census. By 1870 the county reported a census count of 19,982, a 361 percent growth factor.[7] Cole organized his command in this boom-town atmosphere, probably competing with railroad construction entities for transportation and

---

[3]Barnes for Dodge, general order, 10 June 1865, *The War of Rebellion*; Hafen and Hafen, *Powder River Campaigns*, 35.

[4]Twelfth Missouri Cavalry Regimental History, *The War of Rebellion*.

[5]Alfred Sorenson, *History of Omaha: From Pioneer Days to the Present Time*, 149–61; Ambrose, *Nothing Like It*, 132–35.

[6]*Nebraska Republican*, 30 June 1865.

[7]Harrison Johnson, *Johnson's History of Nebraska*, 169.

Col. Nelson D. Cole of the
Second Missouri Light Artillery
and commander of the
Eastern Division of the
Powder River Indian Expedition.
*Courtesy of the Missouri
Historical Society, St. Louis.*

supplies since the army's quartermaster system had failed to deliver needed materials ordered for the journey. General Dodge later wrote of the problems in provisioning the expedition: "The contract for transporting the supplies was made by the quartermaster's department at Washington and not closed until the 1st of May. The contractors were given from that time until the first of December to complete their contract, no time being specified for the delivery of any supplies at designated points earlier than the limit named."[8]

Connor instructed Cole to carry a sixty-day supply of rations.[9] Nelson Cole described the hectic organization of the expedition:

---

[8]Summary report of Dodge, 1 November 1865, Hafen and Hafen, *Powder River Campaigns,* 53.

[9]Cole's official report of 10 February 1865, Hafen and Hafen, *Powder River Campaigns,* 82. The orders that Cole referred to are the informal orders that he received via telegraph during this period, as he would not receive formal orders from Connor until 10 July, after he had been on the trail for ten days.

Brig. Gen. Patrick E. Connor, commander of the District of the Plains and the Powder River Indian Expedition. *Courtesy of the Wyoming State Archives, Department of State Parks and Cultural Resources.*

The command was organized at Omaha City, Nebr. Ter., and consisted of eight companies of my regiment, the Second Missouri Light Artillery (equipped as cavalry), and eight companies of the Twelfth Missouri Cavalry, numbering about 1,400, rank and file, with a train of 140 six-mule wagons. My artillery consisted of one section of 3-inch rifled guns, manned by men of the Second Missouri Light Artillery.[10] Much difficulty was experienced in procuring suitable transportation to accompany the command, and very considerable delay in the movement of the column was occasioned thereby. Most of the mules furnished were unbroken and from two to four years old, utterly unfit for the service required of them, but no others could be procured, whilst the teamsters were in the main worthless.

---

[10]The artillery that Cole mentioned was the three-inch ordinance gun, a rifled cannon that could accurately propel a ten-pound elongated shell a distance of 1,835 yards at five degrees of elevation. The gun was one of the mainstays of the Union Army, along with the Napoleon twelve-pound Howitzer. Cole wrote that "one section of 3-inch rifled guns" went with the expedition (a section was two guns). An artillery company or a battery, as they were called in the Civil War, would normally have six cannons. Thomas, *Cannons*, 39.

The time from June 20 to July 1 was spent in getting these incongruous elements organized into a train. A considerable quantity of commissary stores and a lot of spare parts and materials for the repair of wagons and harness had not arrived when, on June 30, I received a telegram from General Connor not to delay for anything, but to purchase supplies at Omaha City. This I did to the extent of about $15,000. General Connor also directed me to leave no grain behind, but to take all I could get trains to haul. To do this I was compelled to hire citizen transportation.[11]

Cole telegraphed a last-minute message on 29 June to General Dodge regarding his progress in organizing the expedition: "I am delayed here waiting for commissary and quartermaster's stores that have not arrived. I understand from Colonel Myers that they are on steamer Hannibal, which passed Kansas City at 2 P.M. to-day; also in getting my mules shod; they will all be shod to-morrow."[12]

A last-minute drama played out on 29 and 30 June as to who would lead the expedition. Brigadier General Connor had sent Col. Herman H. Heath, Seventh Iowa Cavalry, to Omaha, with the intention of having him as the overall commander of the eastern column.[13] Connor had verbally advised Heath of his plans for the campaign before Heath left Fort Laramie. When Colonel Cole learned of this, he reminded Connor that he had time in grade over Heath, and that as senior officer he should command the expedition.[14] As Heath had been recommended for the brevet rank of brigadier general, Connor assumed that that rank would justify his placement of Heath in command. Connor then telegraphed Major General Dodge and requested that Heath be put in charge. Dodge investigated and responded, "General Heath has not been assigned with brevet rank; until he is by the War Department we cannot assign him."[15] Connor then notified Heath with "General Dodge decides that Colonel Cole is the ranking officer until you are assigned in your brevet grade. Communicate the verbal orders I gave you to Colonel Cole."[16] To Cole he sent "Special

[11]Cole's official report of 10 February 1865, Hafen and Hafen, *Powder River Campaigns*, 60–61.
[12]Cole message to Dodge, 29 June 1865, *War of Rebellion*.
[13]Connor to Dodge, 29 June 1865, Dodge Collection.
[14]Connor to Dodge, 29 June 1865, *The War of Rebellion*.
[15]Dodge to Connor, 29 June 1865, 7 P.M., ibid.
[16]Connor to Heath, 29 June 1865, ibid.

Orders, No. 33, relieves General Heath. You must move your column immediately. . . . Heath will communicate to you the verbal instructions I gave him. I will mail a letter of instructions to Columbus."[17]

On 29 and 30 June the telegrams from Dodge and Connor took on an almost frantic tone to get the expedition on the trail. Dodge to Cole: "What delays you at Omaha? What are you waiting for?"[18] Connor to Cole: "You are authorized to purchase quartermaster's and subsistence stores necessary to complete your outfit."[19] Dodge to Cole: "Don't wait for rations."[20] Success or failure of the upcoming expedition would rest in great part on their transportation, specifically on the condition of their horses and mules.

⁜   ⁜   ⁜

The teamsters that Cole complained about were also called muleskinners. A teamster's job was to keep his wagon, pulled by six mules, under control and moving. The teamster rode on the left rear (nigh wheeler) mule and guided the entire team with a single rein called a jerk line. The difference between an experienced teamster and an inexperienced one was simple—the experienced teamster knew the personality of each of his mules and would have them functioning like a polished drill team, while the inexperienced one would have trouble controlling the team and find them to be obstinate. During this period, mules were in constant demand for civilian and military freighting because they were considered better foragers and were more surefooted in difficult terrain than horses. A pair of mules could cost from two to four hundred dollars, and mules from Missouri were generally considered the best.[21] The standard six-mule wagon weighed about a thousand pounds. The recommended payload over rough terrain, such as the command would travel, was between 1,800 and 2,500 pounds. In reality, the load was much heavier because the term 'payload' does not take into consideration the weight of the wagon, the

[17]Connor to Cole, 29 June 1865, ibid.
[18]Dodge to Cole, 29 June 1865, ibid.
[19]Connor to Cole, 29 June 1865, ibid.
[20]Dodge to Cole, 29 June 1865, ibid.
[21]Randy Steffen, *The Horse Soldier, 1776–1943*, 2:79, 91–93; Emmett M. Essin, *Shavetails and Bell Sharps: The History of the U.S. Army Mule*, 4–6.

teamster and his gear and rations, or feed for the mule team.[22] There were 140 wagons going with the expedition, each pulled by 6 mules, for a total of 840 mules. Allowing for additional mules to pull the artillery, and probably some spares, there were approximately 850 to 900 mules with the command.

The number of mounted men numbered about 1,400, which meant at least 1,400 to 1,500 horses with the command. The prescribed daily diet for each horse and mule was twelve pounds of grain (oats, corn, bran, or barley) and ten pounds of hay.[23] The grain would have to be transported in the freight wagons for the animals, while the grass along the trail would have to substitute for the hay. With only 140 wagons at his disposal, there was no way that Cole could carry along a sixty-day supply of grain for his animals. It is doubtful that they could even carry a thirty-day supply. With a maximum payload of only 2,500 pounds per wagon, it would have taken twice the number of wagons to carry even a thirty-day supply.[24] That payload also had to include items such as rations for the men, ammunition, camp gear and personal items, and spare harness and wagon parts. Colonel Cole would later state, in his report at the conclusion of the campaign, that by the ninth of September, "My stock at this time had been about sixty days without grain and had nothing but grass and cottonwood to live on for that length of time"—that meant the command had run out of grain for their horses and mules by mid-July.[25] Cole's hurriedly pre-pared expedition was now ready to depart on an ill-defined mission into a vast wilderness area.

---

[22]Robert A. Murray, *The Army Moves West: Supplying the Western Indian Wars Campaigns*, 2.

[23]Ibid.

[24]Twelve pounds of grain per day for 2240 horses and mules equals 26,880 pounds of grain daily for the animals. Thirty days times 26,880 pounds of grain equals 808,400 pounds of grain. Dividing that between 140 wagons means 5,760 pounds of grain per wagon. With a maximum payload of 2,000 pounds per wagon, it is extremely doubtful that they had anywhere near a thirty-day supply of grain.

[25]Cole's report of 25 September 1865, *The War of Rebellion*.

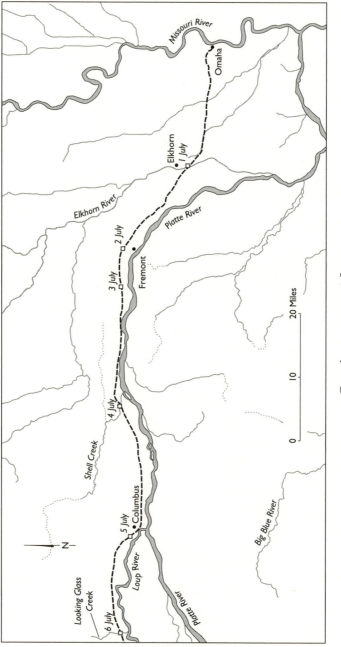

COLE'S ROUTE, 1–6 JULY

Dates indicate night's camping spot. *Maps by Bill Nelson.*

CHAPTER THREE

1–6 July

ON THE MARCH

ON THE MARCH—The 2nd and 12th Missouri Cavalry, for several days past stationed near the city, received marching orders yesterday and left this morning for the Indian country upon the Plains. A battery of two rifled guns accompanies the expedition. Yesterday evening the battalion marched through Farnam Street presenting a splendid appearance. The equipment of the expedition is superior to that of any that has ever preceded it across the plains and we trust that important results will occur.

Nebraska Republican[1]

Imagining the expectations of the members of Col. Nelson Cole's expedition today is difficult. Nobody, except possibly the colonel, had a clear idea of where they were headed or what, specifically, their assignment was. Into this uncertainty the hastily formed expedition departed Omaha City on 1 July 1865. Ten days would elapse before Connor's orders would catch up with the expedition on the trail.

Heading west today out of Omaha, over their approximate route, a traveler passes through Elkhorn, Fremont, and Columbus. These are villages that the expedition passed through in 1865 that are still there today. This is rich-looking agricultural country, and it is not hard to imagine how Nebraska got its nickname, the "Cornhusker State," with its miles upon miles of corn fields. They would initially follow the flat, fertile Platte River Valley slowly as various elements of the expedition came together.

---

[1]*Nebraska Republican*, 7 July 1865.

SATURDAY, 1 JULY 1865

Cole's command had problems before it could leave Omaha. On 1 July Colonel Cole telegraphed General Dodge as the command struggled to get underway:

> My command left this point this morning. I have been compelled to purchase several thousand dollars worth of quartermaster's stores to complete my outfit. My regiment has not been paid for six and eight months and the men are very much dissatisfied. Major Almstedt, paymaster, is at Fort Kearny with plenty of funds.[2] Please direct him to pay my regiment at Loup Fork, at which point I leave the main road. The men need the money for their families and they can express it home from that point; this will save me much trouble. Please let me know by telegraph whether the men can be paid or not.[3]

General Dodge answered Colonel Cole the same day from St. Louis: "I have telegraphed Major Almstedt to meet you at Loup Fork. If he does have no delay over one day and night for payment, as you are over a week behind the time you should have started. Why did you not get your quartermaster's store when you left here? I gave orders that you should go fully equipped."[4]

It was not a very auspicious beginning, as Cole reported trouble getting the expedition underway: "On the 1st of July, after some delay caused by the refusal of two companies of my regiment to move when ordered, the command, with the exception of three companies (which remained to complete their equipment, collect stragglers, and escort the rear trains), took up the line of march toward Columbus, on the Loup Fork of the Platte, following the line of the Pacific telegraph."[5]

The refusal to march by two of Cole's companies may have had a connection with the pay situation. It had become common for volunteer troops at the end of the Civil War to want to go home now that

---

[2]Maj. Henry Almstedt had previously served as colonel of the Second Missouri Light Artillery, Nelson Cole's current command, from November 1861 until August 1863. He was later assigned to the staff of the United States Paymaster. Dennis Northcott, "Guide to Civil War Manuscripts in the Missouri Historical Society Archives."

[3]Cole letter to Dodge, 1 July 1865, *The War of Rebellion*. The Loup Fork, mentioned by Cole, is where the Loup River flows into the Platte River near Columbus, Nebraska.

[4]Dodge letter to Cole, 1 July 1865, ibid.

[5]Cole's official report, 10 February 1867, Hafen and Hafen, *Powder River Campaigns*, 61.

OMAHA, LOOKING NORTHWEST
ON FARNAM STREET AT TWELFTH STREET IN 1867
Farnam is the street that the Powder River Indian Expedition marched out of
Omaha on 1 July 1865. The building on the skyline is the Nebraska Territorial
Capitol Building. *Courtesy of the Nebraska State Historical Society, 20070254.*

the war in the East was over. With their enlistment not up yet, soldiers
had a general feeling that they had not signed up to fight Indians on
the western plains. This had happened previously at Fort Kearny in
Nebraska, and would happen at Fort Laramie and also later on this
expedition, where Cole instructed his company commander to shoot
the first man who did not move when the order was given to move out.
Cole was not unique in his handling of this situation, as Connor had
ordered a cannon loaded with grape shot aimed at rebelling troops at
both Fort Kearny and Fort Laramie to persuade their compliance.[6]

First Lt. Charles H. Springer, Twelfth Missouri Cavalry, recalled his
first day on the trail: "To-day the 1st day of July 1865, the companies of

---

[6]Connor report to Dodge, 21 June 1865, ibid., 38–39.

the 12th Mo. Vol. Cav. and the 2nd Regiment of Mo. Light Artillery started from Omaha, Nebr., and marched about 24 miles to the little town of Elkhorn on Elkhorn [R]iver and encamped for the night."[7]

SUNDAY, 2 JULY 1865

Cole reported that "On the 2nd the balance of the command with the trains followed, as the command marched about 15 miles and encamped near Fremont."[8]

MONDAY, 3 JULY 1865

The wagon train and the rest of the command overtook the main column at Fremont, on the Platte River.[9] Fremont, located about thirty-five miles west of Omaha, was founded in 1856 and named after the famous pathfinder John C. Fremont. Dodge County, of which Fremont is the county seat, had a population of 309 people in 1860.[10]

Lyman G. Bennett's journal began on 3 July. He was traveling up the Missouri River on a steamer to Omaha, to catch up with Colonel Cole and report as a civilian engineering officer for the Powder River Indian Expedition, Eastern Division:

> The steamer being relieved of very much of her cargo at Nebraska City, so lightened her that we made a rapid progress up the river against a current which in many places was quite rapid. A bend in the river would occasionally bring us to the bold high bluffs on either side. The hills, clothed in the richest verdure, were very beautiful to behold. While passing a small place called Wyoming, a Mormon camp, in the immediate neighborhood called every body to the deck to see them. It was early in the morning and numbers of both sexes were at the river half stripped performing their ablutions. On the side of the hill, almost above the boat, temporary sinks were prepared and being used by men and women promiscuously and women made no attempt of concealment from those on the boat or from each other.
>
> Reached Omaha about 3 P.M. We waited on board a long time for hacks

[7]Springer, *Soldiering in Sioux Country*, 5.
[8]Cole's official report, 10 February 1867, Hafen and Hafen, *Powder River Campaigns*, 61.
[9]Ibid.
[10]Johnson, *Johnson's History of Nebraska*, 169, 319.

Lyman G. Bennett as major of the
First Arkansas Volunteer Cavalry
in 1863. *Courtesy of the Wyoming
State Archives, Department of
State Parks and Cultural Resources.*

to come down to take us to town. None coming, I walked nearly a mile to
town.

Yankee Robinson was performing there and every body almost had gone
to the show.[11] Saw Gen. Heath to whom I reported, who ordered me to
report to Col. Cole on his way to the plains. Not a horse or any outfits could
be procured at Omaha. Lt. Amsden & I proceeded by stage to overtake the
command, trusting the march on being mounted on getting there.[12] The
boys composing the Signal party and Mr. Miller, who is to be my assistant
will come on in the morning and overtake us as soon as they can.

---

[11]The *Nebraska Republican* reported in its 30 June 1865 edition: "Yankee Robinson's Great Show
will exhibit in Omaha on the 3rd and 4th prez. The entire concern will be here having one char-
iot drawn by forty horses and many other amusements never before seen in Nebraska. This is
pronounced a superb show, and fulfill all their promises. See their advertisement elsewhere."
Apparently the Yankee Robinson show did not live up to advance billing, as the *Nebraska
Republican* reported in its 7 July 1865 edition: "Yankee Robinson's 'Big Show' has left town. It
was very tame and was only big in bills."

[12]Lt. Frederick Amsden was a member of the U.S. Army Signal Corps. Cole's official report, 10
February 1867, Hafen and Hafen, *Powder River Campaigns,* 91.

Two very pleasant ladies were in the stage on their way to Elkhorn to spend the 4th. Genl. Heath also proceeds to Cottonwood on military business. The ladies kept us awake by their pleasant conversation until midnight when they reached their destination.[13]

Springer reported that the command marched about eight miles, with several stops to allow the extensive train to catch up. They camped on the banks of the Platte. He went swimming with Capt. Charles F. Ernst and five men. Springer then speculated as to the command's destination: "The great question which agitates the minds of our officers and men, except the Colonel commanding is: where is our destination? Are we to march by such a circuitous route to Mexico, to clean out in times to come the Frenchmen, and revel and dance in the halls of Montezuma, with the dark eyed senoritas those delicious Spanish waltzes?"[14]

Springer is probably reacting to camp gossip regarding their destination, as it was unknown to him at this time. The French had taken advantage of the turmoil in the United States during the War of Rebellion and installed an Austrian archduke, Prince Maximilian III, as emperor of Mexico and enforced his rule with French troops. Rumors floated around the Union Army that now that the Confederacy had been whipped, the still-intact army should head south and drive the French out of Mexico.[15]

TUESDAY, 4 JULY 1865

Bennett's journey—and journal—continued:

I dozed and tried to sleep in the stage, but found the effort more fatiguing than trying to keep awake. Many were the bumps; I succeeded from being tilted against the side of the coach. Shortly after sunrise, arrived at the Headquarters of Col. Cole and reported myself for duty. A horse was found for me and I was mounted, also Lt. Amsden. We marched through a fine country for Nebraska, being along the north bank of the Platte and as level as is well could be. The valley is quite well settled and many fine farms are being cultivated. Corn and grass look uncommonly good. Wheat

[13]Bennett diary, 3 July 1865 entry.
[14]Springer, *Soldiering in Sioux Country*, 5.
[15]Joan Haslip, *The Crown of Mexico: Maximilian and his Empress Carlotta*, 364–65.

and oats are rather short. Marched 18 miles and camped on a clear stream of water called Shell Creek, near where it enters the Platte. Wood and grass were plenty. Nearly every soldier stripped and had a good swim. I went in and had a good wash. The day has been excessively hot. An oppressive south wind has blown all day, with a breath that nearly supports raising great clouds of dust and rendering it impossible to keep clean. Fired a motivational salute from the two cannon of the expedition in honor of the glorious 4th.[16]

Springer described Independence Day on the trail: "In the morning of the glorious 4th of July the roar of the artillery woke us up." He then reminisced about war experiences in Tennessee and Mississippi and continued to speculate as to where the expedition was headed. "Where shall we be next year? Still serving Uncle Sam, I suppose. Probably we will spark the fair maidens of Mexico. At present I am sitting at the mess box, while my men are currying their horses, others cooking the frugal supper."[17]

WEDNESDAY, 5 JULY 1865

FORT LARAMIE, July 5—A column consisting of the 2nd Missouri light artillery, equipped as cavalry, and the 12th Missouri cavalry passed Columbus Nebraska to-day, en route for Powder River, to cooperate with the other columns now preparing to march from Laramie against hostile Indians.[18]

Columbus was founded in 1856 by several men from Columbus, Ohio. The 1860 census for Platte County, of which Columbus was the population center, listed 782 people living there.[19] Cole's command marched through Columbus on 5 July. George Bird Grinnell described Nelson Cole's command moving through Columbus: "Cole's new command made a great impression when it passed through Columbus. There were sixteen hundred men, all splendidly mounted and some artillery and it looked like a very effective force."[20]

---

[16]Shell Creek, where the command camped, is just east of present-day Schuyler, Nebraska. Bennett diary, 4 July 1865 entry.

[17]Springer, *Soldiering in Sioux Country*, 6.

[18]*Daily Rocky Mountain News* (Denver), 6 July 1865.

[19]Johnson, *Johnson's History of Nebraska*, 170, 501.

[20]George Bird Grinnell, *Two Great Scouts and Their Pawnee Battalion*, 87–88.

In a 1929 letter Luther H. North recalled meeting with Colonel Cole as the command passed through Columbus: "He [Cole] certainly had a fine command, the best looking lot of horses and the finest mule teams I ever saw. I had been doing a little scouting and guiding for a company of troops stationed here; and Cole sent for me, wanting to employ me to guide his division northwest. I had never been farther than the head of the Loup River, and didn't like to take the responsibility from that point to the Powder River and perhaps to the Yellowstone."[21]

Cole sent a telegram to Major General Dodge, answering Dodge's questions from his last message and giving him an update on their progress: "Arrived at this point [Columbus] to-day, my command in fine condition, and will move as fast as nature of country will permit. I will make up the week I am behind. I made my requisition for quartermaster's stores before I left Saint Louis, and supposed they were shipped on steamer Calypso or Omaha with the balance of my stores. Captain Seely, assistant quartermaster, is responsible for their nonshipment, as he had plenty of time to have shipped them on either of the above mentioned boats."[22]

Bennett was still getting himself organized for the journey:

> It has been a warm windy day, but little more cool and pleasant than yesterday. We left the Platte River and camped on the Loup two miles above its mouth and three miles from Columbus. Met Mr. Jack, an old soldier from the 4th Ark. Cav. and had him detailed as my orderly.[23] Hearing that Maj. Robinson was in town, I rode to Columbus and saw him. He had attempted to come down the Platte from Kearny in a boat, but failed and paid $50.00 to get to Columbus in a wagon. Purchased a pair of shoes, thread, needles, caps and wash bowl. Returned to camp, drew two horses and wrote two letters, one to Mellie & one to Thomas Simpson.[24]

Springer developed a thirst while on the trail: "Near Shinn's Ferry I went to a house where I stopped once in 1861, as I came from Fort Kearney from soldiering and drank 2 glasses of beer."[25]

---

[21]L. H. North letter to *U.S. Army Recruiting News*, 26 November 1929.
[22]Cole's report to Dodge, 5 July 1865, *The War of Rebellion*.
[23]Bradbury, "Biographical Sketch of L. G. Bennett." Bennett had previously been a major in the Fourth Arkansas Volunteer Cavalry. The Fourth Arkansas had two privates with the last name of Jack: Daniel of Company M and John A. of Company L. *Civil War Soldiers and Sailors System*.
[24]Bennett diary, 5 July 1865 entry.
[25]Springer, *Soldiering in Sioux Country*, 6.

No mention is made as to whether the paymaster, Major Almstedt, met the command at Columbus. One must assume that he did, as he had four days to travel the approximately 110 miles from Fort Kearny to Columbus, which is more than enough time to make the trip.

THURSDAY, 6 JULY 1865

A wide, shallow river with a muddy and/or sandy bottom, the Loup River enters the Platte River from the northwest at Columbus, Nebraska. Upriver it divides into three branches, the South Loup, the Middle Loup, and the North Loup. These three rivers dominate central Nebraska for about 270 miles to their headwaters in the north central part of the state. The command moved out along the Loup River to the west of Columbus. Bennett described the march:

> Started ahead of the column in order to transact business with Maj. Robinson. Our march was up the north side [of] the Loup over a level plain thru low bluffs, which skirt all streams in this country, are about 4 miles from the river. A few patches of cottonwood trees fringe the river. Camped at 3 P.M., seventeen miles from Columbus, marching 20 miles during the day. Good grass and wood at this camp. Col. Cole & Major Landgraeber caught 100 or 200 fish of the kind called Bull Heads.[26] We had fish for supper. We crossed a stream called Looking Glass Creek. A man is building a grist mill on it. Lt Amsden stayed at Columbus to wait for his party. I am expecting Miller with them. Am mapping the route as I go along. Rained very hard during the night. The sound of the rain and thunder awakened me and looking out, there was a sort of spray raising from the grass which made it look through my drowsy eyes like water. I thought the whole plain was covered with water and uttered a cry of alarm. The sentinel was walking his beat and taking the storm as a natural consequence and assured me all was well, when I laid down and to sleep again.[27]

Springer went fishing with Private McBeath and "caught some very nice pickerels, but the mosquitos were so bad, we had to give it up."[28]

---

[26]Maj. Clemenz Landgraeber was a member of the Second Missouri Light Artillery. *Civil War Soldiers and Sailors System.*

[27]Bennett diary, 6 July 1865 entry.

[28]Springer, *Soldiering in Sioux Country,* 6–7.

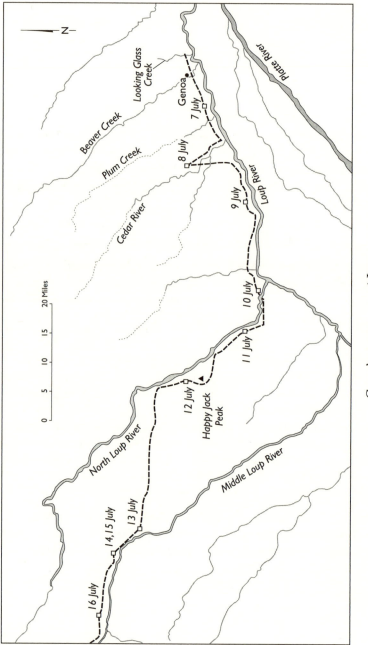

Beaver Creek

Looking Glass Creek

Plum Creek

Cedar River

Genoa

7 July

8 July

9 July

10 July

11 July

12 July

Happy Jack Peak

13 July

14, 15 July

16 July

North Loup River

Middle Loup River

Loup River

Platte River

—N—

0   5   10   15   20 Miles

COLE'S ROUTE, 7–16 JULY

7–16 July

FOLLOWING THE LOUP

FRIDAY, 7 JULY 1865

Twenty miles west of Columbus is the town of Genoa. In 1865 Bennett described the town as "two small log houses" that were trading posts just east of the Pawnee Reservation boundary. Today's Genoa has a population of over one thousand and is located where the Pawnee Agency stood in 1865. The agency had, at that time, what was probably one of the most impressive buildings in all of Nebraska Territory, a three-story brick school building. This newly built structure was part of a United States treaty obligation with the Pawnee tribe to provide them with education.[1]

Cole described how he obtained supplies as the expedition followed the Loup River, "leaving the last vestige of civilization at the Pawnee mission, 110 miles from Omaha City. From the many farms which lie along the Platte a sufficiency of forage was purchased to supply the command; here I also procured a drove of fifty beef-cattle."

In his haste to get the expedition organized, Cole had been unable to find experienced guides. He also worked with an 1857 map that was woefully inadequate for the areas to be traveled. He recalled, "After passing the Pawnee Mission and until reaching the Niobrara River my only reliable source of information was a copy of Lieut. G. K. Warren's map, furnished me by the chief engineer of the department, as

---

[1] *Genoa, Nebraska, Historical Stars*, 5.

the guides I have employed were unfamiliar with the country, having been over its surface but little; yet they were excellent judges of prairie country and were of much value in the selection of favorable ground for the movement of the trains."[2] Luther North wrote of Cole's guide situation in a 1929 letter: "Cole had no guide at that time, but hired George Sard at the Pawnee Agency; he was a clerk from Chicago, and had been there only a short time, knew nothing of the country and was, of course, soon in some difficulties. It was said afterward that Colonel Cole threatened to hang him."[3]

Bennett gives a glimpse of the Pawnee Agency near Genoa:

> Left camp at 6 A.M., the grass was covered with great drops of water, look-ing for the world like crystal beads. It was long and cool at starting, but soon cleared up and the middle of the day was warm. Before we entered the Pawnee Reserve, we passed two small log houses which, I was told, was the town of Genoa. A mile farther was a large three story academy for the edu-cation of the Pawnee Indians. It was a fine building. Several houses were around resembling a small town. I likewise noticed a steam grist mill. Beaver Creak comes in here from the North West and is a fine stream. Larger quantities of corn was planted by the Indians and looked very well. They had finished hoeing it and had gone on a hunt and their two villages nearby was [sic] entirely deserted. I entered some of their houses. Outside they look like a haystack or round bank of earth. Inside they are quite neat. A long narrow passage leads into them. The fire is built in the center, the smoke going out at the top where a hole gives it passage and also furnishes light. There are some 3000 Indians that live in the two villages. All were at the mission. The morning was fine for marching and I enjoyed myself much.[4]

In an unpublished paper by Bennett from around 1875, he wrote an amusing sidelight to the visit to the Pawnee village: "While leisurely prosecuting our researches about the town, Lt. Amsden suddenly exclaimed 'I've made discovery boys and shall flee this place at once.'

[2]Cole's official report of 10 February 1867, Hafen and Hafen, *Powder River Campaigns*, 65. The map that Cole referred to resulted from explorations by Lt. Gouverneur Kemble Warren in 1855, 1856, and 1857. Gouverneur Kemble Warren Papers.

[3]L. H. North letter to *U.S. Army Recruiting News*, 26 November 1929. Luther North might be mis-taken that Cole had no guides by the time he reached Columbus. Mr. Gay and Mr. Raymond are mentioned frequently as civilian guides throughout Bennett's account of the expedition and may have been hired in Omaha. Neither Cole nor Bennett specified when or where the guides were hired.

[4]Bennett diary, 7 July 1865 entry.

'Flea the place' responded Capt. McMurray 'no mortal being can do that more effectually than it is already flea'd.'[5] It required no inspector General to discover that the town was literally alive with fleas that were as voracious and bloodthirsty as Fiji cannibals."[6] He would still be complaining about the Pawnee fleas days later. Bennett's 1865 journal continues:

> Riding occasionally up on the bluff which now come with from ½ a mile to 1 mile from the river and close to the road. The view was grand[;] I could see the Platte river & timber at least 15 miles to the south. Near a small stream called Plum Creek I went back among the hills. The ravine was well wooded with small stunted oaks. The hills—the valleys—the tall grass, the trees, & etc. looked like an enchanted land, and I thought of all the romantic places I had ever read about. We camped near Council Creek on the Loup. It was quite busy for a hour or two fixing a bridge of brush and dirt to cross the train upon. Then went down the river a mile or more and had a good bath. The Col. & Maj. went out and caught some very fine fish. Some of the catfish weighed 10 pounds. We are living high. I like this country much better than any other Nebraska I have seen.
>
> Two Pawnee Indians accompany us as guides. They are hardy bucks with no clothes except a fiery red shirt. Tonight the Q.M. gave them pants. Nearly all the men in the camp has been in the river swimming. Naked men throng the river and its banks. I wonder what the surgeon's wife thinks of soldiering and soldiers? Marched about 13 miles.[7]

Springer, also impressed with the school building, wrote, "In the morning of the 7th of July we started early came to Pawnee Mission, where there is a fine 3 story brick building erected by the Jesuits for the conversion of the natives to Christendom. Here we are at the end of civilization, no more settlements from here, and no more roads to travel." He described the empty Pawnee village: "We encamped at 11 o'clock A.M. on the bank of Loup Fork." After dinner he went to the river, fishing with little success, "and after taking a swim, I returned to camp, and went to bed."[8]

---

[5]Capt. Junius G. W. McMurray, First Missouri Light Artillary, detached from duty as inspector of artillery, Department of the Missouri, was currently serving as Colonel Cole's aide-de-camp. Cole's official report of 10 February 1867, Hafen and Hafen, *Powder River Campaigns*, 91.

[6]Lyman G. Bennett file, Wyoming State Archives.

[7]Bennett diary, 7 July 1865 entry.

[8]Springer, *Soldiering in Sioux Country*, 7.

Colonel Cole, knowing that he was entering a roadless wilderness, sent this reassuring message to Brigadier General Connor: "I purchased everything at Omaha that I required. My command has everything that it needs. When do you expect me at Bear Butte?"[9] One must wonder if he really expected an answer, as from here on there would be no opportunity for further communication other than by messenger. Council Creek, where they camped that night, is six and one-half miles west of Genoa. As Springer said, they were at the edge of civilization, and the command would not see another settlement until the completion of the expedition in late September.

SATURDAY, 8 JULY 1865

Civilian guides who didn't know the country plagued the expedition from the start. On this day, one of these men advised Colonel Cole to take a route north, following the Cedar River, as it would be an easier route for the train than their current path following the Loup River. Cedar River is a winding, shallow stream that enters the Loup from the northwest, just east of present-day Fullerton, Nebraska.

Marching through a roadless wilderness with a large command that included a train of 140 wagons, Nelson Cole and his officers had to anticipate a certain amount of road building and bridging in crossing waterways and rough terrain. By "Anticipating the frequent use of tools in the construction of bridges and cutting embankments [Cole] had organized one of the companies of the Second Missouri Light Artillery as a pioneer company, under command of Capt. N. Boardman."[10]

Bennett described a hectic day:

> Started about 6 A.M. and after half a miles march left the river to the left, taking up the valley of Cedar Creek, which flowed from the North West. One of our guides stated that this road would avoid sand hills and several small creeks which came down from the bluffs, and were difficult to cross. Cedar Creek was pretty well timbered for this country and was a larger clear stream, but full of quick sand. On the maps this is called Calamus

---

[9]Cole message to Connor, 7 July 1865, *The War of Rebellion*.

[10]Cole's official report of 10 February 1867, Hafen and Hafen, *Powder River Campaigns*, 63. Capt. Napoleon Boardman was a member of Battery M, Second Missouri Light Artillery. *Civil War Soldiers and Sailors System*.

Creek, but the Indians and guides called Cedar River. The land was very rich and fine and in time this valley will be settled. An abundance of game was seen, such as elk, deer, and antelope, also prairie chicken and fish. Thanks to Maj. Landgraeber, we had a mess of them tonight.

About 4 miles from our starting point in the morning we crossed a ravine rather difficult for loaded teams to cross. Here I was called upon to make a bridge which occupied about an hour. Co. M, Capt. Boardman's, 2nd Mo. Artillery has been detailed as pioneers and performed the work assigned readily. We tried to cross the stream where we first struck it but could not on account of high banks and quicksand. We tried the 2nd time and failed and after camping at 2 P.M., the pioneers dug a road down the steep bank so that it was feasible crossing. The Q.M. immediately commenced moving his train in order to have no delays the next morning. Three or four wagons were taken over safely, but finally one got set in the quicksand and the mules could not pull it. After unloading it 20 men & the mules could scarcely pull the empty wagon on. Very many of the wagons got set in the quicksand and two or three tipped over and was nearly washed out of sight. A large force of men was detailed to assist. Some of them stripped to the skin, others only partly undressed, and such a shouting, toiling, swearing neither clothed or fully naked crowd I never before saw. It was really interesting to see them work in the water. Sometimes mules would fall down and be dragged along by the others. I watched them until long after night. It was ten o'clock before the train was over. I longed for an artist to take a sketch of the crossing of Cedar River. I have done what I think no man while marching over the plains has never done before—mounted a map for the Col. The scenery has been delightful and entirely new, no white man ever having explored it before us. Marched 13 miles.

In examining for a crossing I rode my horse up and down the river for a mile, sometimes more than belly deep in quicksand and water.[11]

Thus the command ended the day with the wagons mired in country unsuited for the heavy train, and showing little progress for a day's hard work. Colonel Cole probably had some harsh words for the guide who advised them to follow the Cedar River.

SUNDAY, 9 JULY 1865

In the morning Cole made the decision to abandon the Cedar River route and move back to the Loup River: "from the necessity of select-

---

[11]Bennett diary, 8 July 1865 entry.

ing ground passable with the trains, the course changed nearly south."[12] Bennett gave more detail on this change to the route:

> The guide who directed us up Cedar Creek has deserted and we find ourselves among bluffs impossible for the heavy train. The Indians advise us to get to the Loup again. Accordingly our course lies over the bluffs on the dividing ridge in a south west direction. One small stream had to be bridged, but the pioneer party was not long in doing this. We made a substantial bridge in five hours and sloped the high banks on each side. Our road was very crooked on the highest ridges overlooking the whole surrounding country, which is very high and broken, being entirely cut up by ravines. Saw considerable wild game. A Capt. caught two young deer about as large as lambs. Reached the river at 3 P.M. and here marched the road up a bank. Also struck a recent trail following up the river. Plenty of grass, wood and water. No fish tonight.
>
> Lt Amsden and signal party came up today. Certainly until we struck the Loup, very rough and broken, and no trails for us to follow.[13]

The guide who gave the bad advice to take the Cedar River route, and subsequently deserted, was probably George Sard. Recall that Cole had just hired him on 7 July at the Pawnee Agency, and Luther North said that Cole later threatened to hang him. Sard probably took Cole's threat seriously and headed back to the Pawnee Agency, as no mention of his name appears in Bennett's or Springer's journals, while the other two guides are mentioned periodically throughout the journey.

MONDAY, 10 JULY 1865

Colonel Cole received his long-awaited orders pertaining to the expedition's destination and purpose from Connor: "Whilst camped near the mouth of the North Branch of the Loup, Lieutenant [John P.] Murphy, First Nebraska Cavalry, with escort arrived, bringing dispatches from General Connor containing full instructions as to my destination and route, of which up to this time I was entirely uninformed save that I was to move my command up the Loup Fork, where I would receive orders."[14]

---

[12]Cole's official report of 10 February 1867, Hafen and Hafen, *Powder River Campaigns*, 62.
[13]Bennett diary, 9 July 1865 entry.
[14]Cole's official report of 10 February 1867, Hafen and Hafen, *Powder River Campaigns*, 62.

Cole's orders from Connor at Fort Laramie, dated 4 July 1865, read as follows:

Colonel: In accordance with verbal instructions heretofore communicated to you through Bvt. Brig. Gen. H. H. Heath, U.S. Volunteers, you will proceed with your column by the best and most practicable route to the east base of the Black Hills, in Dakota Territory; move thence along the east base of the Black Hills to Bear's Peak [Bear Butte], situate[d] at the northeast point of the hills, and where a large force of hostile Indians are supposed to be camped. From Bear's Peak you will move around the north base of the Black Hills to the Three Peaks [Little Missouri Buttes]; from thence you will strike across the country in a northwesterly direction to the north base of Panther Mountain, where you will find a supply depot and probably part of my command. You will see by the lines marked on the map I enclose herewith [enclosure not found], the route to be taken by you and the other columns of the expedition. If, after you turn the northeast point of the Black Hills, I should desire you to change your course or ascertain your whereabouts, I will make the signal fires communicated to you by General Heath. You will not make the signal fires unless it is to answer mine or in case you require assistance. The Indians will try to impede your progress by burning the grass in your advance or stampeding your animals. The former you cannot prevent, but the latter by side-hobbling your horses and mules, which you must do by all means. You will always have pickets out and send scouting parties out on your left flank and front and scout well the streams and cañons putting out of the Black Hills on your left. You will not receive overtures of peace or submission from Indians, but will attack and kill every male Indian over 12 years of age. It is reported that a large band of Indians are congregated at the base of Bear Butte. You will endeavor to surprise them. In order to do so you should first, through your scouts, find out their exact locality, and reach them by night marches. Hire a number of guides from among the Pawnees if you can. They will all be borne on your quartermaster's rolls as guides, as the general department will not pay scouts. I would enjoin upon you to use all the expedition possible consistent with the welfare of your horses, which you will endeavor to keep in as good condition as possible.[15]

Brigadier General Connor submitted a copy of his orders for Colonel Cole, along with Connor's operational plan for the Powder River Expedition, to the Department of the Missouri on 28 July.[16] Division

---

[15] Connor's orders to Cole 4 July 1865, ibid., 35.
[16] Connor's letter to Maj. J. W. Barnes, 28 July 1865, ibid., 40.

commander Maj. Gen. John Pope, in a letter to Connor's superior, Gen. Grenville Dodge dated 11 August, reacted to Connor's instructions to "kill every male Indian over 12 years of age" as follows: "These instructions are atrocious, and are in direct violation of my repeated orders. If any such orders as General Connor's are carried out it will be disgraceful to the government, and will cost him his commission, if not worse. Have it rectified without delay."[17] Connor responded to this reprimand later in August from his command on Powder River: "The General's [Pope] and your [Dodge] instructions will be implicitly obeyed."[18] Unfortunately this change to the original orders was never communicated to Cole, as his next contact with Connor's column was in late September, days after the final confrontations with the Powder River Indian tribes.

✳   ✳   ✳

The route on the north bank of the Loup became more demanding as Bennett worked with the pioneers to get the wagons through. He described the day:

> A messenger came in from Fort Kearny in the night having traveled 75 miles to find us. What was the import of his messages, I know not. We broke up camp shortly after sun rise and pushed on up the left bank of the Loup. The bluffs in some places approach very near the river and deep dry ravines, difficult to cross, occasionally come down from the mountain, but my pioneers made the pattern practical. We came at length to a muddy slough which was most difficult to cross, we commenced bridging it near the river and found it a big job, finally it was reported that a crossing could be affected above which we availed ourselves of, and we came over. A wild muddy creek was the next impediment. A bridge was impossible, fording was difficult. A few facings of willow helped the matter a little, but the mud was cut so deep that sometimes the mules were completely submerged, would fall down, get tangled up, but finally the train was got over. Left the main Loup and followed up the north branch and camped three miles above its mouth. I was employed all the afternoon exploring the river, sounding it and fixing a ford. A tolerable one is found and we hope to get

---

[17]Pope letter to Dodge, 11 August 1865, ibid., 43.
[18]Connor message to Dodge, 20 August 1865, ibid., 44.

NORTH LOUP RIVER NEAR ITS CONFLUENCE WITH THE MIDDLE LOUP
This is the general area where the command camped on 10 July and
Cole finally received his orders from Brigadier General Connor. *Author's photo.*

the train over without difficulty. Among the standing candidates for public
favor here is fleas. I can endure lice, gullinippers and dog bites very well, but
they are not a circumstance to a Pawnee flea. Have written home.[19]

Springer complained about the weather being cold with a drizzling
rain. He was on guard duty for the train again and worked with the
pioneers: "We built several bridges and helped the train across, we

---

[19]Bennett diary, 10 July 1865 entry. Bennett was still complaining about the fleas from the Pawnee
village visit on 7 July. In his unpublished paper, written in the 1870s, he recalled, "For days they
stuck to us like 'grim death to a deceased African' and our recollection of the Pawnee towns was
frequently sharpened by the bites of these troublesome tormentors." Lyman G. Bennett file,
Wyoming State Archives.

came to a swamp: the teams of the 2nd Missouri Artillery were in front as they entered the swamp. The very first one stuck up to the hubs in the mud." Springer said that the drivers were unwilling to "go into the swamp for fear of getting their feet wet, [and] I ordered my men to strip off. I set the example and plunged into the mire, and by a good deal of exertion, we got the team out." Springer and his men spent the rest of the afternoon working to get the teams through and got into camp at about 8 P.M. After supper, the quartermaster rewarded them for their hard work with a canteen of whiskey.[20]

The area of the campsite, on the north side of the river, is near the bridge over the North Loup three miles north of today's St. Paul, Nebraska, on Highway 281. The confluence of the North Loup and Middle Loup is three and one-half miles downriver from there.

TUESDAY, 11 JULY 1865

The command crossed to the south bank of the North Loup River at the ford that Bennett had selected the previous afternoon and followed it in a northwesterly direction. The reason for crossing the river was, no doubt, because the scouts had alerted Cole to more difficult terrain ahead on the north bank. Bennett and the pioneer company were in for another day of hard work:

> The column commenced moving after six o'clock and crossed the river with little delay occasioned by the teams being driven aside from the road which I had marked out. 40 or 50 men were detailed to assist who stripped and soon pushed them all over. The guides appear to know as little about the country as we do and the first thing they did was to lead the column into the hills. A nearer and much better rout[e] lay along the river bottom. Capt. Boardman and I directed a portion of the command to go that way. About five miles we came to an impassible slough and ascended the bluffs to get around it, thence over a level plateau. At two points deep narrow ravines intersected it and we had no way of avoiding them or crossing without building bridges which we soon did. Should this country ever become settled, we have made a good road for the people to follow. We saw a herd of about 200 elk, which made off as fast as they could trot when they saw us. We also saw many deer, but did not get a shot at them.

---

[20]Springer, *Soldiering in Sioux Country,* 8.

After selecting a place for encamping, I reconnoitered the country for three or four miles ahead and found it good traveling. Our bridging operations are on [the] most too common to suit all hands on this march. But it must be done. Our last bridge was over a deep ravine. We filled it up six or seven feet with logs & brush, then shoveling on dirt was able to readily cross the command and teams.

One feature in crossing the river this morning was about 75 naked men in the water to assist the teams that got stalled. When the doctor's ambulance went over, in which was his wife, the men all stood at attention with "arms" presented. It is suggested that government provide the men with breech clouts to tie their —— up, like Indians and not cause a too severe shock to the ladies['] modesty.

Several deer have been killed this afternoon and we have a fine roast of venison for breakfast, which Maj. Landgraeber obtained. The Maj. is a fine genial honest Dutchman and we have many hearty laughs at his expense. The Maj. likes whiskey and as it is customary to give a dram to those who have been at work in the water, the Major after returning from bathing calls for his dram because he has been in the water.[21]

Springer again worked with the pioneers: "The next morning as the 11th of July dawned, we crossed the north arm of Loup Fork. As I am permanently detailed as pioneer for our train I superint the crossing of our teams. The bed of the river is mostly quicksand and the banks miry. After a good deal of hard work and the breaking of several wagon tongues, we affected the crossing."

The command camped early and Springer went fishing with bugler Joseph Hewey and "caught some very nice catfish, enough to make us a nice mess."[22]

WEDNESDAY, 12 JULY 1865

Lyman Bennett also worked with the pioneers as the command moved up the south bank of the North Loup. Several formidable obstacles were encountered, slowing the pace of the train. He described a trying day:

Left camp at 5½ A.M., our rout leading over the smooth bottom bordering the river for about five miles, when we struck a ravine coming down

[21]Bennett diary, 11 July 1865 entry.
[22]Springer, *Soldiering in Sioux Country*, 8.

from the hills. Where it entered the river and not 10 feet from it, the beavers had built a dam and raised the water two feet above the river. In their dam was an abundance of fish and while we were improving the road across the dam, the idle ones of the party caught large numbers of fish. About half a mile further, we came to a like stream flowing down from the hills, and hemmed in so close by the bluff that we had to cross by driving into the river and out again on the same side. It required no little digging to get a passage way down into the river. For about three miles more the way was over the dry plain skirting the bluffs. The grass was crisp and dry like hay and cracked under our feet. The grass in this country is all drying up, and there being little if any rain it cures in the sun like hay and remains good feed for buffalo and stock all winter. We came at length to another ravine and beaver dam more difficult to cross than the last. After miring horses, being scratched by the brush and bruised about for some time, exploring a passage, we at length found one next [to] the bluffs above the dam, and while the men were improving the crossing, I went ahead to explore a mountain which rose up before us. After clambering among rocks and crawling along the side of the hill, I found it utterly impossible to pass near the river and sent back to Capt. Boardman to find a way over the hills while I crossed and recrossed the river to find a ford, for if a way over the hills could not be found, fording the stream was our only recourse. Horse fell through the quick sand several times, wetting the sides and on my return I found that a way had been found over the hills and ridges and the party on the march. We went into camp and shortly after the command came up. Marched 10 miles. Found plenty of choke cherries. An Elk was killed by the men and a piece sent to our mess.[23]

Making an assessment of the route traveled on 12 July was made more difficult because neither Bennett nor Springer recorded the miles that the command had moved upriver the previous day. Probably on 11 July, after the river crossing, they went into camp near present-day Elba, Nebraska. The first two streams that they encountered on 12 July would be Auger Creek and Munson Creek. Eight miles further, the command would have been stalled by Davis Creek. While the pioneers improved the road around it, Bennett moved ahead and explored for a route around the "mountain which rose up before us." That mountain is Happy Jack Peak, directly in the line of travel three miles ahead of Davis Creek. While not much of a mountain by western standards, it is the only hill in the area that fits Bennett's descrip-

---

[23]Bennett diary, 12 July 1865 entry.

tion.[24] After moving around Happy Jack Peak, the command went into camp near today's Scotia Junction.

Charles Springer reported, "Some fool set fire to the prairie as we came to a rather big creek. My men went to work lively, and we had just crossed our last wagon when the fire reached the bank." With a smooth road ahead of them, Springer decided to go hunting with one of his men. While chasing an antelope, his horse became mired in a creek bed. As the horse struggled to get out, Springer was unhorsed with his left foot stuck in the stirrup, and he was dragged about fifty yards with the horse running at top speed. "I thought 'Good by Springer' but luckily the grass was long and thick it only cut my hands." He was able to shake his foot loose, "and I lay on the grass bleeding." Fortunately, he was not seriously hurt, and the horse ran a short distance and came back. They headed back, arriving in camp about sundown.[25]

THURSDAY, 13 JULY 1865

The terrain encountered along the North Loup continued to present obstacles for the wagons and challenges for Bennett and the pioneers. He described the day: "A bright warm morning and camp was broken up at 6 A.M., the pioneers as usual in advance. We followed up the river four or five miles and coming to a stream flowing from the west and being difficult to cross it. It was determined to strike across the divide to the main Loup."[26]

Bennett continued:

> After a mile or more of travel we entered the hills following for a short distance an old trail supposed to be that of Lt. Smith of the Topographic Engineers, who made a survey in this region in 1857.

---

[24]Happy Jack Peak is named for a pioneer, Jack Swearengen, who lived near there in the 1870s. During that time, it was used as a lookout for hostile Indian war parties, as at 2,057 feet it is the highest point in the area. The north face of the peak has been excavated to allow today's railroad tracks and Highway 11 to run along the riverside, but Bennett's train had to go around the hills to the south to get by.

[25]Springer, *Soldiering in Sioux Country*, 9–10.

[26]This could have been one of two creeks: Mira Creek, which runs at the northwest side of the present-day town of North Loup, or Dowell Creek, which is about three miles northwest of the town. Today's Mira Creek doesn't look that challenging to cross, while Dowell Creek presents a deep gully, at places a canyon, and would be a formidable obstacle.

Deer, Elk and Antelope were found in great numbers and sometimes would run across our line of march but a short distance from the column. The men would sometimes open on them by platoons & companies, which sounded much like a young battle, but rarely killing any game. Of course I tried my hand at shooting at the animals but with my usual luck. A few Antelope were killed. Our guide shot one through the heart and wounded another.

Large numbers of men are accustomed to leave the command and straggle off in search of game. The Col. had flanking parties out to pick up stragglers and when caught they were dismounted and made to go on foot under arrest. Forty or fifty were thus collected and tramped along under the boiling sun, sick enough of straggling.[27] About 20 miles from camp we ascended a high steep ridge being the main divide between the North Branch and main Loup. And then commenced one of the most crooked ziggy routs of the whole march winding over the divides with deep ravines on either side and discovered many trails made by wild animals and, in one, fresh Buffalo tracks. One dead Buffalo was found near the road. The Indians had fired the grass and miles of the hills were black and bare, the grass being all burned. Most of the command neglected to fill their canteens and suffered much for want of water. The animals were nearly exhausted, when we reached the Loup at 5 P.M. and plunged headlong into the stream and it seemed they would never drink enough. Indians had camped near our camp and at no distant date. Of course, they are hostile Indians, as none other are in this region. We have made 27 miles march, being the farthest we have went in a day since the expedition started over a rough barren and parched up region.[28]

Springer wrote, "July 13th Doctor [George W.] Corey (our regiment surgeon) told me we had to march about 30 miles across country before we came to water, and surely so it proved to be. . . . We struck what is supposed to be the middle branch of the Loup Fork about 5 o'clock P.M. There the men and horses rushed in the water and drank." Colonel Cole had high praise for Springer's company for their work as pioneers, which was conveyed to him through Col. Oliver Wells, regimental commander of the Twelfth Missouri. Colonel Wells said he was pleased and would send the company a canteen of whiskey.[29]

---

[27]Capt. Samuel Flagg of Second Missouri, Battery B, reported, "Private James Craig deserted July 13, stealing two horses fully equipped." Perhaps Private Craig was one of the stragglers who had to march many miles on foot in the hot sun. Flagg's official report of 20 September 1865, *The War of Rebellion.*

[28]Bennett diary, 13 July 1865 entry.

[29]Springer, *Soldiering in Sioux Country*, 10.

Where they picked up the Middle Loup River is another best-guess situation that depends on the angle that they came across country. By measuring mileage back from the mouth of the Dismal River, which they would pass on 19 July, it appears that they came to the river north of today's Arcadia, Nebraska.

FRIDAY, 14 JULY 1865

A new element of danger was introduced to the command as Bennett recalled an uneventful day followed by chaos after dark:

> The march was not resumed until 8 A.M. in order to give the stock as much rest as possible. The rout was up the left bank of the Loup in a northwesterly direction. Fortunately we had no bluffs to climb, the road leading along the bottom, which in some places was two miles wide. Country dry and sandy. The pioneers had but one place to repair at the crossing of a small dry creek bed. The work was but slight and no delay to the column was caused. But little timber along the Loup and few wild animals were seen. The Indians have burned much of the grass in the valley and on the bluffs.
>
> We marched but nine miles and camped on the bottom where [there] was excellent grass. In the evening a thunder shower came up, but very little water fell, enough to wet the grass and make it disagreeable getting about.
>
> About nine o'clock at night I had lain down and was just going off into dream land when a commotion among the stock awakened me and peering out into the darkness a confused moving mass of horses and mules was observed in full tilt down along the lines towards the lower part of camp. A stampede had commenced among the stock in the upper part of camp, and as they passed along the lines, reinforcements were added until the whole camp was in commotion. Those that were fastened to wagons or picket ropes reared and kicked, and many broke loose and joined the frightened throng. Most of the stock was hobbled and it was amusing to see the awkward plunges they made. The pickets on the lower end of camp was aroused and tried in vain to stop the surging column, some foolishly fired their carbines which added to the fright and speed of the animals. About two thirds of the stock of the command in this manner broke loose and cleared out. Mounted men were sent after them and collected a large number, but large numbers escaped and were traced many miles on the line of march. Some men were trampled on while sleeping and seriously injured. Tents were run over and torn down and the tattered fragments but

added to the wild circus of the flight. It was a wild scene. Their flights over the ground was heard a long distance and resembled the deep roar of a tornado. My horse was missing among the others and it was no use hunting for him in the darkness.[30]

Springer had gone fishing after dinner, but that ended quickly due to the oppressive heat and gnats and mosquitoes. He "killed a blowing viper, one of the most poisonous of snakes and returned to camp. In the evening I lit a candle and set in the wagon reading, when the thunderstorm broke loose in all its fury, the rain came down in torrents; all at once I heard a noise, as of a herd of buffaloes or horses galloping: I looked out of the wagon, and saw all our horses at top speed going down the river. Stampede, the terror of the lives on the plains." Springer woke his company and was out all night rounding up the horses. In the dark his horse stepped in a prairie dog hole, and Springer was unhorsed again. "I got my ribs bruised and had to give up the chase."[31]

Capt. Samuel Flagg also reported the night's events: "On the night of July 14, while camped on the bank of Loup Fork, by some cause unknown a general stampede occurred. Recovered all our horses except eight."[32] The stampede probably took place near present-day Comstock, Nebraska, with thunder and lightning the apparent cause.

Saturday, 15 July 1865

Colonel Cole made a decision to stay in camp for the day while parties were sent out to retrieve the horses and mules. Bennett had a chance to catch up on his mapping and recorded what went on in camp during an idle day that also included visitors:

> The horse question agitated the camp this morning and as soon as it was light enough to discern objects on the plains, parties were out in search of missing property. Some were found at no great distance and small squads were being brought in. My horse had not gone more than a mile and like a sensible beast gave up the chase and went to grazing. Orderly Jacks had him back by sunrise. No one knows the cause of the stampede. Probably some mule with more devil than work in him sent the evil spirits into the herd, as was done to the swine in bible days, and away they all went, devils and all.

[30]Bennett diary, 14 July 1865 entry.
[31]Springer, *Soldiering in Sioux Country*, 11–12.

Lt. Amsden of the Signal Corps was sent upon a high hill ½ mile away with a telescope to see if he could discover horses in the distance. Arriving at his position and making his observations without discovering horses, he signaled with a flag the results of his observation. A soldier saw the signal and not knowing he was out, came running to the Col. and informed him that Indians were on the bluff waiving a flag of truce. Of course the mistaken zeal of the soldier produced a laugh among those who knew the secret.

Parties with horses kept dropping into camp all day until all but about fifty horses were recovered; some of them went fifty miles before being overtaken. In the evening Little Chief, the chief of the Omahas with two half breeds came into camp with about 20 horses and mules. He had found them 30 miles away and brought them to us. The Omahas were hunting on the north branch and saw the column as it passed, but did not reveal themselves, and had escaped our notice. When they found the stock they concluded to follow up and see who we were. Coming in sight of camp, his Indians were afraid of being killed and secreted themselves in the bluffs while their chief and the two half breeds came to camp. When assured of being treated friendly the remainder of his party was sent for and came into camp and remained over.

Little Chief was an old man dressed in a suit of broadcloth the same as the whites. On each shoulder he wore an epaulet like the Generals in former times and suspended from his neck was a large silver medal worth five or six dollars with the head of President Fillmore on one side and an inscription on the other. Many of his Indians were dressed in old fashioned grenadier or bombardier coats, fancifully decorated with gold lace, bell buttons, and tinselry. They were the best looking Indians I ever saw. Of course a crowd was constantly around them to gaze and talk with them. It required an enormous amount of provisions and coffee to do them. They acted as if they had had nothing to eat in a month. A little whiskey touched their sympathies the best and they gave many grunts of satisfaction with the Major who gave them the liquor.

I have improved this idle day in platting up my notes and making maps. Still I am somewhat behind. One can do but little while constantly on the march.[33]

Springer spent the night retrieving animals. "I returned to camp about 11 o'clock A.M. the next morning. Today the command layed [*sic*] over, and a good many horses were brought in, but my stallion 'Charley' my good beautiful Charley not amongst them."[34]

---

[32]Flagg's official report of 20 September 1865, *The War of Rebellion.*
[33]Bennett diary, 15 July 1865 entry.
[34]Springer, *Soldiering in Sioux Country*, 12.

SUNDAY, 16 JULY 1865

Bennett reported on the day's travel:

> Marched 12 miles in a northwest direction along the north bank of the Loup. Separate parties had not returned who were out in search of missing stock and we camped early for them to come up. By night all were in, but few animals were brought in. Our losses foot up about 40 horses and mules. Lt. Amsden of the Signal Corps is short two mules but as his load is light, he hopes to get along with the two that are left.
>
> Portions of our rout was quite sandy. We make a road that will never be obliterated, and selecting the best places. Should this ever become a thoroughfare, I believe the line will be where we now pass. Timber is getting scarce and the Loup is materially smaller. Still there is an abundance of wood and water for camping purposes.
>
> Col. Cole is badly poisoned with ivy and one of his eyes is swelled until it is entirely closed. Have seen but little game and none has been caught today.[35]

Springer wrote, "We received orders to march at 6 o'clock accordingly we started. The men, who had lost horses in the stampede, were ordered to go with the wagons as pioneers, as I had extra horses, only three of my men had to walk." With the horse-hunting parties still out, the command did not march far, so that the search parties could catch up. "I went fishing again and catched a nice 'Hickory shad', also my orderly sergeant caught a blue catfish, weighing about 5 pounds." Charley was still missing.[36]

Cole's command continued its trek northwest through central Nebraska Territory, now entering the infamous Sandhill country.

---

[35]Bennett diary, 16 July 1865.
[36]Springer, *Soldiering in Sioux Country,* 12.

CHAPTER FIVE

17–25 July

THE SANDHILL COUNTRY

The sand areas, or hills, so often spoken of, are also found in the western portion of the State, chiefly along the Upper Loups and the Niobrara, and some of their tributaries: also on the south side of the Platte, where they run parallel with the stream, and are from one to six miles wide. In the northern part of the state, however, they cover much larger areas. These hills are composed of fine sand, pebbles and gravel, and in some places are covered with nutritious grasses, and are stationary, while in other places, again, they are entirely barren, and the sand so loosely compacted that the wind is ever changing their form.

This sand region has never been thoroughly explored nor properly investigated. Some scientists have undertaken to account for these hills by the theory that the winds in the course of ages have blown the sand from the bars on the rivers; but there are many difficulties in the way of this theory, as in many places the hills are composed of pebbles and stones that could not well have been moved by the wind.

Numerous important streams rise in this sand region of the northern part of the State, among which are the Loups, the Elkhorn, Cedar and Calamus flowing southward, and the Pines, Evergreen, Plum, and Fairfield Creeks, flowing northwardly to the Niobrara.

Harrison Johnson[1]

MONDAY, 17 JULY 1865

The command entered the Sandhill country of north central Nebraska. Very little has changed since Harrison Johnson's description of the country was written in 1880, except that cattle have replaced the buf-

---

[1]Johnson, *Johnson's History of Nebraska*, 75.

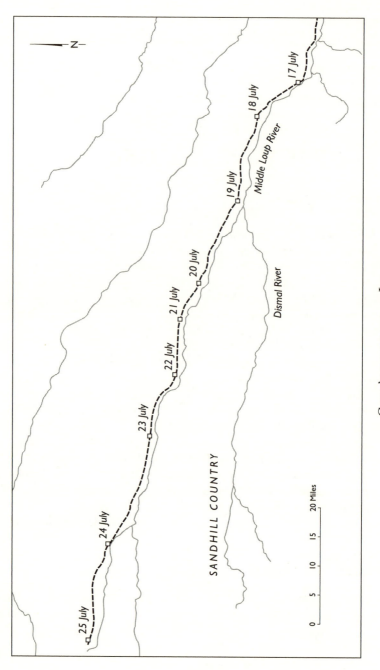

COLE'S ROUTE, 17–25 JULY

falo that used to roam this region. Bennett wrote of an uneventful but productive day's march:

> Commenced the march at 6 A.M. The road at times was more than a mile from the river. Our course was very straight and over good roads. We were able to avoid sand hills and bad places and accomplished 20 miles by 1 P.M. and camped on a fine bottom where wood and grass were in abundance. The wood was on the same side [of] the stream that the camp was. Generally wood is on the opposite side and the men wade after it in all kinds of costumes from the simple one given by nature to a shirt and a pair of drawers. I have laughed to see careful men, before starting into the river, carefully roll up their pants above the knees and before half way across, find the water waste [sic] deep, not only wetting their pants but every garment about them. It rained during the night. The soil is so sandy that no amount of rain can make it muddy.[2]

Springer described a countryside growing bleaker while wondering if the Yellowstone River was the possible destination. He mentions that "Signs of Indians are here plenty, old camps and carcasses of buffaloes lately killed, but we have not seen any Indians yet, except the day before yesterday when a chief of the Omahas with 4 warriors and a Chief of the Caws with one warrior visited our camp."[3]

Tuesday, 18 July 1865

The command continued northwest into the sandhill country, as Bennett described a wet morning:

> The rain continued in the morning and for a time it was doubtful if a movement would be made. About 9 A.M. it stopped raining, but a mist was swept over the ground, nearly as bad as rain in wetting ones clothes. The tall grass in camp was loaded with water and I got my feet and clothes completely soaked. We marched fourteen miles over tolerably fair roads. In some places they were sandy and heavy for the wagons. The sand hills are approaching nearer the river than heretofore and some times rise up from the very banks, and so loose that a horse can get among them with difficulty. Near our camp were fresh signs of Indians. Those accustomed to them said that these tracks were not more than 24 hours old. They had

[2]Bennett diary, 17 July 1865 entry.
[3]Springer, *Soldiering in Sioux Country,* 13.

evidently left in haste showing that they had become aware of our approach and fled, taking every precaution to hide their trail and going off in every direction among the hills. A party was sent out who found that their different trails united about 8 miles away and that they had went north. No clue could be had of what tribe they belonged to.

Our Pawnee guides have given me the name of Pohote the Willa, which when translated into English means the hill climber. This arises from my frequently climbing hills to take observations.

Very little wild fruit has been found in this region. I have found some today entirely new to me called sand cherries, growing on a vine much like a strawberry vine on the poorest, most sandy and desolate places. The fruit is nearly as large as tame cherries, black when ripe and rather bitter to the taste, but after all not bad to eat. They can be gathered in bushels on the sand hills. Occasionally a patch of Choke Cherries is found on low bushes and are very fine. Wild grapes are sometimes found but very sour, green and small. Rained most of the day.[4]

Springer was officer of the day. After the march, "one of my men caught several fine catfish, one of them weighing about 7 pounds. I had a good supper."[5]

WEDNESDAY, 19 JULY 1865

The daily mileage total reported by Bennett was not calculated very scientifically so far. Although odometers on wagons were in use in this era, none were installed on any of the train's wagons until later in the expedition.[6] At this point of the journey, miles traveled were estimated by taking the pace of the train multiplied by the time traveled. The variable here is that this doesn't take into account the time lost while

---

[4]Bennett diary, 18 July 1865 entry.

[5]Springer, *Soldiering in Sioux Country*, 13–14. Springer is now one day out of synch with Bennett's journal. To make this timeline work, I have moved Springer back one day to fall in line with Bennett. I made this decision because I believe that Bennett's diary was written in real time, whereas Springer's appears to be transcribed from notes at a later date. Colonel Cole's report generally coincides with Bennett on dates. I believe that Springer became confused with his notes and added an additional day on 18 July. Bennett is very methodical with his note taking, including heading each day's entry with the day of the week, month, and date, while Springer's style is a looser, sometimes rambling style. Springer's diary moves back in phase with Bennett's timeline on 1 September 1865, as he records two September firsts.

[6]Bennett diary, 24 August 1865 entry.

the pioneers cleared the roadway ahead in rough terrain, stream crossings, etc. Under these circumstances, Bennett's estimates of miles
traveled were reasonably accurate. He described the day's march:

> Commenced the march at 5½ A.M. The sun came up clean and bright and
> the air was just cool enough for marching and we made good progress over
> very good roads, skirting the sand hills. The valley is getting very narrow
> and in places there is but little room for the road between the bluffs and
> river, there again the valley swells out and there is a fine basin, an
> amphitheater surrounded with sand hills. Patches of timber, mostly on
> islands are scattered at intervals along the river. We passed the mouth of
> Dismal River, a large stream coming into the Loup from the south.
> Marched seventeen miles and camped in the bottom near the river bank,
> wood and grass plenty. There are several species of grass here entirely dif-
> ferent from any that grows on the prairies in the states. Some species is
> very tall and fine. Rained during the Afternoon.[7]

The Dismal River enters the Middle Loup River from the southwest, less than a mile east of today's Dunning, Nebraska. From this
point on, the Middle Loup diminishes in size quite rapidly, although
it still has miles to go before its headwaters.

According to Springer, "The weather was extremely hot and cloudy.
After pitching headquarters, my bugler Joseph Hewey went fishing and
caught two catfish, each weighing about 6 pounds; toward evening we
had a hard rain, but it didn't last long." Later that evening he joined
seven other officers out for a "good joke":

> I always enjoy a good joke, and wouldn't allow a good opportunity to slip
> by; I went with them to camp 'E' of our regiment. Capt. [Jefferson] Miller
> who commands the company is a member of the church, don't take any of
> the ardent, and even don't swear; although I am no great friend of all this
> neither, but people must excuse a soldier, and I know they do, if once in a
> while in case of provocation he slips one of them 24 pound rifled oaths, but
> this Miller professed and all occasions proclaimed that he was strictly a vir-
> tuous man. Now he had a women in the company as laundress, who run
> away from her husband, who at the time was very sick; some of our offi-
> cers always on the "look out" for something "new" heard the rumor that
> Captain Miller paid that woman who was sleeping in the wagon noctur-
> nal visits, and that was what the officers were after to ascertain; accord-

---

[7]Ibid., 19 July 1865 entry.

ingly we went, armed with lighted candles to his wagon, acted drunken, raising the cover at once all around the wagon, and calling Captain Miller to join our fun. There we found this muster of man in bed with the woman. We all broke out in an indescribable laughter. Captain Miller looked thunderstruck; He was so confused that he couldn't say a word, only stammered: gentlemen; gentlemen.[8]

At least two women traveled with the expedition, the laundress who slept with Captain Miller and Doctor Corey's wife, mentioned earlier by Bennett on 11 July. Springer also told of the doctor's wife in his 5 September entry. Although no evidence of other women traveling with the expedition has surfaced, Civil War regulations allowed up to four laundresses per company.[9] With sixteen companies between the two regiments, the probability of other women traveling with the expedition was strong.

First Lt. William Rinne of Battery C, Second Missouri Artillery, reported, "Private Nicolas Thomason, with one horse and equipment, was missing while detailed on flanking duty and was supposed captured by Indians on the 19th day of July."[10] Indian signs were discovered the following day, so that may have been the case. One must wonder, though, if Private Thomason might have deserted, as Private Craig had on 13 July.

THURSDAY, 20 JULY 1865

Signs of an Indian war party were discovered and another stampede occurred on the day's march, as told by Bennett:

---

[8]Springer, *Soldiering in Sioux Country*, 14–15.

[9]"Four laundresses are allowed to each company, and soldiers wives may be, and generally are, mustered in that capacity. They are then entitled to the same quarters, fuel, and rations as a soldier, and the established pay for the washing they may do for soldiers and officers." August V. Kautz, *The 1865 Customs of Service for Non-commissioned Officers and Soldiers*, 12–13, item 11. Louis LeGrand, *The Military Hand-Book and Soldiers Manual of Information*, 35–36, states, "Washer Women: . . . Their duties are those of washer-women to the men. The price of the washing is prescribed, and is paid out of the soldier's monthly pay. The women are liable to be discharged or 'drummed out of camp' in event of any gross misconduct, drunkenness, or breach of camp etiquette. Each woman is required to have a certificate of good character from headquarters before she can assume duty within the lines."

[10]Lieutenant Rinne's official report, 20 September 1865, *The War of Rebellion*.

The Loup is getting more narrow and rapid. Is very crooked and full of islands. Timber is disappearing and the fuel is now mostly brush. Marched 18 miles and camped in a dry pretty valley with plenty of grass but little wood. A few fish were caught, mostly small.

We found signs of Indians. At one point were marked in the sand three horse shoes and a stick pointing to the north. Our Pawnee guides interpreted this as an indication that a war party had been there, had been up the two branches of the river but met no enemies. The horse shoes indicated that of few horses had been stolen and the stick; that they had gone northward.

A stampede of horses occurred this afternoon, but the men were out and stopping most of them, about fifty escaped. Men are out after them and will no doubt bring them all back.[11]

After the day's march, at 7 P.M. Springer was reading a book at his campsite. "I start up from my seat, throw down the book, and see the horses of the 2nd Missouri Artillery galloping furiously through our camp. In a moment I saw what it was; a stampede." He sprang to action and helped bring back the horses, which "were nearly all recaptured a few hours afterward."[12]

FRIDAY, 21 JULY 1865

In the aftermath of the second stampede, a new element was introduced that may have had a connection as to the cause of the stampedes, as Bennett described the events:

> The parties in pursuit of horses not returning, we laid in camp until 2 P.M., and then only marched three miles to a place where there was plenty of grass. Wood, I fear, has disappeared except a little brush which suffices to cook with.
>
> When ready to start, a number of men in Co. H refused to go any farther. The Col. went to the Co. and ordered the Lt. [Phillip Smiley] in command to move out and shoot the first man who disobeyed.[13] The Lt. mounted his men and then told them that the first son of a b—— who refused to march when he gave the order, he would shoot. The threat had

---

[11]Bennett diary, 20 July 1865 entry.

[12]Springer, *Soldiering in Sioux Country*, 15–16.

[13]Second Lt. Phillip Smiley was a member of Battery H, Twelfth Missouri Cavalry. *Civil War Soldiers and Sailors System*.

the desired effect and none fell back. Arriving at camp, a court marshale [*sic*] was called and the men tried. What the result is has not transpired. I hope it will be severe enough to put a stop to the spirit of insubordination which exists, and I am sorry to say among some of the officers. Col. Cole however is a man of energy and determination and will not be rode, even by officers. No game has been seen for two days.[14]

The Loup is here a deep narrow stream flowing rapidly over a pebblely bed. A short distance above [is] the hill that is in so close that we will have to travel over the bluffs.

Capt. Montgomery came back with all the horses but three.[15] He went fifty miles for some of them. It seems that the devil gets into the horses. I have worked hard all day on my platts [*sic*] and still there is much to do.[16]

In the morning Springer found out that there were still forty horses from the Second Missouri and ten horses from his own regiment missing. The command spent the morning in camp waiting for the search parties to come in. "At 1 o'clock we started, the bugle sounded forward, but no forward movement was made, and at last we heard that one company of the 2nd Missouri Artillery had refused to march any further, but they finally concluded it's best for them to go."[17]

Saturday, 22 July 1865

Bennett described a wet, miserable morning:

A cold damp disagreeable day for marching. The rain continued to drizzle all the time we were on the road, completely saturating our cloths and wetting to the skin. Twice we were obliged to leave the river and toil over the bluffs for some distance. The hills shutting in the valley until it was impossible to pass thru. We marched 8 miles and camped at 3 P.M. The rain ceased, but the grass was wet and disagreeable getting around. The stream is getting smaller and very crooked with frequent patches of timber. I observed some cedar in the cañons, among the bluffs I found some wild currants that were very large and fine, also choke cherries and acres of wild

---

[14]The mutiny probably took place in the vicinity of today's Thedford, Nebraska. The results of the court martial are not known, as Cole made no mention of the incident in either of his official reports.

[15]Capt. William C. F. Montgomery was in Battery H. *Civil War Soldiers and Sailors System.*

[16]Bennett diary, 21 July 1865 entry.

[17]Springer, *Soldiering in Sioux Country,* 16.

cherries. The currants were as large as grapes. Another stampede occurred among the horses, but few escaped. Parties are out after them. In the evening Lt. Amsden sent up two rockets to indicate to the parties that were out, where our camp was. It was terribly dark. Marched 17 miles.[18]

Springer complained that "The weather was very cold and a fine drizzly rain come down constantly; as someone had stolen my Indian rubber coat I got soaking wet, and felt very chilly." After dinner at about five o'clock, another horse stampede occurred. Springer speculated on the cause of the stampedes, writing, "The 2nd Mo. Art. men are making the horses stampede, maliciously and willfully in order to turn the expedition to the nearest military post; they are dissatisfied, they have in all their soldier life never been out of Missouri; now for the first time they have to leave the flesh pots of Egypt and came down to the right hard soldiering, they want to back out."[19]

Springer may have been right about the Second Missouri causing the stampede to sabotage the expedition. What better way to cause the expedition to abort than a loss of its animals? Colonel Cole probably had to look no farther than Battery H of his own regiment for the culprits who had attempted to sabotage the mission.

Sunday, 23 July 1865

The Loup continued to get smaller and the valley had all but disappeared, as Bennett described the day:

> Resumed the march at 5½ A.M. The road leading over the bluffs it is found impossible to ascend the valley any higher. The bluffs are precipitous and approached very near the river. In short, it is no longer a valley but a cañnon [sic]. Occasionally the bottoms widen out affording room for camping purposes. The water is cold and clear and quite rapid with numerous patches of timber upon the banks. If this continues we shall not lack for wood. The roads are very crooked winding around the irregular hills and sometimes up and then down the steep sides. Of course we make our own roads. Getting on some high points the views were magnificent, especially when they overlook the river valley.

---

[18]Bennett diary, 22 July 1865 entry.
[19]Springer, *Soldiering in Sioux Country*, 16–17.

I have not been very well today, but hope to wear out any disease that may get hold of me. Marched 15 miles.

About noon the clouds cleared away and the sun shone out bright and pleasant. Tonight it is raining again.[20]

MONDAY, 24 JULY 1865

Bennett wrote about some horses and mules beginning to wear down:

> Reveille was sounded long before daylight and the camp in a bustle of preparation for marching. We eat breakfast in a hurry, saddled in a hurry and was off shortly after five. It took some time to get the train up the hills from the valley where we camped, it being steep and sandy.
>
> We left the river at some distance marching among the irregular hills which cover the country everywhere. It was cool and pleasant marching. Our road was a repetition of the same devious windings as yesterday among the hills. Nothing of note occurred on the way, the march was steady and uninterrupted. A few horses and mules gave out and were left. The stock which gives out are those which stampeded and have been run down and over tasked. One fellow seeing a horse left behind, pulled the saddle from the one he was riding and put it on the abandoned animal and sent his own horse ahead. His newly acquired steed would not go and he had to foot it a mile or two and carry his saddle on his back until he caught up with his own horse.
>
> Saw several deer and antelope, a few were killed. Camped on the bluffs overlooking the Loup which here is a small creek, not more than ten or twelve feet wide, sending down the stock for water. Wood plenty, grass poor. Marched 17 miles.[21]

Springer reported, "We cannot follow the river bottom anymore, but have to take up in the hills." He took a five-mile walk with Private McBeath after arriving in camp and found signs of an old Indian camp, "killing a big viper on the way home."[22]

TUESDAY, 25 JULY 1865

As the command neared the head of the Middle Loup River, which they had been following for weeks, Cole recalled the firewood situa-

---

[20]Bennett diary, 23 July 1865 entry.
[21]Ibid., 24 July 1865 entry.
[22]Springer, *Soldiering in Sioux Country*, 17–18.

tion: "When near the head of the Loup wood entirely gave out and the command was forced to resort to buffalo chips, of which a very limited quantity could be found. Bog peat was also used as substitute for wood, of which there was considerable quantities found on this part of the route."[23]

Bennett gave a good description of the monotonous sandhill country:

> We were off in good time, striking off among the bluffs. The hills are arranged the most singular I ever saw being dotted irregularly over the country without violating all known laws in relation to hills. There are no continuous ranges. The valleys are of all shapes and sizes; are entirely distinct from each other. One would think in the neighborhood of a stream, ravines would lead into it from the surrounding country. Not so, however one is as apt to run away from the river as into it. This soil is less sandy today and the roads were tolerable hard, the wagons cutting in but little. The guides know no more about the country than I do and today lead us off our course and we performed at least five miles of additional travel in getting to the river to camp. Reached the stream about 2 P.M. Plenty of grass but not a stick of wood or brush. The men picked up buffalo chips for fuel. The creek is very small with marshy banks, is no more than 3 or 4 feet width and heads about 5 miles above. More game was seen today than anytime in the march.
>
> Antelope and deer were plenty. A wolf was caught. The flanking party reports a trail of ponies and horses going north. Also five ponds of water and good grass off from the river. Marched 18 miles.[24]

Springer described the terrain as endless sand hills and sand plains, which made for "weary and tiresome marching. . . . [G]ood water explains the presence of so much game."[25]

The Middle Loup branches into three smaller streams near its headwaters. The command probably followed the northernmost of these streams, simply because it fits their line of march. They were now approximately ten miles north of today's Whitman, Nebraska, in what is still an inaccessible, primitive area. Springer's description of endless sand hills and plains is right on the money. It is tedious to drive through today, even in a matter of hours, making it hard to fathom traveling through it for weeks at ten to fifteen miles per day.

---

[23]Cole's official report, 10 February 1867, Hafen and Hafen, *Powder River Campaigns*, 63.

[24]Bennett diary, 25 July 1865 entry.

[25]Springer, *Soldiering in Sioux Country*, 18–19.

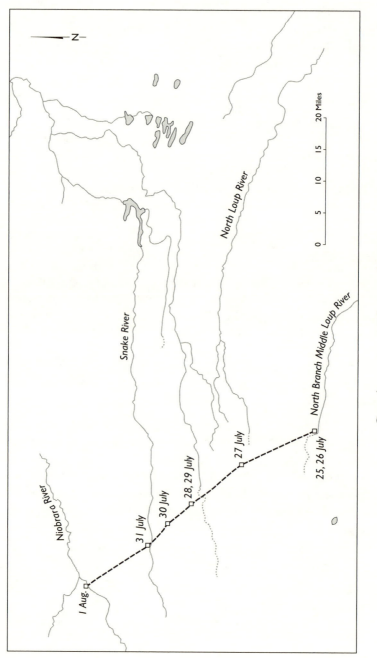

COLE'S ROUTE, 26 JULY–1 AUGUST

CHAPTER SIX

26 July–1 August

TO THE NIOBRARA

WEDNESDAY, 26 JULY 1865

With his command at the head of the Middle Loup, in barren country, with inadequate maps and incompetent guides, Colonel Cole pondered his next move. A wrong decision could bring disaster down on his command. He reported:

> I had many misgivings as to the practicability of moving a command as large as mine across the country from the head of the Loup to the Niobrara River, as my information was, in effect, that the region to be traversed was a barren, sandy desert, without fresh water, wood, or grass. To be positive, I lay in camp one day for the purpose of scouting for the best route. I sent two parties, one on Lieutenant [G. K.] Warren's trail, who returned reporting that the route impassable for trains, with but little grass and ponds of brackish water. The other party sent to the north or more direct line to the Niobrara River, reported a practicable route with excellent grass and water in abundance.[1]

Colonel Cole assigned Lyman Bennett to lead the party north toward the Niobrara. Lieutenant Amsden of the Signal Corps headed the party to the west. Bennett described the day:

> The Loup was found to head about five miles above camp and six miles up the valley and not more than a mile above where the stream commences there is not the first indication of water.

---

[1]Cole's official report, 10 February 1867, Hafen and Hafen, *Powder River Campaigns*, 63–64.

The Col. sent me out with a party of men to explore the country to the north towards the Niobrara in search of water and grass as well as a feasible rout.

Another party under Lt. Amsden was sent further west near the route pursued by Lt. Warren in 1856. I took a course over the hills bearing N 35 W noting the hills and valleys over which we passed as well as on either flank. About five miles out we came to a small shallow pond in a large valley with fine grass. As water was the grand item of my search, I took note of the miserable water hole and pushed on just over the ridge and about a mile and a half was another small water hole in a similar valley. A wet marsh was near the pond with a narrow dry ridge between. Over another ridge and another valley was found excellent grass but no water. The country is a succession of high ridges and narrow valleys running nearly east and west with small ponds and good grass in the valleys. The ridges are sandy and generally impassible, we were lucky enough to find practicable passes over the ridge. About noon the horses were much fatigued and we stopped at a water hole to rest. Mr. Raymond, the guide, went ahead about two miles and found a good size lake with brush and one Box Elder tree on the banks. Satisfied with this important discovery, we took the back trail for camp. I had the men march by file in order to make as distinct a trail as possible. By winding about the valleys and hills we found an excellent route for a road. Reached camp about 4 P.M. The Col. was well pleased with my report but forbore to decide which rout to take until Lt. Amsden's return. I saw considerable game mostly antelope but no buffalo or sign of Indians. At dark Lt. Amsden and his party was not in. The QM Lt Thorn was also missing.[2] One of the cannon was hauled upon the hill overlooking camp and fired every ten minutes in order to attract the attention of the missing ones and direct their course. Signal rockets were also sent up making a fine display. About 10 o'clock Lt. Amsden came in. He had traveled about 20 miles finding no water except near camp and night coming on he had resolved to camp out but the firing of our guns attracted his attention and he came in. Lt. Thorn came in about 12 o'clock. He had been lost among the hills and made the entire circuit of our camp having traveled 75 miles and when our signals were discovered, he was 10 miles south of us. Springs are near the camp with excellent water.[3]

Springer spent the day hunting antelope without success. After hunting he rode with the flankers and promptly got lost in the sand

---

[2]Lt. George R. Thorne of the Second Missouri Light Artillery was the acting assistant quartermaster and acting commissary of subsistence. Ibid., 90.

[3]Bennett diary, 26 July 1865 entry.

hills. His party wandered for several hours and did not get back to camp until 6 P.M.[4]

THURSDAY, 27 JULY 1865

In the morning Colonel Cole decided on Bennett's route and the command headed north, as Bennett described the day:

> The Col. decided upon the rout explored by me and at an early hour the camp was aroused and the march commenced. We left the Loup Valley above where the last trace of water was found. We have thus followed up a long river for near 300 miles from its mouth to its very source and above. At first it was near a half mile in width, gradually it lessens in width and volume until it becomes a narrow rapid creek flowing down a deep cañon. Then a mere rivulet that can be easily stepped over with marshy banks. I never before followed a stream so closely as this.
>
> Our road was a good one today. The train came all right, keeping nearly up with the column. A few antelope and deer were killed and we obtained a little for our mess. We reached the lake and finding the grass on the other side, we camped there. Some one set fire to the dry grass and weeds bordering the lake and a big fire was the consequence, which required the whole command to put out. The lake we called Lake Raymond from our guide who first discovered it.
>
> After dinner Col. Cole and I took a ramble over the bluffs to explore the country and discovered another finer lake than the first, which I called Lake Cole from the Col. It was a fine sheet of water. Plenty of water fowl and some were shot. From the bluffs magnificent views were attained of the surrounding country. I found some cherries and enjoyed myself much in galloping over the hills.
>
> In front of camp is a fine bottom with excellent grass. Marched 16 miles & ½.[5]

Springer recalled the day: "[T]raveled very near due north, left the valley of the Loup Fork, and came over the same ground where I had been the day before; we encamped on a nice lake. The weather was very hot, and towards evening it commenced raining hard. There is not a particle of wood to be found. Buffalo chips are very scarce also,

---

[4]Springer, *Soldiering in Sioux Country,* 19–20.
[5]Bennett diary, 27 July 1865 entry.

but we managed to cook with but little fire. Game of every description in abundance."[6]

The country that Bennett described still looks much as it probably did in 1865. Unfortunately the names of the lakes—Lake Raymond and Lake Cole—did not survive, and as there are hundreds of lakes and ponds in the area, it would be difficult to identify the site.

FRIDAY, 28 JULY 1865

The expedition continued to probe its way north through the sand hills, as Bennett recorded the day's activities:

> Capt. Boardman was sent yesterday to explore the route of today. As the stock is getting worn down, we marched but 8½ miles today, winding among the hills and through fine valleys. One large dry basin, evidently the basin of a lake was surrounded with a strip of timber which was like an oasis in the desert. Although this is a miserable desolate country, yet there are some magnificent scenery. It is strange and entirely different from anything I have ever seen. We camped on a small stream running northeast. The water was dark and filthy but was the best we could get. Valleys, hills, lakes, ponds and marshes are the characteristics of the country. No game found. Marched 8½ miles.
>
> I noticed around Lake Raymond a parapet of earth formed by the action of the wind and water, by the grass and refuse matter in the lake floating to the shore and there remaining, forming in the course of ages a high embankment nearly as singular and perfect as if formed by the hand of man. This dike or parapet runs nearly around the lake and is from two to four feet high.[7]

Springer was not happy as he described the campsite: "We marched only 10 miles and encamped, rather mean ground not a particle of wood, the water is scarce and nasty." In the evening the mood lightened up as bugler Vetter sang sentimental songs that included "The Last Rose of Summer," "Washington's Grave," "In the Times When I Was Hard Up," "You Want to be a Soldier Badly," and "Come and Serve Old Uncle Sam." His descriptions conjure up an image of soldiers gathered around a campfire, far from civilization in the sandhill

[6]Springer, *Soldiering in Sioux Country*, 20–21.
[7]Bennett diary, 28 July 1865 entry.

country, listening to sentimental songs sung by one of their own. Springer also "observed some kind of fireworks on the summit of a high hill. Somebody is lost among the dreaded sand hills."[8]

SATURDAY, 29 JULY 1865

Although Bennett complained about the water at their campsite, the command lay over a day while the stock grazed on the good grass that was available: "We did not march today, but remained in camp on Boardman's Creek. This stream is named after Capt. Boardman who discovered it yesterday and is a tributary of Snake River. There is no map or account of the steams and lakes we have met with on this route; hence we are adding to the geographical knowledge of the region."

The name "Boardman Creek" did survive, and it flows from the west and enters the Snake River north of Mullen, Nebraska, into today's Merritt Reservoir. Bennett continued:

> I have worked at my plats all day and have worked up my notes considerably but am still behind. There is a great deal of topography to put in here. We have splendid grass and our stopping in camp today is on their [the stock?] account. There is however no wood and the men are searching the country over for buffalo chips. Fuel is also obtained from cherry roots. On the sand hills the winds blow the sand entirely away leaving the roots to dry up and die. Considerable fuel is procured from this source. The weather today is bright and warm, but not as hot. Capt. McMurray went on a reconnaissance and found a stream of cold pure water about 8 miles ahead. This is a godsend in a region of sand and dirth.[9]

Springer took advantage of the layover and went hunting. He killed several ducks but was unable to retrieve them from the lake. He spent the afternoon patching his wardrobe.[10]

SUNDAY, 30 JULY 1865

Connor's left, or west, column of the Powder River Indian Expedition departed Fort Laramie on this day, heading northwest toward the

[8]Springer, *Soldiering in Sioux Country*, 21–22.
[9]Bennett diary, 29 July 1865 entry.
[10]Springer, *Soldiering in Sioux Country*, 22.

headwater area of Powder River. Their purpose was two-fold: first, to establish a post on Powder River that would be used as a base of operations now and in the future against the Indians; and secondly, to rendezvous with the two other columns at Panther Mountain in southern Montana. As with the other two columns, they were to attack and punish Indians as they found them.

Connor's command was made up of three companies of the Eleventh Ohio Cavalry, one company each from the Seventh Iowa Cavalry and Second California Cavalry, and a detachment of fourteen men from Cole's Second Missouri Light Artillery. There were also four companies of the Sixth Michigan Cavalry, which numbered about two hundred men. Their role would be to build and man the fort on Powder River. The command had a battalion of seventy-five Pawnee scouts under Capt. Frank North and seventy Winnebago and Omaha scouts commanded by Capt. E. R. Nash. Capt. Henry E. Palmer, acting assistant quartermaster for the command, summed up the expedition: "Not Including the Michigan troops, we had, all told, 404 soldiers and 145 Indians, together with about 195 teamsters and wagon masters in the train." Their train had 185 wagons.[11]

Nelson Cole's eastern column continued to feel its way toward the Niobrara River, as Bennett was chosen to lead a party ahead to determine the route to the river:

> We marched to McMurrays Creek, a clear cold and beautiful stream of water. The best I have found since the expedition commenced. The ridges and hills are higher and more difficult to cross thru here heretofore and the valleys are magnificent with excellent grass. The Col. directed me, with a party of men to go to the Niobrara and note the distance, country & etc. After riding about 8 miles over high steep ridges and fine valleys, we entered a range of the worst sand hills we have yet encountered. After winding among thru and climbing over them, I was surprised to find a large clear stream of water flowing rapidly eastward. It was not large enough for the Niobrara and we concluded it must be Snake River. The maps place the mouth 100 miles east and running but a short distance in the country. Thus we have added another item to the geographical knowledge of this country. Crossing this creek we made our way over the coun-

---

[11]Capt. H. E. Palmer's account, 30 July 1865, Hafen and Hafen, *Powder River Campaigns*, 108–109.

try and ascending a high hill saw the bluffs of the Niobrara in the distance. We estimated it at five miles, but when we came to ride over the country, found it to be near 10 miles. Antelope and deer were numerous and the boys expended many shots uselessly at them. On reaching the Niobrara, we found a fine spring of clear cold water. The river is perhaps 50 yards wide with a rapid current and very clear and pure. I had a good bath and it was some little time before the whole party came up. I observed ledges of calcarions [calcareous] rock and rough rock and pebbles in the bottom of the river. There is plenty of wood along the river principally Cottonwood, Box Elder, Ash & Elm. Pine and Cedar grew in the bluffs a mile beyond the river. The banks are high and steep. Above them the country is very level and will have good roads. It was late as we set out on our return and rode fast to get back to camp before dark. One or two of the horses broke down and were left behind the men coming back in on foot. It was dark before we reached camp and we got a little off our track but heard the bugles sounding tattoo and made our way without further difficulty. The Col. was preparing to send up rocket signal to direct us. I was very tired and went immediately to bed after supper. Marched 8 miles.[12]

Springer wrote that the command "Marched about 5 miles and encamped in the valley where the head of the Snake River is. . . . [P]rettiest streamlet imaginable, so nice, clear and cold."[13] This was actually the stream discovered by Captain McMurray; the Snake was thirteen miles further.

MONDAY, 31 JULY 1865

Cole moved the command to the Snake River and described the firewood situation: "Scarcely any wood found in this section until reaching the Snake River where there was an abundance of cedar."[14]

Bennett reported difficulty in finding a good trail through this section of the sand hills: "Left camp on McMurrays Creek at 6 A.M., the column winding over the hills in a crooked course. Owing to the difficulty of getting through the sand hills, we traveled about five miles more than was necessary a direct road would have taken us. The Col.

[12]Bennett diary, 20 July 1865 entry.
[13]Springer, *Soldiering in Sioux Country*, 22.
[14]Cole's official report, 10 February 1867, Hafen and Hafen, *Powder River Campaigns*, 64.

84   *POWDER RIVER ODYSSEY*

and I went ahead to find a road through the sand hills and while out the column found another road and were in camp before we returned. My horse came near giving out and I was obliged to ride another. Marched 13 miles."[15]

Springer recorded, "We marched 15 miles through some awful sand-hills, and I arrived at the headwaters of the Snake River at 1 o'clock P.M. where we pitched camp. . . . My black servant, Sam was lost hunting, among the sand-hills."[16]

Tuesday, 1 August 1865

The Niobrara River runs from its headwaters in eastern Wyoming across northern Nebraska and empties into the Missouri River about thirty-six miles west of Yankton, South Dakota. The command set out for this landmark on the journey, as Bennett observed:

> Capt. McMurray's Aid de Camp procured a cedar post and with a jack knife smoothed it and then cut letters giving the date and circumstances of the expedition, and set it in an elevated position near the crossing of Snake River. Should others pass through after us, they will here find a record of our travel.
>
> Commenced the march early over hilly country, but not as rough as what we have previously passed through. By winding among the hills we found a good road and after about six miles travel came to a smooth plain. While the column was halted, I endeavored to discover the mouth of Antelope Creek with a telescope. I saw a depression in the hills at the point we were aiming at which I judged to be the creek. Our guides thought differently and the column diverged from its course to the right and after about 4 miles travel on a good road over the level plain, we struck the Niobrara River at a ford where again food was found and about three miles above Antelope Creek, thus proving that I was correct in the location of the stream. A crossing was soon affected and camp formed on the bluffs overlooking the north bank of the river. Lt. Amsden & I took a fine bath in the clean limpid waters of the Niobrara. The country changes here materially from that we have been marching over. The sand hills disappear. A hard clayey soil affords a good road bed and the hills are more gentle swells over which a wagon can pass anywhere. The grass is stunted and

[15]Bennett diary, 31 July 1865 entry.
[16]Springer, *Soldiering in Sioux Country*, 23.

the region sterile and dry. The bottom of the Niobrara is very narrow and confined between high rocky bluffs affording but little room for trees which line the bottoms where there is room for a foot hold. In the bluffs I discovered a few pine & cedar. In the bottom was cottonwood, ash, and hackberry, with a variety of shrubbery. I found large quantities of wild cherries and wild currants. The currants were very firm and while the pioneer men prepared the crossing, I picked a hat full which made an excellent desert at dinner. There were two varieties of currants, one yellow the other black and as large as large goose berries. The weather has been quite warm. A strong south wind has prevailed this afternoon.

We have marched 18 miles. This is my birthday, I am 33 years old.[17]

Cole reported, "Where we struck the Niobrara timber was very plenty. . . . Grass was scant, and with my large number of animals it was difficult to obtain sufficient for one night."[18]

Springer wrote that Sam and Private Coulder came back from hunting after supper. "[T]hey had lost their course, and never struck our trail until 12 o'clock today."[19]

The command camped on the bluffs overlooking the north side of the Niobrara River three miles up river from where Antelope Creek empties into the river. This is in an area known today as Coburn Canyon, about nine miles northeast of where Highway 27 crosses the Niobrara, south of Gordon, Nebraska.

---

[17]Bennett diary, 1 August 1865 entry.
[18]Cole's official report, 10 February 1867, Hafen and Hafen, *Powder River Campaigns*, 64–65.
[19]Springer, *Soldiering in Sioux Country*, 23–24.

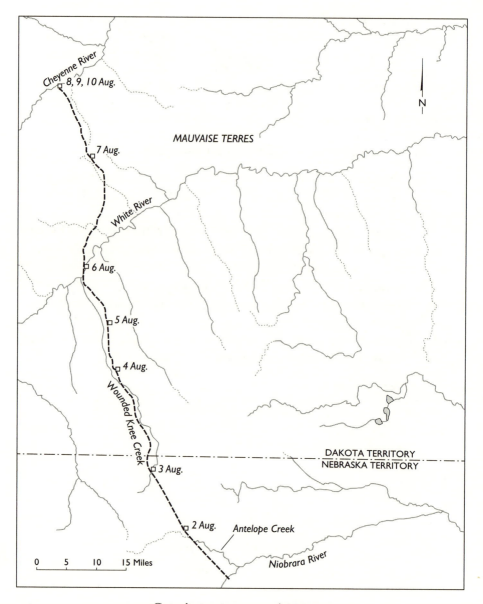

Cheyenne River

8, 9, 10 Aug.

MAUVAISE TERRES

7 Aug.

White River

6 Aug.

5 Aug.

4 Aug.

Wounded Knee Creek

DAKOTA TERRITORY
NEBRASKA TERRITORY

3 Aug.

2 Aug.

Antelope Creek

Niobrara River

0 5 10 15 Miles

N

COLE'S ROUTE, 2–10 AUGUST

CHAPTER SEVEN

2–10 *August*

MAUVAISES TERRES

For centuries humans have viewed South Dakota's celebrated Badlands with a mix of dread and fascination. The Lakota knew the place as mako sica. Early French trappers called the area les mauvaises terres à traverser. Both mean Bad Lands.

Badlands Official Map and Guide[1]

Nelson Cole's command prepared to move northwest into present-day South Dakota, with their route to take them along the eastern slopes of the Black Hills. Their projected path would take them north for several days following Wounded Knee Creek. Where the creek empties into the White River, they would cross and enter into a spectacular scenic area known as Mauvaises Terres, or the Badlands. This is an area of desert landscape made up of multi-colored buttes, peaks, and gullies. It is also a terrain virtually devoid of the grass and water so necessary to sustain their already worn-down stock.

WEDNESDAY, 2 AUGUST 1865

Cole described the landscape where the command traveled: "From the Niobrara our route lay over a gently rolling prairie toward the bluffs at the head of Wounded Knee Creek."[2] This is the same Wounded Knee Creek that twenty-five years later would be forever associated with the

---

[1]*Badlands Official Map and Guide* (National Park Service, U.S. Department of the Interior, GPO 472-470/40143, Reprint, 2001).

infamous Wounded Knee massacre of 1890, which marked the end of the Indian war period in American history.

The command traveled in a northwesterly direction, following the bed of Antelope Creek. Bennett recorded the day:

> We started early this morning, I on foot. My horse got loose during the night and the guard took him up and I could not get him. I went perhaps a mile on foot when the Col. ordered his orderly to bring a horse. Wind from the north and quite cold. The road was hard and smooth, the country quite level. What hills there were very gradual to ascend. There were immense quantities of game all over the plain. The flankers would drive them onto the column and the men would fire and drive it back. The poor frightened animals ran backwards and forwards until quite exhausted and it was not uncommon to see an antelope with his mouth open and so tired he could scarcely go. An immense quantity of ammunition was expended and perhaps 50 deer & antelope shot. One antelope in streaking though the column actual[ly] ran against a man and through [*sic*] him down. We reached a low piece of ground when one or two springs were found and halted and finally camped. The Col. went ahead and found a creek, but returned too late for us to reach it. Clear but cool day. Marched 12 miles.[3]

Springer complained about the weather: "A cold north wind blew over the level plain and went chilling through my light blouse. My overcoat is stolen. We traveled north-west by west, through the most desolate country I think, I ever saw." Springer described the men firing at the antelope: "[A]lthough there were strict orders prohibiting all shooting, . . . the men could not resist the temptation and fired anyhow. Sometimes it sounded like a lively skirmish. Col. Cole was chafing in anger, but he is not a particular favorite of officers or men, we don't mind him at all. I bet he thought the 12th Mo. Cav. is a rough set."[4]

Cole recalled, "The first night's camp was made at the head of Antelope Creek, a small marsh from which in a number of springs a considerable amount of water rises."[5] Cole's description and Bennett's mileage estimate puts the campsite near today's Gordon, Nebraska.

[2]Cole's official report of 10 February 1867, Hafen and Hafen, *Powder River Campaigns*, 65.
[3]Bennett diary, 2 August 1865 entry.
[4]Springer, *Soldiering in Sioux Country*, 24–25.
[5]Cole's official report of 10 February 1867, Hafen and Hafen, *Powder River Campaigns*, 65.

THURSDAY, 3 AUGUST 1865

The command continued northwest from their camp at the head of Antelope Creek. Their next destination was Wounded Knee Creek, which starts in northern Nebraska and flows north into South Dakota. The G. K. Warren map shows both creeks, so this path was by design. Bennett described the countryside:

> It was a bright pleasant morning and the column was under way shortly after sunrise. Winding over the swelling plain, the army looked like a huge serpent stretched over the plain.
>
> After nine miles travel we came to a range of hills, the dividing ridge between the White and Niobrara rivers. The wind suddenly commenced blowing and sweeping over the hilltops, penetrating the thickest clothing. We found ourselves among the hills and ravines at the head of Wounded Knee Creek. The ravines were deep and some time was spent in looking up a road running between the ravines. Three miles of wending over the hilltops brought us to the creek and it required considerable work by the pioneers to construct a road down the bluff and a bridge over the stream. After crossing we went into camp where plenty of wood and grass could be obtained. While the tents were being put up, I rode five miles in the advance to explore the road for tomorrow and as far as I went found excellent roads.
>
> A few miles from camp Indian signs were discovered about two or three weeks old. Dr. Leary & his orderly while rambling among the ravines came upon a deer. The orderly fired but supposed he had missed him. Dr. Richardson came upon him soon after and found him badly wounded and killed him & brought it into camp.
>
> Among the ravines is considerable pine of a small size and poor quality. The timber on the stream is Elm, Box Elder, Cottonwood, Ash and Willow.
>
> About ten miles ahead of us is a high Butte on the right of the line of march called Porcupine Tail Butte. It is a splendid land mark and can be seen all over the country. But little game seen today. Marched 13 miles.[6]

After going into camp, Springer went exploring among the trees along the creek. It reminded him of his native Germany. "In the evening we had for supper, baked beans, stewed venison, tea, coffee, and sourkraut [sic]. . . . We are living high, fresh meat, game or fish every day."[7]

---

[6]Bennett diary, 3 August 1865 entry.
[7]Springer, *Soldiering in Sioux Country*, 25.

The command moved northwest and went into camp on Wounded Knee Creek near the Nebraska–Dakota Territory border. The country becomes more rolling here, with deciduous trees along the creek and pines on the hills. Bennett accurately described Porcupine Butte, a prominent landmark in the area that was shown on the G. K. Warren map.

FRIDAY, 4 AUGUST 1865

The command continued traveling northwest down the valley of Wounded Knee Creek. Moving north, the bluffs along the valley become higher and the pines increase considerably. It is beautiful country. The valley narrows and the ground becomes increasingly broken. Bennett described the march:

> Marched at 6 A.M. The morning was foggy, but the wind soon cleared it away and I was able to take the bearings without difficulty. For five miles the road was among the sand hills and was of course crooked and rough but not very bad. Striking the creek bottom we had a fine road. Thirteen miles brought us to a high range that shut the valley in close, so that it was impassable. We were more than an hour in looking up a road over the bluffs. The Col. did the principle part of the work of exploration. The guides lay down and went to sleep. For the most part, they are a humbug and know as little of the country as we, and take no pains to explore the road.
>
> We had a hard time getting up and over the hill through a drizzling rain. We went into camp ¾ a mile from the foot of the hill in a fine location. The bluffs on the opposite were very singular and fine being perpendicular and of the same material as Chimney Rock on the North Platte. This country is rich in petrification. I have seen some fine specimens of wood and bone and vegetables.
>
> Marched 17 miles. Rained this afternoon considerable.[8]

Today's highway crosses the creek numerous times, and it is not hard to imagine the difficulty getting the wagons through here when it was roadless. The 4 August campsite is about five miles north of the town of Wounded Knee, the site of the Wounded Knee massacre.[9]

---

[8]Bennett diary, 4 August 1865 entry.
[9]Michno, *Encyclopedia of Indian Wars*, 351.

SATURDAY, 5 AUGUST 1865

The command continued following Wounded Knee Creek as the valley narrowed and became more difficult for the trains. Bennett described the route:

It was very foggy in the morning owing to the rain last evening and I could get my compass bearings with difficulty. Capt. Boardman's pioneers were sent in advance to repair the roads. About two miles from camp the road ran upon the side of a steep hill and considerable work was required and even then it was not as good as it should have been. Above the road the hard clayey bluff arose a hundred feet almost perpendicular, while below was another perpendicular cliff, at the foot of which ran the creek. The rocks and cliffs and crags were wild and romantic while the pines moaning in the breeze added to the impression of wilderness of the region. In the rocks were imbedded large quantities of bones, mostly in fragments and solid as the rock itself. One of the Headquarters wagons, while passing this place, was tipped completely over. This was the only accident of the day, though we had a bad road most of the way. At one point we dug a road four feet deep up a steep bank. Among the crags on the opposite side of the valley, I noticed one with a tall perpendicular shaft running up about a hundred feet, which we called Light House Rock, and another with a formation like a dome on some public building, which I called Dome Rock. Our road was very crooked and we marched only seven miles. Bright and pleasant day. Camped on Wounded Knee Creek where was plenty of wood and excellent buffalo grass.

I noticed several varieties of fine wild flowers entirely new to me. Among them is a sort of milk weed with a white border around the leaves which was very beautiful.[10]

Lt. Charles Springer wrote of an incident involving one of the privates, who caused a small sand avalanche that stampeded some of the horses. The private was arrested and dismounted, or forced to walk for a few days. "The weather turned towards noon, very warm, the sky cleared off, and the sun lit up the magnificent scenery. Some of those hills resemble chimneys, houses or old castles, it would be worth something for an artist to look upon."[11]

---

[10]Bennett diary, 5 August 1865 entry.
[11]Springer, *Soldiering in Sioux Country*, 26–27.

Lt. Col. Samuel Walker of
the Sixteenth Kansas Cavalry.
*Courtesy of the Kansas State
Historical Society.*

This part of the valley gets even more difficult with rough terrain.
Today's road moves up on the bench land above the creek bed to the
east to avoid the hills and gullies below. Springer's description of the
hills with stone outcroppings as "magnificent" is an accurate one.

✻   ✻   ✻

The center column of the Powder River Expedition finally left Fort
Laramie on 5 August. Lt. Col. Samuel Walker marched his command
northward toward the Black Hills. Walker's departure was hardly
uneventful. Shortly before they were to depart, on 30 July members of
Walker's regiment, the Sixteenth Kansas Volunteer Cavalry, refused to
march, citing that their enlistments would expire while they were on
campaign. Connor's loyal California troops lined up two howitzers

---

[12]George F. Price, Acting Assistant Adjutant-General, to Connor, 31 July 1865, *The War of Rebellion.*

"loaded with grape and canister," thus persuading the rebelling troops to proceed on the expedition. Seven of the ringleaders were arrested, put in irons, and court-martialed.[12] Walker reported the command getting under way: "I on the 5th of August 1865 left Fort Laramie with 10 Squadrons of my Regiment, a detachment of the 15th K. Vols. with two Mountain Howitzers commanded by Lieut. Gill & a train of thirteen wagons to haul forage as far as the Black Hills where they will be sent back."[13] Walker's command consisted of about six hundred officers and men.[14] His orders from Connor read, "You will proceed with the companies of your regiment, now at this post, as the center column of the Powder River Indian Expedition by the route marked on the map herewith transmitted, via Rawhide Creek through the Black Hills, across the headwaters of the Little Missouri, in a northwesterly direction to Powder River to a point nearly opposite to the north end of Panther Mountain, and thence in a westerly direction to the general rendezvous of the four columns of the expedition on Rosebud River."[15]

The rest of the letter is identical to the 4 July orders to Cole, including the controversial order to "kill every male Indian over 12 years of age."

SUNDAY, 6 AUGUST 1865

The command continued down Wounded Knee Creek, with the day's destination being the White River. Bennett wrote:

> We resumed the march down Wounded Knee Creek, following the valley which occasionally widened out into pleasant grassy savannas with the creek winding from side to side of the valley and generally fringed with a growth of trees and brush. Occasionally the bluffs and creek prevented further progress when a road would be sought out along the side of the hills until a favorable place could be found for a descending into the valley and marching over level roads. After an hour or two marching we found the ground wet and in many places muddy from recent rains, the creek too was

---

[13]Walker's official report, 25 September 1865, Hafen and Hafen, *Powder River Campaigns*, 92. Second Lt. Edward Gill was in Company H, Fifteenth Kansas Cavalry. *American Civil War Research Database.*

[14]Hafen and Hafen, *Powder River Campaigns*, 25.

[15]Connor's orders to Walker, 28 July 1865, ibid., 42.

high and muddy. The rain of the 4th which scarcely reached us here drenched the whole surface and we found ravines that are usually dry, now a flowing stream and the loose friable soil ready to sink our horses in to their knees, obliging us to build a few bridges. As we approached White River, the hills sloped more gradual and we found it easy traveling along their sides and over them. About noon we came upon a hill overlooking White River Valley, which was about a mile and a half wide.

Reaching the river, we found it thick and muddy and nearly white as milk, occasioned from the washing of the recent storm. A sediment of soft mud had been deposited on each bank from two to three feet in depth, miring the horses and stalling the wagons so that it was necessary to build a corduroy road from the water to the bank above. The trains all came in in good order and crossed the river.

At this point we entered the Bad Lands or "Mauvaises Terres" or in other words the Devils Land and judging from appearances a few miles away from the river, it is the devil's own country. The Col. and I mounted our horses, just at night and rode out two or three miles returning after night. The moon shone beautiful and it was a fairy night. Marched 15 miles.[16]

Springer recalled: "[W]e traveled about 18 miles, over very ruggy grounds, and but very poor grass. . . . [W]e camped on the banks of White River, the river was high through recent rains, and the water looked rather milky. The crossing we affected where the old trail from Fort Pearce [Pierre] to Fort Laramie crosses but the bottom and bank were very miry."[17]

Cole wrote of the White River crossing: "The crossing of the White Earth River was rendered very difficult by recent rains, which having submerged the banks made them almost impassably miry, compelling the construction of corduroy roads before the trains could be gotten over."[18]

The valley widens out considerably for the last miles before Wounded Knee Creek empties into the White River. As they were following the creek, they probably crossed the White River to the west of where today's highway bridge is and camped on the north side.

[16]Bennett diary, 6 August 1865 entry.

[17]The G. K. Warren map shows the route from Fort Laramie to Fort Pierre. Springer, *Soldiering in Sioux Country*, 27.

[18]Cole's official report of 10 February 1867, Hafen and Hafen, *Powder River Campaigns*, 65–66.

THE WHITE RIVER IN SOUTHWEST SOUTH DAKOTA
Bennett and Captain Boardman's pioneers built a corduroy road
near this point for the wagons to cross on 6 August 1865. *Author's photo.*

MONDAY, 7 AUGUST 1865

The command prepared to move through some of the most desolate
yet strikingly beautiful terrain that they would encounter on the entire
expedition. Much of this spectacular landscape is within the bound-
aries of today's Badlands National Park. Bennett recorded the day's
travel:

> We broke up camp quite early and were marching at 5½ A.M. For the
> first four or five miles we had a level [road] over Genl. Harney's old trail.
> In places the ground was soft and muddy, especially in going through the
> Prairie Dog towns, where the earth had been dug up. Sand has entirely
> disappeared and the clay, which is usually hard as a rock was now soft and

MAUVAISES TERRES, THE BADLANDS OF SOUTH DAKOTA
Cole's expedition passed through here on
7 and 8 August 1865. *Author's photo.*

muddy. There must have been an enormous amount of rain fall here. We
soon entered the Bad Lands and here the earth was perfectly bare with not
a particle of vegetation for a mile or two and strewn over with fragments
of rock, generally feldspar, lava and iron rocks. I collected many fine specimens, many entirely new to me. Occasional arising out of the plain would
be a high mass of baked clay in the form of a pyramid column or temple
crown with tall tapering spires and minarets and cut by the wind and storm
into variety of fantastic shapes. One we called Temple Rock, another
Lighthouse Rock, another Cupola Rock, Dome Rock, Hell Gate, Pyramids Rock and such other names were bestowed. Poets may sing of
Lehming Rock and scientific explorers dwell with rapture on them, but no

mountain or other scenery I ever beheld can come up to this wildness and in strange beauty. It was grand in the extreme.

My horse came near giving out as it was with difficulty I got him into camp. The day was quite warm, in fact the warmest we have had. Occasionally through the openings in the surrounding crags, glimpses could be obtained of the Black Hills looming in the distance. Camped at Ash Spring after marching 16 miles.

Had I time I would visit more of this strange region and its geological formation. I have many fine specimens and will someday when I have time write upon this subject. This is truly a level of desolation. No game exists here that I have seen. Fresh Indian signs have been discovered in the shape of pony tracks making off towards the Black Hills. We may expect to come in contact with the red skins at any time from now on.[19]

Cole wrote, "On the passage through the 'Badlands' no water fit for use was found save at Ash Spring, where some old holes were cleaned out, which afforded sufficient for the time.[20]

Springer appeared to be in awe of the spectacular scenery:

For me to describe through what kind of a country we traveled is impossible. Sergt. Kelley gave about the best description, not exaggerated at all, he said: that God the Almighty, when he created the world, did not have time to come out here his 6 days were too short consequently he left it, in the original chaos, and the bible tells us how it looked. Mountains half clay, half rock, reaching toward the skies, in all imaginable shapes; hardly a sign of vegetation or animal life, nothing but bare ground. . . . If I had my way I would call it the "Valley of Death." . . . Our horses are falling away amazingly, the mules in the teams are getting very weak, because the grass is very scarce. . . . We encamped at an oasis in this desert, called Ash Springs.[21]

The command's route probably mirrored today's Highway 44, as it moved north through this stunning but difficult terrain. Although today's maps do not list "Ash Springs," there are two springs located along the line of travel at about the right distance of Bennett's mileage calculation. They camped about five miles south of present-day Scenic, South Dakota.

---

[19]Bennett diary, 7 August 1865 entry.
[20]Cole's official report of 10 February 1867, Hafen and Hafen, *Powder River Campaigns*, 66.
[21]Springer, *Soldiering in Sioux Country*, 27–28.

Tuesday, 8 August 1865

Bennett described another day in the Badlands:

The day opened without a cloud and as the sun mounted to the meridian, it became extremely hot. The greater portion of the Bad Lands, being bare and destitute of vegetation, reflected the rays and added to its intensity. The horses and mules were so much affected by the heat that many teams gave out entirely and the trains did not all arrive until late at night.

A mile from camp the road led down a steep bluff which required much skill in descending to prevent accidents. A few of the officers struck off from the road to the right to collect specimens among the bare cliffs near the head of Bear Creek. I went a short distance with them, but my duties on the road prevented my going far from the line of march. I obtained some fine specimens of rock and petrification and saw the fragments of a petrified turtle that was, when living, at least three feet across his shell. Others of the party found one that was at least ten feet across. Tis said that there is a place where the fossil turtles are piled on the top of each other and one is 30 feet across. They have been washed down from the cliffs and are more or less mutilated, but yet enough remains to get the outlines and size. Mastodon bones were also found, one as large as a man and Dr. Richardson found a wolf's head imbedded in the rock and about entire. Quite a number of enormous teeth were also found. This is really the most singular region imaginable and the French voyagers were right in terming it Mauvaises Terres or the Devil's own.

At length we ascended a long steep hill and left the valley of death behind and found a level smooth road to Cheyenne River. Game began to appear, the first since entering the Bad Lands.

Near the Cheyenne was a high steep hill down which we descended into the valley. The Cheyenne is a large stream now much swollen and muddy from recent rains. The water is thick with the soil that has washed from the neighboring hills.

It was late when we reached camp and everybody was used up. I lay down on my cot and did no platting or other work but eat my supper. Thankfully we are now out of the Bad Lands and for one, I have had enough of them. Marched 15 miles.[22]

The terrain from Ash Springs to the Cheyenne River is described very accurately by Bennett. The head of Bear Creek, where the offi-

---

[22]Bennett diary, 8 August 1865 entry.

cers collected specimens, is three miles south of today's Scenic, South Dakota. The campsite on the Cheyenne River may have been within a mile or two east of today's highway bridge.

Springer wrote, "[C]ame through another valley like the one described, only the hills were higher and in a still more phantstic [*sic*] confused mass; the sun hid itself behind a dark cloud, not a breeze stirred, the heat was intense and suffocating. . . . We progressed but slowly, the animals gave out." The country finally changed as grass began to appear. The command arrived at the Cheyenne River about 4 P.M. Springer described the water as "very muddy not fit for use, until settled."[23]

WEDNESDAY, 9 AUGUST 1865

Colonel Cole decided to rest the animals and men by remaining in camp on the Cheyenne River. Bennett took advantage of the time to catch up on his mapping:

> No movement today. The teams and horses are too much in need of feed and rest to push them very far [in] this hot weather. I have progressed very finely with my plats. Also selected a place for crossing the river. The water is more like mud than any Illinois mud hole and generally the bottom of the river is covered with mud from one to four feet deep. It was some time before I could find a hard gravel bottom all the way across. On the opposite side is splendid grass, an abundance of wood and a fine camping ground. Quite a number of large elk were brought in as well as deer and other game. Elk are in great abundance on this stream and the whole command is feasting on elk meat. Nothing of any account has occurred in camp today aside from preparing a ford for crossing. Weather hot. We are now near 700 miles from Omaha.[24]

Springer spent the morning reading, and after supper he went exploring downriver about eight miles. Back in camp, four men of the Twelfth Missouri were arrested by Colonel Cole for some confusing issue over hunting, and their two elk were confiscated. Two captains

---

[23]Springer, *Soldiering in Sioux Country*, 28–29.
[24]Bennett diary, 9 August 1865 entry.
[25]Springer, *Soldiering in Sioux Country*, 29–30.

from the regiment went to Cole and defused the situation, as the Twelfth Missouri was in a fighting mood over this.[25]

THURSDAY, 10 AUGUST 1865

Cole had the command move across the river at the crossing that Bennett had selected the previous day. He decided to lie over one additional day. "On the south fork of the Cheyenne there were limited quantities of grass, but wood and water in abundance. It was necessary to pull the wagons up the high bluffs with drag ropes to attain a high plateau over which the route now took its way. To purpose this and to give the animals rest I lay here two days, moving hence August 11."[26]

Bennett wrote of another day at the Cheyenne River:

> The grass being exhausted about our camp and there being any amount of the most excellent quantity on the opposite side of the stream, the camp was moved about a mile. The ford proved an excellent one and there was no delay with the train or column crossing. The bluffs however were very steep so that the teams could not ascend them with their loads. Heavy details of men were made and ropes attached to the wagons and with 25 or 30 men to assist each team, the train was soon all up.
>
> Our camp was an excellent one with trees and shade and a fine level surface, really the best camp since the expedition commenced.
>
> Made considerable progress with my plats. An expedition sent out to Elk Creek reports seeing a buffalo. My horse is too lame and used up to go further and I will oblige to leave him.[27]

Springer spent most of the day reading Byron's *Werner* and other poetry.[28]

❊   ❊   ❊

Only six days out of Fort Laramie, Walker's center column already experienced difficulties. They traveled north from Fort Laramie, probably following a close proximity to the route of today's Highway 85. "In

---

[26]Cole's official report of 10 February 1867, Hafen and Hafen, *Powder River Campaigns*, 66.
[27]Bennett diary, 10 August 1865 entry.
[28]Springer, *Soldiering in Sioux Country*, 30.

six (6) days march we reached the South Cheyenne [River]," wrote Walker. "We found but little grass but poor water   From Raw Hide [Creek] to the Cheyenne the country is very barren & sandy   Traveled forty two miles without any water   Found the Cheyenne at last, half dying   Got plenty of water, but brackish. It made many of our men sick   Several died from the effects of it. Here we fed our last corn[.]"[29]

Applying the same math used to calculate the needs of Cole's command, it is doubtful that Walker's column carried even enough grain for a full ration for six days for their approximately six to seven hundred animals.[30] Walker, no doubt, sent his wagons back to Fort Laramie at this time.

It is a coincidence that Walker and the Sixteenth Kansas were on the South Cheyenne on the same day as Cole's expedition, only about eighty-five miles to the west in Wyoming.

---

[29]Walker's official report, 25 September 1865, Hafen and Hafen, *Powder River Campaigns*, 92.

[30]Six hundred horses and mules at twelve pounds of grain per day per animal equals 7,200 pounds of grain. Six days' worth of grain would be 42,000 pounds; divided by thirteen wagons, this would total 3,323 pounds per wagon. Remember that the maximum recommended payload for the freight wagons was only 2,500 pounds and that includes such vitals as ammunition and rations for the men.

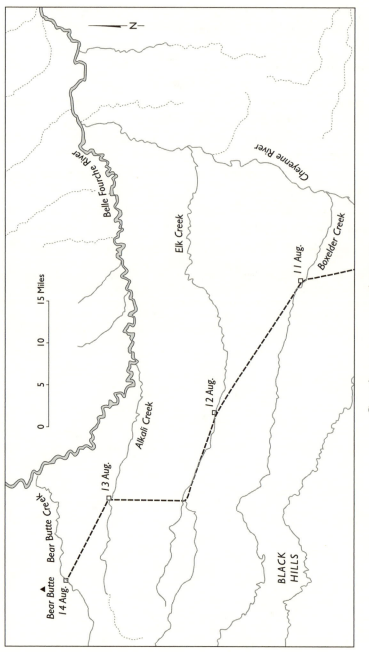

Cole's route, 11–14 August

CHAPTER EIGHT

11–14 August

MARCH TO BEAR BUTTE

B ear Butte would be on the horizon for several days, as the command was once again in motion after their three-day rest on the banks of the Cheyenne River. The mountain stands just north of the Black Hills, six miles northeast of today's Sturgis, South Dakota. It rises 1,253 feet above the surrounding plains, 4,426 feet above sea level. While not a tall peak by western standards, its religious significance to the northern Plains Indians, particularly the Cheyenne and Sioux, cannot be measured.[1]

FRIDAY, 11 AUGUST 1865

Bennett described a day of easy travel for the recuperated stock:

> The column did not start until six A.M. and after all the regimental trains had been taken up the bluffs, we then struck off over the plain which was level for some miles, then low hills with a gentle slope that did not impede the teams in the least. We found pools of water on the highest prairie, but it was some what tinctured with alkali. The road was covered with coarse smooth gravel and was as hard and smooth as a macadamized road. We reached Elk Creek about noon but found nothing but the dry bed of the stream. To all appearances it was perfectly dry. Cottonwood and other timber grew upon the banks and there was every indication of water. This had more the appearance of being a stream and not being one than any I

---

[1]Jerry Oehlerking, "The Dick Williams Story: If Bear Butte Could Speak," 22–25.

ever saw. After a thorough search, water was found in pools in the creek bed sufficient for the stock. In a low ravine, wells were dug for the use of the men and good water obtained. Marched 14 miles.[2]

Springer gave his observations on the day's campsite: "We finally came in sight of a strip of timber which proved to be Elk Creek. After coming down the hill, we had to cross the about 3 miles wide bottom, and then we only found a puddle of muddy water. We pitched camp then I went to work and commenced digging a well." After several tries Springer was rewarded with "a vein of clear cold and well tasting water."[3]

Both Bennett and Springer identified this campsite as Elk Creek, but perhaps they were mistaken. The creek they camped on was probably Boxelder Creek, as it is within the mileage estimates given by both Bennett and Springer for the day—Bennett fourteen miles, Springer twelve miles. The real Elk Creek would have been a march of twenty-eight miles. The command would have had to cross the Boxelder streamed to get to the real Elk Creek, and neither Bennett nor Springer mentions a crossing.

On 31 October 1865 a letter from a person identified only as Jay, a special correspondent to the *Missouri Democrat*, was published in Denver's *Daily Rocky Mountain News.* Dated 30 August 1865, the letter described the march of Cole's column from the South Cheyenne to the Powder River. Jay, either an officer or a civilian employee with the expedition, wrote, "From South Fork Cheyenne we moved over a beautiful rolling highland prairie, along the base of the Black Hills to Bear Butte, crossing and camping on a number of tributaries of the Cheyenne, some dry, save water standing in holes, others running very fine."[4]

✳   ✳   ✳

After sending his wagons back at the Cheyenne River camp, Walker's column continued north, now using a pack train for ammunition, rations, and camp gear. He briefly described the march: "In Twenty six (26) miles reached Beaver Creek at the base of the Black Hills

---

[2]Bennett diary, 11 August 1865 entry.
[3]Springer, *Soldiering in Sioux Country*, 30.
[4]Hafen and Hafen, *Powder River Campaigns*, 355.

Found scarcely any grass, had to cut cottonwood to feed on[.]"[5] The twenty-six miles traveled from the Cheyenne River would place Walker's command approximately five miles west of present-day Highway 85 at Beaver Creek, about nine miles southwest of today's Newcastle, Wyoming.

SATURDAY, 12 AUGUST 1865

Bennett was fascinated by the abundance of fossils in the area. His excitement was evident in his description of the day's travel:

We broke up camp shortly after sunrise, starting earlier than at any time since being on the march. About three miles from camp we found several good springs furnishing water sufficient for the command. The road was over a gently rolling prairie for ten miles and traveling was excellent. I observed on the slopes of the hills regular rows of grass covering most of the country and looking much like a closely mowed meadow where the swaths are visible. Reaching the divide separating Elk and Bear Creeks, the bluffs toward the latter were quite steep, but a good road was found to go down them. On these bluffs I collected a number of fine specimens, among which were pieces of isinglass, fine specimens of petrified wood, also shells and portions of the internal structure of monstrous marine animals. I observed fragments of shell fish that must have been ten or twelve feet across. The whole range of hills in places were entirely composed of the remains of these monsters. Exposure to the air and storms had pulverized them and others were broken in large fragments, yet the outlines of turtles and large shell fish could be distinctively traced. I found portions of vertebrae of some marine animal, beautifully coruscated with joints and sutures. For miles, our horses, at each step, crushed and ground to atoms the remains of a past but once living ago. Only think of the mountains of fossils that for ages have been moldering away and becoming portions of the soil until but faint outlines here and there indicate that the earth and rocks we are treading upon was once living and animate matter. This is truly a singular region. Here are indication of volcanic action and a deluge strangely commingled marine fossils and formations from heat laying side by side.

We camped on Bear Creek, a dry steam except puddles of water in holes. At times this is as large as a river and the dry channel is in many places 100 feet wide and 20 feet deep with a small growth of Box Elder, Cottonwood,

---

[5]Walker's official report of 25 September 1865, ibid., 93.

and Ash timber. On an Elm tree was the remains of an Indian child nicely folded up in Buffalo robes and blankets. The surgeon and Capt. McMurray took it down and examined the contents. Hot day, the sun pouring down upon the dry and dusty earth. Bear Butte is plainly in sight. Two short days march will bring us there. It is a very prominent land mark. We are now within 15 or 20 miles of the foot of the Black Hills. Marched 14 miles.[6]

Springer sighted Bear Butte. "About 10 o'clock we came in sight of a mountain, isolated from the long chain of hills running from north to south, that mountain is called Bear Butte and is the place where we should meet General Connor's command. About 12 o'clock we encamped on Bear Creek, which contains very nice water but it tastes swampy."[7] It must have been camp gossip that Springer thought that they were to meet Connor's command at Bear Butte. Evidently Colonel Cole had not yet communicated their destination to all of the officers of the expedition.

The 12 August campsite probably was on the real Elk Creek. Current maps do not list a Bear Creek in this area, although the Warren map shows a Bear Creek in the line of march.

✳   ✳   ✳

Walker rested his command at Beaver Creek, while he sent his scouts ahead: "[L]aid up one day to send scouting parties into the Black Hills Saw many signs of Indians but all old   Scouts returned reported no grass to be found[.]"[8]

SUNDAY, 13 AUGUST 1865

The command continued its march toward Bear Butte as Bennett described a windy day:

> It was a bright pleasant morning when we commenced to march. But after an hour or two a high wind arose from the north, nearly blowing us off our legs. I scarcely ever saw the wind more powerful. Afternoon it began to abate and we progressed with more speed and comfort.

---

[6]Bennett diary, 12 August 1865 entry.
[7]Springer, *Soldiering in Sioux Country*, 31.
[8]Walker's official report of 25 September 1865, Hafen and Hafen, *Powder River Campaigns*, 93.

Our course for ten miles was west, moved up Bear creek until it ran out and there was no more of it. We then went north across a divide to a creek that has no name. There was but little water in it in holes in the creek. Had plenty of wood but little grass. We called the creek Minni Wak sa Creek or Broken Water. We traveled 19 miles.[9]

The creek with no name is called Alkali Creek on modern maps.

※   ※   ※

Walker continued his trek north around the western edge of the Black Hills. "[T]he next day marched North west along the base of the Hills to a fork of Box Elder Found some water in holes but not one bit of grass[.]"[10] Pvt. Alonzo D. Waln[11] said that "the party camped on Beaver, Iron, and Sand Creeks, on the Belle Fourche and Red Water during their sojourn."[12] As there is no Box Elder Creek on the G. K. Warren map and no such listing on the current maps of eastern Wyoming, the creek that they camped on was probably Iron Creek. Twenty miles northwest of the Beaver Creek campsite would put them on that creek, in the vicinity of today's Osage, Wyoming.

MONDAY, 14 AUGUST 1865

Cole's command had seen Bear Butte on the horizon since 12 August, and it had been their target since then. Generals Pope, Dodge, and Connor had stated in earlier orders and correspondence that the hostile tribes would likely be found near Bear Butte; however there was no indication of their recent habitation of the area. Cole remarked on arriving at the landmark, "Moving northwestwardly from here over a high rolling country we crossed quite a number of sinking creeks, trib-

---

[9]Bennett diary, 13 August 1865 entry.

[10]Hafen and Hafen, *Powder River Campaigns*, 93. The Box Elder Creek that Walker camped on should not be confused with Montana's Boxelder Creek between the Little Missouri River and Powder River, which both commands camped at later. This is also not to be confused with the Boxelder Creek in present-day South Dakota where Cole's command camped at on 11 August.

[11]Pvt. Alonzo D. Waln was a member of Company H, Fifteenth Kansas Cavalry; *American Civil War Research Database*. Walker reported "a detachment of the 15th K. Vols. with two (2) Mountain Howitzers commanded by [Second] Lieut. [Edward] Gill," as part of his command. Hafen and Hafen, *Powder River Campaigns*, 92.

[12]Irma H. Klock, *All Roads Lead to Deadwood*, 8.

utaries to the forks of the Cheyenne, arriving at Bear Butte on the 14th."[13]

Bennett also described the arrival at camp and the subsequent adventure of climbing the peak:

> We left camp at 6 A M taking a line for Bear Butte. For four or five miles we had a gradual ascent and a very fine road. When on the table the plain was very level and smooth and we made a bee line for the Butte for three miles, when coming to a ravine, the course was changed northerly to the south branch of Bear Butte Creek, where we found fine water, grass and wood. The valley was about a mile wide but, over the whole was drift wood indicating a high stage of water at no very recent date. We camped about three miles from the foot of the Butte and after dinner a party of officers with myself set out for the Butte. We galloped over the plain and up the side of the hill as far as we could go with horses, then dismounting and leaving them with orderlies. We climbed up the steep rocky bluff until we stood on a pinnacle and was astonished to find a deep valley between us and the main peak. There being no other alternative we clambered down and then up up up [*sic*] the precipitous rocky side until finally we were upon the topmost height of Bear Butte. I never saw a finer view. South of us was the Black Hills and all around the naked plain covered with streams. At the foot of the Butte was the two creeks & our camp 3 or 4 miles off looking very tiny. The men in camp looked like mere specks. Bear Butte is about ten miles from the Black Hills and rises out of the level plain 1500 feet. All around is level. This is holy ground for the Indians and many were the presents to the great spirits in the shape of beads, arrow heads, rings, etc., that had been left there. Quarts of beads were picked up by the men. On the way back we found a very fine spring of ice cold water. I found some specimens of iron ore and some very fine gypsum which if in the United States of America would be of immense value. In addition to this while on the plain I found some shells and Orthaseran fossils.
>
> I fired a pile of rotten wood on the Butte which offends the Col. some-what. But it soon burned down and at night could be seen but little. This has been an interesting day for me. Still no trace of Indians. About 20 miles north of the Butte a large dust was observed which was supposed to be caused by a herd of buffalo. Marched 14 miles.[14]

Springer climbed Bear Butte with Pvt. Theophilus McBeath. "Col. Cole and staff also were there." Springer described the view: "[F]rom

---

[13]Cole's official report of 10 February 1867, Hafen and Hafen, *Powder River Campaigns*, 66.
[14]Bennett diary, 14 August 1865 entry.

BEAR BUTTE
This view is looking from the general area where
the command would have camped on 14 August 1865.
The tree line of Bear Butte Creek is in the foreground. *Author's photo.*

the top a splendid view far into the Black Hills presents itself; in the
north west we could see the 'Inyan Kara Peak' and the 'Little Missouri
Buttes.'"[15]

The probable camp location is about three miles southeast of Bear
Butte on Bear Butte Creek's east bank. The valley looks much like
Bennett described it, except cattle ranches now occupy the terrain
with fenced pastureland.

Jay described the Bear Butte camp in glowing terms:

Grass good and plenty; at Bear Butte Creek especially fine and in very
large quantities, and for the first time, in a week or more, we found really
good water.

Bear Butte had been for three days before reaching it, in sight, and as
soon as reached we climbed, of course, by hundreds. It is a lone peak, surrounded by comparatively flat country, rising to an altitude of 4500 feet
and with sides inclined at no place less than forty-five degrees, generally

---

[15]Springer, *Soldiering in Sioux Country,* 31–32.

from sixty to eighty degrees. To reach the top requires several hours of very hard pulling and hauling among the loose stones and pines, with which the sides are covered. The path is an Indian improvement on a mountain goat path, and must be two miles long from end to end. Once on top a level, crescent shaped space is found, covered by rocks and pines. Among the latter are pyramids of sticks and stones, hair, rings, arrows, beads, and other articles offered to the Great Spirit, by penitent savages for their many misdeeds.

The view from the butte is magnificent: the Black Hills to the south stretching away in the distance; the bluffs of the North Cheyenne to the north, and unknown mountains to the west.[16] The soil of all looked barren, but the cause may be drouth. Along Bear Butte Creek the soil looked better than elsewhere and the grass was most abundant.[17]

✳   ✳   ✳

Without the encumbrance of the wagons, Walker's command continued to make good time but was still struggling to find adequate forage and water for their rapidly deteriorating animals. "Started at 3 AM to try and find grass Entered the Black Hills but a pretty good road marched twenty seven miles before we could find a particle of grass or water   Found some grass but miserable water in holes[.]"[18] Walker's probable route would take them west of Inyan Kara Mountain, with their campsite five to six miles north of the peak. Private Waln, of the Fifteenth Kansas, recalled that the command spent "some time in the Inyan Kara Region."[19]

---

[16]Those unknown mountains to the west that Jay mentioned are the Bear Lodge Mountains of today's Crook County, Wyoming.

[17]This letter was printed in the *Rocky Mountain News* on 31 October 1865. Hafen and Hafen, *Powder River Campaigns*, 355–56.

[18]Walker's official report of 25 September 1865, ibid., 93.

[19]*Black Hills Daily Times* (Deadwood, S.D.), 14 October 1879.

CHAPTER NINE

15–19 August

REDWATER RESPITE

TUESDAY, 15 AUGUST 1865

"From here [Bear Butte]," wrote Cole, "I moved to the northwest, intending to reach the valley of the Belle Fourche River and follow it some distance."[1] What Cole omitted from his abbreviated report of the day's march is that once again bad advice given by one of the guides delayed the command. Bennett gave more detail for the day's travel:

> Leaving our camp on the south fork of Bear Butte Creek we struck directly across a ridge in a northwesterly direction and into the valley of Butte Creek which we followed for a short distance and then crossed the creek and entered the low hills bordering the creek on the north and was progressing very well over a fine road when one of the guides came back and informed us that the road could be much improved by striking more north. Accordingly the course was changed and soon was among hills ravines and rough broken ground over which it was almost impossible to cross and entirely out of our course. The Col. was mad at the guide who had led him off his course and some sharp words were offered. We finally came to White Wood Creek and camped. This steam was nearly dry, but there was good grass and an abundance of Oak trees along its course. This is almost the only Oak I have seen on the march. It is short and of a poor quality. We had an excellent camp. The sun however was high and it was disagreeable working on the maps.
>
> No indication of Indians have as yet been seen. Where are they is the inquiry. The country is for the most part dry and sterile. The hills are bare

---

[1]Cole's official report of 10 February 1867, Hafen and Hafen, *Powder River Campaigns*, 67.

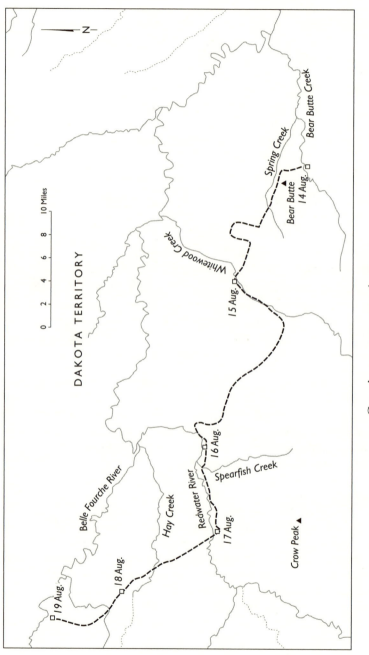

DAKOTA TERRITORY

Bear Butte Creek

Spring Creek

Bear Butte

14 Aug.

Whitewood Creek

15 Aug.

16 Aug.

Spearfish Creek

17 Aug.

Crow Peak

Redwater River

Hay Creek

Belle Fourche River

18 Aug.

19 Aug.

10 Miles

0   2   4   6   8

COLE'S ROUTE, 15–19 AUGUST

and composed of dry clay. A cloud of dust is raised on the march. This hides the column from view. In the bottoms along White Wood creek the soil is rich but too dry for successful cultivation. Marched 12 miles.[2]

The Butte Creek that Bennett described following after leaving their camp on Bear Butte Creek is no doubt today's Spring Creek. The creek, in the general location where the command would pick it up, runs northwest for several miles and then turns to the southwest. The command followed the creek on the south bank until it turned to the southwest, then crossed it and continued in a northwesterly direction, which would have taken them directly to Whitewood Creek over good ground, had it not been for the unfortunate advice from one of the scouts to head north into rough terrain. The probable location of the camp on Whitewood Creek was near where the creek crosses the boundary line between Meade and Lawrence Counties. Looking back from there over relatively flat country, Bear Butte is prominent on the skyline to the southeast.

"On arriving at White Wood Creek," Cole wrote, "one of its [Belle Fourche River's] tributaries, I found a more practical route to the west."[3]

WEDNESDAY, 16 AUGUST 1865

The command left their campsite on Whitewood Creek and moved southwest following Cole's newly discovered route along the creek for several miles. They then passed through a gap in the hills and moved in a northwesterly direction, and as Cole said, "pursuing it, reached a mountain stream called by traders Red Water."[4] Bennett described their route to the Redwater River, effusive in his description of this beautiful stream and surrounding area:

> Our course was changing southwest today to get on the route as planned. And also to avoid some hills in front for a few miles. It soon was rocky but not very rough. We soon came among the spurs of the Black Hills and found small quantities of timber on the hills. Further on the peaks were clothed with pine that looked tall and excellent for lumber or timber for 12 miles.

[2]Bennett diary, 15 August 1865 entry.
[3]Cole's official report of 10 February 1867, Hafen and Hafen, *Powder River Campaigns*, 67.
[4]Ibid.

The road was very good and direct. When we ascended a long hill of easy grade and suddenly came to a steep rock precipice on the other side. No place could be found to go down into the valley so the column turned to the right in a northerly direction over the side and down a ravine and finally struck a lazy stream of pure water flowing with current from the Black Hills. In the bottom was excellent feed and our stock luxuriated in the tall grass.

Some very fine fish were caught from the stream. This is the most beautiful and finest stream I have seen. From three to five deep and rippling over the rocky bottom singing an anthem for ever. There is more of these rocky recesses among the Black Hills. There was much dispute about this creek. Some contended that this was the North Cheyenne. But its size and the course it ran convinces me to the contrary.

This beautiful valley resembles the Rolling Stone in Minnesota and should this region even be settled, here will be a fine location. A few deer were killed. The trains came in in good time though suffering from want of water. We crossed two dry creek beds. I like this country, rough as it is, far better than the plains where the earth is parched and vegetation scarcely exists. Marched 18 miles.[5]

The command moved southwest, following Whitewood Creek until it reached the gap in the hills. They moved west through the gap, then turned and moved in a northwesterly direction, crossing what is today Highway 34, and traveled several miles west of present-day St. Onge, South Dakota. The country is, as Bennett described, "a long hill of easy grade." They reached the edge of the bluffs, and had to move north to descend into the valley of the Redwater River. The command camped on the south bank of the river, in the area where Highway 85 crosses the river between Spearfish and Belle Fourche, South Dakota.

Springer commented on the day: "We marched 20 miles and encamped on the South Fork of the La Fourche or Belle Fourche River, which is a beautiful stream on some places 10 feet deep and as clear as crystal." Springer and at least fifty men went swimming.[6] He was mistaken about the identity of the river, which is understandable when one looks at the G. K. Warren map, as many of the waterways and lakes where they camped or crossed over, including the Redwater, are not shown on it.[7]

---

[5]Bennett diary, 16 August 1865 entry.
[6]Springer, *Soldiering in Sioux Country*, 32–33.
[7]G. K. Warren map of 1857.

Correspondent Jay described the Redwater River: "Two or three days brought us to 'Red Water,' a mountain steam which flows from the center of the Black Hills into the Cheyenne River. The current was rapid as a mill race, clear as crystal, and full of fish, which sported about, near the surface, seemingly waiting for the line to draw them out. Its branches are numerous and the volume of water carried out by it immense."[8] The Redwater River is perhaps the clearest mountain stream in the area, being fed by Sand Creek and Spearfish Creek, which both come from the interior of the Black Hills.

THURSDAY, 17 AUGUST 1865

Bennett, in one of his most colorful descriptions, provided a glimpse of the command in high spirits as it marched west in the beautiful Redwater Valley:

It was a cool fine morning for marching and with the romantic scenery around of mountains looking protectively down upon us. A swiftly flowing stream of pure water murmuring over its rocky bed and a belt of luxurious vegetation fringing the stream so inspired the command that they went singing joyously along, unmindful of those left behind and the scenes of dreary wilderness we had passed through. Our course was up the valley of the creek nearly west. Three or four miles from camp we crossed a large stream coming from the mountains and emptying into the main stream we were following. Another small stream was crossed which rises from the base of Crow Peak which arose in solemn grandeur about four or five miles to the south. We called this stream of pure limpid water Peak Creek from its issuing from the mountain. I observed that the bluffs were composed of a red sandstone rock which crops out from the hill sides. The soil was of a reddish color of the nature called mulatto soils in the state, only this was dry and of a deeper red. The bluffs at times narrows the valley down to small dimensions and then again it would widen out to a considerable area. Coming to a stream flowing from among the hills across the prairie several of us searched for a crossing. My attention was attracted by the sound of falling water and hastening to the spot found a splendid cascade where the stream plunges over a ledge of rocks a height of seven or eight feet. Above the waterfall was a good crossing over which the command passed. The stream was cold and limpid and falling over the rocks in a succession

[8]Hafen and Hafen, *Powder River Campaigns,* 356.

of cascades as water leaped foaming into the main river. It was a most beautiful stream and I could not admire it too long. The stream had its origin in a lake or pond little more than a mile where it entered the river. The lake was about 300 yards across and in the center was a cavity perhaps 80 yards across out of which the volume of water came rushing up. This was a most singular place. The lake looked much like the crater of an extinct volcano and the hole where it came up was several hundred feet deep and could not be sounded. We called the stream Cascade Creek. I subsequently learned that in the Black Hills was almost inaccessible valley four or five miles long and a mile across and surrounded with a perpendicular wall of rock within was several ponds, large springs and many small streams issuing from the rampart of rocks. These sank into the ground at the lower extremity of the valley and often flowing under the surface of the earth final[ly] came out at this place and formed Cascade Creek. The valley in the mountains where the waters have their source is called Vasques Hole from one Vasques an Indian trader and trapper who succeeded in descending into it and caught large numbers of beavers there.

Around the margin of the lake were large beds of matter resembling ashes and alkaline deposits in which one would sink over his shoes in being dry and light as ashes. In the stream were water plants and many of them petrified and turned to stone. I collected some specimens that were very beautiful. Many of the rocks around are of an alkaline formation and many very singular in appearance. We camped here and after dinner I was sent with the guides to explore the road ahead. We found a practable route over the ridge into the next valley where was a small stream nearly dry. In climbing up the hills I got a good place to make observations. I found some of the most singular fossils I ever saw, being sharp at the end and some like a fish or serpent and of all sizes from that of a rice straw to two inches in diameter. Of course a number was collected for my home cabinet. Returning to camp I had to nearly swim my horse in crossing the streams and was glad to find that several fish had been caught and served up for the mess. They were most excellent and weighed from two to five pounds apiece.

This is the most romantic country I have yet seen. I learned the main stream was called Red Earth river. We named the various creeks Rapid Creek, Clear Creek, Peak Creek, and Cascade Creek. Marched 6½ miles.[9]

Springer rode on the left flank with his men during the march into the mountains. One of his men killed a buffalo, which they butchered

---

[9]Bennett diary, 17 August 1865 entry.

COXES LAKE NEAR THE SOUTH DAKOTA–WYOMING BORDER
Crow Peak is in the background. The command camped
near here on 17 August 1865. *Author's photo.*

and carried as much meat as possible to camp. He described the spring-fed lake where they camped as "The prettiest for water, right where we camped, there is a lake with a great spring in the center where the water boiles [*sic*] up as in a cauldrum [*sic*], and cool and sweet." Springer still thought that they were following the Belle Fourche River.[10]

The correspondent, Jay, described the scene:

> We camped on the 17th of August at the mouth of one branch, a mile long, one succession of cascades and rapids during the entire distance, which takes its rise in a single spring, boiling up in the center of a small lake. The lake is about an [*sic*] hundred and fifty yards across and scarce knee deep, and in the center a hole of unfathomable depth, like an enormous well, fully thirty feet across, sends out a column of crystal water. The

---

[10]Springer, *Soldiering in Sioux Country,* 33–34.

lake is in a circular valley; all the rocks about it are volcanic, in fact everything tends to the impression that this is the crater of an extinct volcano.
Ashes lie in beds several feet deep, in which horses sink at every step; the
air, when filled with dust, is sulphurous.

Along the Red Water, the bluffs are red sandstone or red clay, all of
them covered more or less with pine. In the bottoms, boxelder and cottonwood line the river bank.[11]

The day ended on a somber note, as Springer reported, "In the
evening Lieut. [Capt. Sydney] Bennett's Negro servant was playing
with another colored boy all at once he staggered, fell down and died
instantly."[12] No mention of the cause of death is made.

The first creek crossed, described by Bennett, is Spearfish Creek.
The next creek, called Peak Creek by Bennett, is today known as
Chicken Creek. Bennett's Cascade Creek is now called Lake Creek.
The wondrous lake/pond described by Bennett, Springer, and Jay is
Coxes Lake, located just east of the present Wyoming–South Dakota
border, a few miles east of Beulah, Wyoming. The lake has been
enlarged by an earthen dam, but the crater in the middle of the lake is
very prominent. Today it is a popular fishing spot in western South
Dakota. While it no longer emits a column of water in the center of the
lake and Cascade (Lake) Creek does not put out the volume of water
described by Bennett, it is still spectacular. Crow Peak, described by
Bennett and shown on the G. K. Warren map is very prominent in the
background to the south.

FRIDAY, 18 AUGUST 1865

The command crossed the Redwater and moved northwest over the
divide separating the Redwater and Hay Creek drainages. It is a gentle slope Bennett described as "an excellent road." Their line of march
took them across present-day Highway 24 at the Wyoming–South
Dakota border. The command then crossed Hay Creek near where it
divides into North and South Forks, and followed the North Fork.
They proceeded northwest about four miles and went into camp in the

---

[11]Hafen and Hafen, *Powder River Campaigns,* 356–57.
[12]Springer, *Soldiering in Sioux Country,* 33–34. Capt. Sydney J. Bennett of Company A, Twelfth
    Missouri Cavalry, should not be confused with Lyman G. Bennett, the civilian acting as engi-
    neering officer for the expedition.

flat open area where Pine Draw Creek intersects with the North Fork. The day's march proved easy, as Bennett described the eventful day:

> We made our way over the ridge over a most excellent road requiring but little work by the Pioneers. Found large beds of gypsum and any amount of fossils. Descending into the valley we followed it up about four miles and camped. The stream was dry except occasional puddles standing in the bed. The ridges and bluffs here are covered with pine, much of which is dead from fires.
>
> While walking through the grass in the bottoms in search of my horse, which had strayed during a temporary halt, I came upon a rattlesnake that sprang at me, but fortunately missed me by a few inches. I was startled at first but finally returned and killed my serpent.
>
> Today Col Walker & several men from the 16th Kansas came in having made their way from Ft Laramie thru the Black Hills and met us here. They saw the dust rising from our marching column and took us for Indians and prepared for fight. But ascertaining that we were white men, they came to camp. We had a pleasant reunion. They had seen nary Indians among the mountains. Had been on the road over two weeks and did not dream of meeting with us. Their column is a day's march behind ours and for a few days will follow our trail. They had a large mail for the command, but nary letters for me. Marched 10 miles.[13]

Colonel Cole told of the meeting with Walker: "While camped in one of these valleys on Pine Creek Lieutenant-Colonel Walker, Sixteenth Kansas Cavalry, with a small party, rode into my camp, having left his command at our camp of the preceding night on the Red Water."[14]

Springer complained to his diary about Cole's direction of the expedition in crossing the Redwater that morning. He said that they waited two hours for the pioneers to prepare the crossing, which should have been done the day before. "I think Col. Cole never commanded an expedition before, the way he managed some things." After the command went into camp, Walker's party showed up. "A party of 15 men belonging to the 16th Kansas Cav. arrived in camp in the afternoon." Springer received three letters, one from "my Katie."[15]

While it is true that Cole had never commanded an expedition before, Springer's frequent complaining about the colonel is perhaps

---

[13]Bennett diary, 18 August 1865 entry.
[14]Cole's official report of 10 February 1867, Hafen and Hafen, *Powder River Campaigns*, 67–68.
[15]Springer, *Soldiering in Sioux Country*, 34–35.

unwarranted, and at times he comes across as immature and uninformed. Probably the seasoned veterans of the Twelfth Missouri Cavalry, who had seen considerable action in the East, resented being put under the command of an artillery officer. Colonel Cole and the Second Missouri Light Artillery were only recently converted to cavalry and had no field experience as such. To date, Lyman Bennett had not criticized Cole at all and seemed very supportive of his management of the expedition. Being eight years older than Springer and more experienced in life, Bennett could be viewed as an objective observer. If Cole were showing incompetence, such as the guides were, Bennett surely would have written about it.

Jay described the meeting of commands:

> Across the first ridge we struck Pine Creek and followed along its bank and camped, getting water from pools in the bed.
> We had scarcely been in camp an hour when Col. Walker, one of the Sixteenth Kansas Cavalry overtook us with a few of his men, bringing the mail from Fort Laramie.
> We, of course, were glad to see him, as the latest arrival from the "world," and still more rejoiced when we got our papers and letters from home.
> The Sixteenth Kansas had come from Laramie through the Black Hills, and arrived in sight of us as we left camp in the morning. We knew nothing of each others whereabouts until they rode into camp; for a start six hundred miles apart, over different portions of country, it was rather a close hit.[16]

❖   ❖   ❖

Walker wrote of his meeting of Cole's command: "Forty miles north of Devils Bute [sic] we fell in with Col. Cole's Column who had been compelled thus far west to get grass and water[.]"[17] The two commands' meeting place on Pine Draw Creek in northeastern Wyoming is closer to thirty-one miles northeast of Devils Tower (Devils Butte). Walker's estimate of the distance and of the direction of the meeting

---

[16]Hafen and Hafen, *Powder River Campaigns*, 357. Springer corresponded with Katie Robertson of St. Joseph, Missouri, and referred to her as "my dear Katie" during the Powder River Expedition. Her brother, Pvt. George W. Robertson, served with Company L of the Second California Cavalry, which rode with General Connor's western column.

[17]Walker's official report of 25 September 1865, ibid., 93.

place has been quoted in virtually all accounts describing this event, but forty miles north of the butte would place the meeting west of the Little Missouri River, northwest of Alzada, Montana, on ground where neither column set foot.

Walker entered the Black Hills on 14 August in the vicinity of Inyan Kara Mountain, about thirty miles from Cole's 18 August campsite. Although he was descriptive in his observations of the geology, Walker did not specify any travel or campsites until he met Cole on 19 August, when he said, "from that through to the North Cheyenne we found very good grass and water."[18] Walker had been traveling about twenty-five miles a day prior to entering the hills, so it appears that he allowed a day or two for the stock to recover. Pvt. Alonzo D. Waln recalled that one of their campsites was on Sand Creek, which would put them just a few miles west of Cole's 18 August campsite at Coxes Lake.[19]

SATURDAY, 19 AUGUST 1865

Bennett described the route to the Belle Fourche, or North Cheyenne, River:

> Our course in the morning for about three miles was up the valley in a northwesterly direction, until the creek ran out, then we turned north, upon the ridge and followed it several miles overlooking another creek which ran north and empties into the Cheyenne. There was no water in this creek where we crossed it but there was a splendid oak grove. The timber being about as thick as it could stand. Our road was generally a good one. We reached the Cheyenne shortly after ten. It was a small muddy stream at the present time but there were indications that at times it is a large body. At present is only about three feet deep with high soft banks that wash with every storm. Grass was scarce but wood and muddy water was plenty. I passed the afternoon reading up on news from the papers received last night. Marched 10 miles.[20]

---

[18]Ibid.

[19]Klock, *All Roads Lead to Deadwood*, 8. Klock's information came from a newspaper article in the *Black Hills Daily Times*, "One of the Pioneers," 14 October 1879.

[20]Bennett diary, 19 August 1865 entry. The river referred to as the North Cheyenne is more commonly called the Belle Fourche River, as noted on the 1857 G. K. Warren map, which refers to it as the Belle Fourche River. The river's headwaters are in the Pumpkin Buttes of central Wyoming. The river winds its way in a northeasterly direction, eventually coming together with the South Cheyenne River in central South Dakota, and then flowing northeast to the Missouri River.

The command left their camp on Pine Draw Creek, traveling in a northwesterly direction. Cole's command probably followed the north fork streambed until it ran out. They then moved north and traveled on a ridge overlooking a creek running north. The dry creek that they then crossed, and where Bennett described the "splendid oak grove," today is called Oak Creek. Several miles further they would enter the wide Pine Creek Valley, which they traveled about four miles, reaching the North Cheyenne River where they went into camp.

Springer wrote:

> [E]ncamped on the north fork of the Cheyenne River, the one mentioned before was only a tributary to the Cheyenne. The weather was excessively hot and sultry, the dust enveloped the marching column in a complete cloud, and we all came to camp like a lot of chimney sweeps. . . . The river is muddy and yellow and not over 15 feet wide. The banks thickly covered with willow. According to what Col. Wells told me (and what authority he is everybody knows it) we are marching to the panther mountain, there to meet General Connors [sic], and that is 10 days march; in case we don't meet him there we go through to Laramie in 15 or 20 days from this. Now I don't believe anything of this and we will see how things develop themselves.[21]

⁜   ⁜   ⁜

Walker was vague in his report of his movements, covering two to three days with this limited description: "[F]rom this to the North Cheyenne the country began to get barren and water scarce   had to feed principally on cotton wood   found some little grass on the North Cheyenne[.]"[22] His command appeared to be marching a day behind Cole's column at this time, following the same route. They likely did not reach the North Cheyenne until the following day, 20 August.

---

[21]Springer, *Soldiering in Sioux Country*, 35.
[22]Walker's official report of 25 September 1865, Hafen and Hafen, *Powder River Campaigns*, 93.

CHAPTER TEN

20–25 August

ON THE LITTLE MISSOURI

SUNDAY, 20 AUGUST 1865

The expedition broke camp, crossed the Belle Fourche River, and headed northwest in search of the Little Missouri River. The head of the Little Missouri is in the Three Peaks, or Little Missouri Buttes, area, west of Devils Tower in Wyoming. The river flows northeast and eventually empties into the Missouri River in North Dakota. Bennett described what turned out to be an exciting day:

> We left camp at 6½ A.M. The trains started earlier and was over the river before the column moved. We were glad to bid good-by to the Cheyenne and this land of desolation through which it flows. On gaining the summit of the hills on the north side, which were at least 1½ miles from the river, I was struck with the scene of peculiar desolation everywhere presented. The hills descended about 1½ miles into the dry valley of a stream emptying into the Cheyenne. On the dividing ridge between the two streams were mounds or hills irregularly cluttered over this country entirely composed of a thin shale which looks as if blackened by fire and then pounded up and heaped by the hand of men. Not a particle of vegetation grew on these mounds which are evidently caused by volcanic action. I never saw a more desolate or forbidding region. The valley was equally desolate. Nothing but cactus and sage brush grew in the valley. The creek was not running there was considerable water standing in holes that were sometimes ten feet deep and clear and wholesome. In this region the soil is very soft and subject to being washed by rains. I passed over places which looked dry but my horse would get mired while crossing and

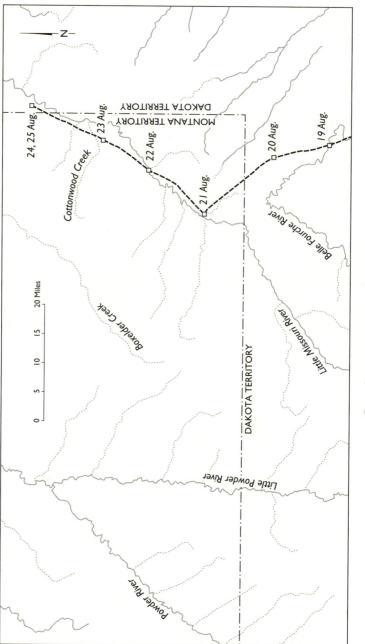

COLE'S ROUTE, 20–25 AUGUST

at one time I thought my horse would never get out. Sometimes on the dry plain the horses would sink into the dust over their hoofs.

After a march of nine miles we pitched camp in the edge of a grove of pine. There was plenty of wood and water but a scarcity of grass. The Col. sent me with a small party in search of the Little Missouri River. We started in a northwest direction and after a few miles, ascended the bluffs on the other side of the valley. Such a scene of desolation I think I never saw. It surpasses the Bad Lands, no vegetation and nothing but dry ravines guide us, crags & etc.

Acres upon acres of marine fossils were piled upon each other and covered the ground for miles. The country was so cut up with gorges worn by water that it was impossible to cross. In going in any direction, [the] first one [that] would meet with would be a cut 30, 40 or even 50 feet deep and perhaps not more than 25 feet across. Changing our course a few degrees to the left, we found better traveling, but still very rough. While going around a hill I was informed that a bear was on the other side. I at once mounted to the top of the hill and sure enough, saw a grizzly slowly making his way among the ravines as unconcerned as though there was no danger near. In fact he did not see us. Some of the boys came up on the other side and when he saw them, off he went in a lope. Coming to a ravine he climbed down as handy as a man and came up on the other side and set off again at a rapid pace, when a bullet was sent through his flanks. He turned and was making towards the man who had wounded him, when another bullet was sent through his heart and with a deep moan he fell and died. I had to make considerable detours to get to him, but was the first on the ground and his bearship stone dead. He was a young grizzly bear perhaps two or three years old and weighed 500. I left all the party except one to skin and take care of the bear while I went to the ridge and there discovered the river about 6 to 8 miles distant. It was too late to go further and I returned and assisted in dressing the bear and then fastening his head to my saddle, started to camp with meat, hide and all.

We had gone about 4 miles when another old bear and her cub was seen. Three of the men galloped off towards them and were quite close before discovered. They then started off, but the boys headed him towards us. He tried to get to the woods but the boys headed him off and he came down the valley towards us. But Sargt. [sic] [Thomas M.] Hamilton's horse got mired in the mud and another one of the boys rode between the bear and us and headed him toward the Sargt. who was fast in the mud and his gun under the horse. The bear made for him, but the Sargt. made his escape on foot and the bear escaped to the woods and got away. So much from a foolish boy being along with us. Bear & cub both escaped into the woods.

Arriving at camp, our bear made quite a sensation. This is my first bear adventure. Sargt. Hamilton is a brave man and did not but come near falling a victim to the foolishness of another. Marched 9 miles besides the bear expedition.[1]

Springer commented on the campsite: "The night was clear and beautiful, but the mosquitoes in such numbers, that sleeping was out of the question. Some bear growled around the camp, and was shot at by the sentinels but everything else quiet as the grave."[2]

Cole's command crossed the Belle Fourche and went over the hills bordering the river valley and then probably followed the Kirkpatrick Creek bed northwest and camped in the vicinity of today's Colony, Wyoming. The black shale mounds that Bennett described are very prominent on the hills that the command passed over leaving the Belle Fourche Valley. The great bear hunt probably took place a few miles northwest of the campsite.

Scurvy among the men now became a serious concern, as Capt. Samuel Flagg reported that on "August 20, Private J. Clark died in hospital, of scurvy."[3]

✳   ✳   ✳

Walker's cavalry rested a day on the Belle Fourche River, possibly in the general area that Cole's command had camped on the previous day. They probably followed Cole's route through this rough terrain, as it would have been the most practicable route to the Belle Fourche in the vicinity. He decided to scout the route to the Little Missouri while the command rested for the day: "lay up here [Belle Fourche River] one day to send scouts Northwest to see if any grass could be got   Our guides knew nothing of the country from this out and our horses were getting weak   Col. Cole has struck north to the Little Missouri[.]"[4] Walker pointed out that he suffered from the same affliction that plagued Cole since the start of his journey—guides who knew nothing of the country.

---

[1]Bennett diary, 20 August 1865 entry. Sgt. Thomas M. Hamilton was a member of Company M, Second Missouri Light Artillery. *Civil War Soldiers and Sailors System.*
[2]Springer, *Soldiering in Sioux Country*, 35.
[3]Flagg's official report of 20 September 1865, *The War of Rebellion.*
[4]Walker's official report of 25 September 1865, Hafen and Hafen, *Powder River Campaigns*, 93–94.

MONDAY, AUGUST 21, 1865

Cole described the route to the Little Missouri River, as well as two deaths that occurred within the command: "From the Cheyenne I moved up one of its tributaries to its head, thence down a small stream to the Little Missouri River, over a comparatively level country but with little water, however. Timber covered all the ridges and cedars filled the canons. Scurvy had now begun to develop itself, and one of the command died of this disease. One of my Pawnee guides also died of apoplexy or some kindred cause."[5]

Bennett also wrote about the deaths in camp:

> When camp was aroused this morning Lo Willacore, one of our Pawnee guides was found dead in his bed. He ate a hearty supper of bear meat and went to bed as well to all appearances as any of us, but this morning he was dead. The other Indians mourn considerably and has taken his bow, arrows, etc. to convey to his friends in the tribe. There was also a soldier died, was buried near a tree on an elevated piece of ground. These are the first deaths in the command except a Negro a few days ago.
>
> After passing up the valley to the ridge, we crossed over into another valley which led to the Little Missouri River. We had a long march of 21 miles. The day was hot and the dust thick and disagreeable. Reaching the river we found considerable water in pools but only a small steam flowing over the riffles. There was but little grass. The region was a very desolate one with little vegetation except sage brush and cactus. We saw many sage hens, a bird like a prairie chicken, a little larger with dark breasts. There were many old Indian signs but none of a recent date. Elk and bear sign were also plenty. Marched 21 miles.[6]

Lieutenant Springer and Capt. Charles F. Ernst had a dinner of black-tailed deer stew, biscuits, and strong coffee.[7] Springer described the evening: 'The stars shine brightly, although I did not sleep last night while on picket, I don't feel sleepy yet, friend Vetter will give us a song before we go to bed, which reminds of better days, long gone by, when we gathered around a glass of beer at St. Louis."[8]

---

[5]Cole's official report of 10 February 1867, ibid., 68. The creek bed that the command followed down to the Little Missouri was probably Five Mile Creek, which goes into the Little Missouri five miles north of today's Alzada, Montana.

[6]Bennett diary, 21 August 1865 entry.

[7]Captain Ernst was a member of Company D, Twelfth Missouri Cavalry. *Civil War Soldiers and Sailors System.*

[8]Springer, *Soldiering in Sioux Country,* 35–36.

TUESDAY, 22 AUGUST 1865

The command marched in search of grass for their hungry animals. Bennett reported, "We followed down the Little Missouri River in a north east direction. The road was very good. We followed an old Indian trail that was well worn. A few fresh Indian sign was discovered, all leading northward, as if skedadling from us. We went into camp at II A.M. Plenty of wood and water but little grass. Windy and dusty. Marched 12 miles."[9]

Lieutenant Springer described an Indian burial site: "We found several scaffolds erected, where Indians were buried upon. Near one there was a circle cut in the ground alongside the scaffold and 5 buffalo heads set around it, with noses toward the center. A small tin cup was also hung on one of the poles; at another scaffold the Dr. Bennett of the 2nd Mo. Art. had the buffalo robe opened where the corpse was sewed into and found the medicine bag filled with all kinds of stuff."[10]

Jay also talked about Indian signs: "On the east bank of the stream, fresh signs were seen of very great numbers of Indians. Trails covering the width of a mile, scarce three weeks old, fresh camp fires from which the ashes were not yet blown by the wind, etc. Numerous scaffolds on which the Sioux bury their dead were seen in the valley. Curious to know something of their funeral customs I examined several."[11]

❊   ❊   ❊

After laying over a day on the Belle Fourche, Walker and his command followed Colonel Cole's trail toward the Little Missouri River. "Scouts returned and reported no grass and an impracticable road Started on Col Cole's trail   reached the Little Missouri in twenty six miles over a barren, hilly broken road   found but little grass on the Little Missouri some water in holes[.]"[12] Without the encumbrance of wagons, his command could move at a faster pace than Cole's train, and he covered the distance to the Little Missouri in one day, while Cole had taken two.

[9]Bennett diary, 22 August 1865 entry.
[10]Springer, *Soldiering in Sioux Country,* 37. Springer seemed confused as to what Lyman Bennett's role was with the expedition, as Bennett was not actually a doctor.
[11]Hafen and Hafen, *Powder River Campaigns,* 358.
[12]Walker's official report of 25 September 1865, ibid., 94.

WEDNESDAY, 23 AUGUST 1865

Colonel Cole faced deciding between heading west to Boxelder Creek and staying on the Little Missouri in hopes of finding grass for the animals. Bennett described the day:

> A scout of sixteen men were sent to try and find the Box Elder fork, a stream supposed to be from 15 to 30 miles westward. The road was level, the region entirely destitute of vegetation. The earth was dry and parched. My ideas of the cause of this desolation is owing to an absence of moisture and rains except at certain seasons when it pours down and runs off carrying much of the soil from the hills and depositing it upon the plain where all the vegetation that has started is covered up and killed out. We camped on a creek coming in from the west and about two miles from the river which we crossed in the morning. Discovered fresh Indian sign. Marched 11 miles.
>
> In the afternoon Lt Kelly came across a grizzly bear and killed him.[13] I have not learned the particulars. Another bear was seen but not interfered with. Our expedition in search of the Box Elder found the stream, but very little grass and it was decided to follow down the Little Missouri another day where it was reported grass was plenty, stop one day for the stock to recover and then cross over to the Box Elder. While at the Box Elder our exploring party were quietly resting and grazing their horses. It appears that Col Walker of the other command sent a similar expedition to ours who discovered our men and took them for Indians and put back to their camp as fast as their horses could carry them, in fact so fast that all their horses played out except one and the next day it was currently reported all through the command that the 16th has met the Indians and had a fight.[14]

Springer complained about Colonel Cole's choice of campsite: "[F]or we are encamped about 4 miles from the river on a bare desolate spot. What Col. Cole's intention is, in taking us away from the river bottom with our already poor animals, I or nobody else can define."[15]

The creek that Bennett described and the campsite that Springer complained about is Cottonwood Creek. Its tree-lined creek bed runs almost parallel to the Little Missouri River for several miles before emptying into that river from the west.

✳   ✳   ✳

---

[13]Second Lt. Hiram L. Kelly was a member of Battery A, Second Missouri Light Artillery. *Civil War Soldiers and Sailors System.*

[14]Bennett diary, 23 August 1865 entry.

[15]Springer, *Soldiering in Sioux Country,* 37.

As Walker's command trailed the other column down the Little Missouri, Cole sent back a message relaying his scouts' observations on their exploration of the route to Boxelder Creek. Walker decided to move his command northwest to Boxelder Creek in spite of the scout's report of onerous conditions across the country to be traveled: "[M]arched one (1) day down it [Little Missouri River], received a dispatch from Col. Cole stating he should go down the Little Missouri for several days before he should cross to Powder River as his Scouts had reported Bad Lands and no grass for 25 miles but I determined to try it[.]"[16]

Thursday, 24 August 1865

Grass for the animals was a growing concern for the command on the Little Missouri. Colonel Cole wrote, "So short were my animals fed that I kept scouting parties out all the time in search of grass, which on the third day was found in plenty."[17]

Up to this time the reporting of mileage traveled by the command was mainly guesswork. From this point on, the method of calculating mileage would now be improved and done more scientifically, according to Bennett:

> Moved down the river along the west bank over a good road but barren and desolate with no sign of vegetation except cactus and sage brush and even those were dry and shriveled. Capt. McMurray, who by the way, is very ingenious, a capitol fellow and a particular friend has spent considerable time in the construction of an odometer. Today for the first time it was attached to a wagon wheel and found to work admirably. Hereafter I hope to depend less upon guessing out distances.
>
> We reached camp at 11 A.M. to our agreeable surprise found plenty of grass and fine camping ground. It was good to see our half starved and exhausted animals pitch into it. A poor soldier died today and was buried in this far off region. His disease was scurvy which is affecting quite a number of men. Marched 11 miles.[18]

---

[16]Walker's official report of 25 September 1865, Hafen and Hafen, *Powder River Campaigns*, 94.
[17]Cole's official report of 10 February 1867, ibid., 68.
[18]Bennett diary, 24 August 1865 entry. The device that Captain McMurray built no doubt counted the revolutions of a wagon wheel, and Bennett was able to convert that information to miles traveled. Odometers had been around for many years, with Ben Franklin given credit for designing a simple one for his carriage to measure the mileage on postal routes. In 1847 Mormon pioneer William Clayton invented a more complex device that he called the "Roadometer." Tad Walch, "Odometer Tallied the Progress of Pioneer Wagons," *Deseret Morning News*, 22 July 2006.

Springer observed, "[A]s 'Boots and Saddles' [bugle call] sounded half of our horses could not be found." They had straggled off in search of grass. Springer was ordered to go with his company and round them up, which he accomplished in an hour or two.[19]

The campsite for 24 and 25 August was located about three to four miles south of present-day Camp Crook, South Dakota, on the west side of the Little Missouri, just east of the today's South Dakota border.

✳   ✳   ✳

Walker moved his command away from the Little Missouri northwest toward Boxelder Creek. "[S]tarted North west   reached Box Elder in twenty eight miles over a barren, broken country   found some stagnant water in holes but very little grass   but feeding along the stream for some miles and cutting cottonwood we got enough for two days as I wished to send a scout to try to find a pass through the Bad lands to Powder River[.]"[20] As Walker was not consistent in the reporting of campsites, dates, and mileage, his path probably mirrored the same general route that today's State Highway 323 takes over a gentle divide between the two drainages. The mileage is pretty close to Walker's twenty-eight miles, depending on the angle of the crossing.

Friday, 25 August 1865

Colonel Cole gave the orders for the command to rest one day, giving the stock a chance to recuperate and feed on the good grass available at this campsite. "Whilst lying by one day to graze and rest the wearied animals and to make some necessary repairs, I sent a scouting party to the westward to discover some practicable route in the direction of Powder River. They proceeded as far as Box Elder Creek, a tributary of the Little Missouri."[21]

Bennett reported essentially the same: "Remained in camp recruiting men and animals. A party which was sent down the river reported mountains on each side the river which gradually closing in narrows

---

[19]Springer, *Soldiering in Sioux Country,* 37.
[20]Walker's official report of 25 September 1865, Hafen and Hafen, *Powder River Campaigns,* 94.
[21]Cole's official report of 10 February 1867, ibid., 69.

the valley. Another to Box Elder reported that stream 20 miles distant and a good road."[22]

Springer went hunting downriver with six men and his servant, without success. "The Sioux had many of their warriors buried near river and I found two pipes or calumets which I took home with me." The mosquitoes were very active and all of the party suffered.[23]

Captain Flagg reported another death from scurvy: "25th of the same month [August] Private Christian Senft died of the same disease."[24]

Cole then readied his command for their next major destinations, first to Boxelder Creek, then northwest through an almost unknown and poorly mapped country toward Powder River.

---

[22]Bennett diary, 25 August 1865 entry.
[23]Springer, *Soldiering in Sioux Country,* 37.
[24]Flagg's official report of 20 September 1865, *The War of Rebellion.*

CHAPTER ELEVEN

26–31 August

PERILOUS CROSSING

SATURDAY, 26 AUGUST 1865

Colonel Cole made the decision to move west toward Powder River, by way of Boxelder Creek. His scouting party confirmed that the creek was about twenty miles to the west. Bennett described the day's travel:

> Left our fine camping ground at an early hour and marched across country towards Box Elder. The road is a good one, and for 13 miles to the summit of the divide there was plenty of grass and fine scenery. Mountains towered up on either side at the distance of from two to three miles and their rocky precipitous sides and peaks were cut by storm frost and wind until they resembled old ruins. One in the distance was like a church with gable and steeple like the real church. Crossing the divide and descending into the Box Elder Valley, we again found a dry dusty and sterile region without grass, except a very little along the stream which was dry except in puddles. The day was hot, the march long and tiresome and I suffered from a sick headache and for a few hours was very sick. Dr. Anderson gave me a dose of medicine which relieved me.
>
> I found some curious specimens, petrified vegetables roots and also some peculiar rock. Dr. Anderson found a jaw bone different from that of any animal now living and full of teeth. Marched 20 miles.[1]

As the command left the Little Missouri and headed northwest, Springer described the "high towering mountains in phantastic [*sic*] forms." According to Springer the water in Boxelder Creek was "hot

---

[1]Bennett diary, 26 August 1865 entry.

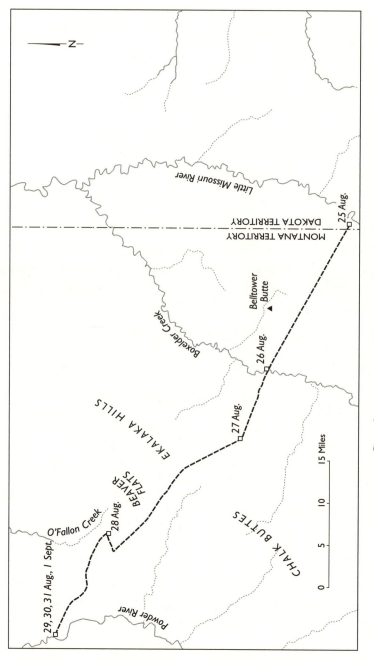

Little Missouri River

DAKOTA TERRITORY
MONTANA TERRITORY

Belltower Butte

Boxelder Creek

EKALAKA HILLS

BEAVER FLATS

O'Fallon Creek

CHALK BUTTES

Powder River

25 Aug.

26 Aug.

27 Aug.

28 Aug.

29, 30, 31 Aug, 1 Sept.

0   5   10   15 Miles

COLE'S ROUTE, 26 AUGUST–1 SEPTEMBER

and bad tasting." An abundance of deer and elk were killed. "Col. Cole arrested some of our men, but could not get them away from their companies, as they were arrested for killing elk. There will be a blow up the morning somewhere. I hope nothing serious will occur, although I would like to see Col. Cole somewhat vexed about it."[2] Cole described Boxelder Creek, but made no mention in his report of the arrest incident. "In the valley of the Box Elder there was a moderate quantity of grass, its timber consisting of box elder, cottonwood and red willow. On the bluffs adjacent there were many pines and cedars. The stream was not running, but water in pools was standing in the bends."[3]

Cole's command moved northwest from their camp on the Little Missouri, over country that still looks much like Bennett's description, with mountains on both sides. Today's Tie Creek Road follows the path that the command traveled. The peak he described as "like a church with gable and steeple" is today called Belltower Butte. It is located on the divide between the Little Missouri and Boxelder drainages about twenty-five miles southeast of present day Ekalaka, Montana. Approaching the summit from the east, Belltower Butte appears very prominently on the right as Bennett described. After the command crossed the divide, they no doubt followed Catamount Creek (a dry creek bed today) down to its junction with Boxelder Creek, where they camped.

SUNDAY, 27 AUGUST 1865

Cole's command crossed Boxelder Creek and moved up one of the streams coming in from the west, probably Buffalo Creek or Lone Tree Creek. They camped after marching less than ten miles because of the uncertainty of grass and water ahead. Cole described the day's travel and addressed the scurvy issue:

> Moving from here westward up the valley of a small creek, a tributary of the Box Elder, I camped on its head, with scant grass obtained by scattering the stock over a considerable area of the country. Scurvy had now become prevalent in the command, and the absence of anti-scorbutics

[2]Springer, *Soldiering in Sioux Country*, 38.
[3]Cole's official report of 10 February 1867, Hafen and Hafen, *Powder River Campaigns*, 69.

made it desirable to discover something as a substitute for the ordinary vegetables. One of the men now fortunately discovered that the yellow, washed clay on which we were camped contained a small bulbous root, which on examination proved to be a species of onion. . . . [T]hey had a good effect on the men, who dug and ate them with avidity.[4]

Bennett wrote of a dry, sterile landscape:

Left Box Elder crossing the river in a north western direction across a most miserable country as far as vegetation was concerned, but level for travel-ing. We went only nine ½ miles not knowing what the country was far-ther and choosing to stop where grass could be found rather than risk find-ing it ahead. Found plenty of good water in a branch leading into Box Elder. Saw traces of a large herd of buffalo which has passed within a few days. I should like to know their business in this dreary region. Finished reading *Very Hard Clash*. Marched 9½ miles.[5]

Springer's men sighted "a couple of Indians"—the first the command had seen since the visit by Little Chief and the Omahas on 15 July—and gave chase, but did not catch them. They "left Box Elder and marched 8 miles to a little creek without a name." Springer shot an antelope.[6]

❋   ❋   ❋

Walker's Sixteenth Kansas was on the Boxelder for two days waiting for the party that he had sent ahead to find a practicable route to Pow-der River. He then decided to move his command towards Powder River and find out what became of his scouts:

[W]aited the two days and the Scout not returning   started on their trail marched this day twenty four (24) miles over the worst country I ever saw not one particle vegetation was to be seen   the whole earth seemed to be one heap of burnt ashes   our horses would sink to their knees at every step   Killed this day ten (10) head of horses to keep them from falling into the hands of the Indians as small parties were now watching us found our scout camped on a small stream that entered into Powder River found some water and grass in the bed of the stream   they pronounced it impossible to reach the river that way without tremendous digging[.][7]

---

[4]Ibid.
[5]Bennett diary, 27 August 1865 entry.
[6]Springer, *Soldiering in Sioux Country*, 38–39.
[7]Walker's official report of 25 September 1865, Hafen and Hafen, *Powder River Campaigns*, 94.

BELLTOWER BUTTE

On 26 August 1865, while crossing from the Little Missouri River to Boxelder Creek, Lyman Bennett described the unusual shapes of the mountains: "One in the distance was like a church with gable and steeple like a real church." He was describing Belltower Butte, at the divide between the two drainages, shown here. *Author's photo.*

Walker's route taken for the crossing was probably in a northwesterly direction to the south of the Chalk Buttes and into the Powder River Breaks, a rough badland country requiring about twenty-five miles of demanding travel to the Powder River Valley.

MONDAY, 28 AUGUST 1865

The expedition was about to experience its most demanding day yet on the trail. Cole's command moved northwest toward the gap between the Chalk Buttes on the left and the Ekalaka Hills on the right. Bennett, riding with the lead elements of the command, described the terrain ahead:

The road in our advance has only been explored 12 miles with no signs of grass and water, but is supposed that both these indispensables requisites could be obtained within 20 miles and it was resolved to push on and trust to luck to find a camping place. We had a good road and an easy grade upon the divide over a dry barren country destitute of vegetation except prickly pear and cactus. Nine miles from camp there was a mountain a mile left of our line of march. Dr Anderson and myself ascended the mountain and had a grand view of the country for twenty miles around. Before us to the west was the Valley of Desolation, a wide stretch of valley filled with gorges, canons, perpendicular walls of rock, crags, cliffs, & torn and jagged and rent in all conceivable shapes and forms. To all appearance it was impossible to pass over it and we turned our course to the right skirting this wild scenery.[8]

The mountain that Bennett and Dr. Anderson climbed is the north-ernmost butte of the Chalk Buttes. The view from there to the west that Bennett described as "the Valley of Desolation" is a badlands area known as the Powder River Breaks. From there it is approximately thirty miles over very rough terrain to Powder River. The expedition's course was wisely shifted to a more northerly direction that took it onto Beaver Flats, a level plain west of today's Ekalaka, Montana, that is tree-less except along creek beds, which are few. The main creek in the area is Little Beaver Creek, which flows northeast and eventually into the Little Missouri River in North Dakota. O'Fallon Creek, which flows north to the Yellowstone, also rises out of this area. Bennett continued:

While on the mountain we saw a buffalo leisurely strolling across the plain about a mile distant. Dr. Corey and his orderly were in the advance and also saw him and dashed after him. Mr. Buffalo soon saw his pursuers and set off at a canter, the two horses after him and gaining on him, after a mile or two overhauled him and got a shot at him and finally killed him. The sun passed down its hot and scorching rays, no water or grass could be found and both men and beast began to suffer. Still we pushed ahead slowly over the rolling plain. Lt Hoagland was sent ahead to find a camp and sent back word that he had found some water.[9] We hurried ahead in the direction indicated and soon came to the rough breaks near the head of a stream running north. In the ravines where the creek exists was a

[8]Bennett diary, 28 August 1865 entry.
[9]Lt. Abram S. Hoagland was a member of Battery K, Second Missouri Light Artillery. *Civil War Soldiers and Sailors System.*

thread of brush and timber. We followed it down three miles and found two pools of muddy and brackish water, which was used up long before half the command had been provided with water. There being no more and no grass in this place, we changed the course westward and endeavored to reach Powder River but on reaching the region of the bluff, we found it impassable. We skirted the precipice for two or three miles looking down for hundreds of feet into the gorges below but no opening for by which we could get down & night coming on, we were obliged to turn back to the creek we had left. While looking over the desolate valley before us, occasionally a buffalo could be seen on the bare ridges or in the dry ravines looking as unconcerned as though none of his human enemies were near. Some of the boys climbed down the steep rocky side of the chasm and killed some of them. I learned that during the day 7 buffalos and one bear had been killed. The sight of a huge buffalo killed on the line of march attracted the attention of the whole command and was something new for us greenies.

Reaching the creek we found no water and following it down until dark, we still found none and was obliged to stop from fatigue. No tents were pitched. Officers and men stretched themselves down on the ground and worried out the night. Horses, mules and most of the men had had neither water or anything to eat for twelve hours and were nearly worn out with hunger and thirst. It was the first really severe march without these we had had. We have at times had a scarcity of a miserable quantity, but never before entirely without. It was resolved to push on at daylight and by some means get down the precipice into the valley and on to the Powder River. We slept on the ground, but the night was warm and we suffered no inconvenience from it. Marched 30 miles.[10]

Springer wrote, "We marched until 6 o'clock P.M. when we came to a valley, where we could see down from the bluffs but such a scene our eyes never beheld. It was something terrible grand and wild romantic, it appeared as if nature in a terrible rage and madness had thrown these big steep hills and huge rocks immense boulders with a gigantic hand into such a confusion." They could see a tree line in the distance that was probably Powder River.[11]

Cole's report summed up the hardships of this most demanding and frustrating day:

[10]Bennett diary, 28 August 1865 entry.
[11]Springer, *Soldiering in Sioux Country,* 39–41.

COLE'S DESCENT TO POWDER RIVER
Possible location of Cole's wagon road used in the descent
to Alkali Creek and Powder River on 29 August 1865. *Author's photo.*

From here to the westward I moved over a gently undulating country, without water save that in a couple of holes, which, with its brackish taste and thick consistency, was almost unfit for use. Nearly night the head of the column arrived at the edge of a cliff in sight of Powder River, distant about six miles across a strip of "Bad Lands," which was a part of "Les Mauvaises Terres" of the Yellowstone River. This cliff was hundreds of feet in height and no place of descent could be found. That this rough, broken region could be traversed after being attained seemed impossible; in no event could an attempt to reach the river that night be a success. This being patent I moved into the valley of O'Fallon's Creek, near its source, and fortunately discovered a small pool, containing possibly half a dozen barrels of brackish water, which the buffalo had been within a short time wallowing in. The intense heat of the day, along with the dust laden air, had created too strong a thirst among the men to hesitate at drinking the water discovered, although it was impregnated with the excrement of these animals. Of forage there was none to be had, and the stock had to be tied up the entire night without water or grass.[12]

To the west, the impassable Powder River Breaks blocked their descent to the valley of Powder River, but now only about ten miles distant. The command spent a sleepless night in a dry camp in the northwest corner of Beaver Flats.

⁑   ⁑   ⁑

Walker was still in the Powder River Breaks fighting the terrain to get his command to the valley floor and Powder River: "I lay up one day to find a road   found a pretty good road by digging."[13]

TUESDAY, 29 AUGUST 1865

In the morning at first light, a search was resumed for a trail to get through the Powder River Breaks to the floor of valley below them. Colonel Cole described the desperate situation: "After some search my guides discovered an Indian tepee trail leading down to the lower plain. By cutting along it and across divides and through canons I was enabled to get the trains advanced about 3 miles by night. . . . After getting the trains thus far I left them with a guard and moved the men, with all the animals, to the river for the purpose of reaching water and grass, of which the stock was so much in need."[14]

Bennett, as always, gave a more detailed account:

> As soon as day began to dawn and it was light enough to distinguish objects, Boots and Saddles was sounded and the march commenced. Capt. McMurray and Mr. Raymond had late the evening before discovered a pass down the bluffs which they thought could be made practicable for the train and command to go down. Accordingly the column was headed in that direction.
>
> One of the guides was half a mile ahead & when near the top of a hill, we saw him put spurs to his horse and almost at the same moment a large

---

[12]Cole's official report of 10 February 1867, Hafen and Hafen, *Powder River Campaigns*, 69–70.
[13]Walker's official report of 25 September 1865, ibid., 94.
[14]Cole's official report of 10 February 1867, ibid., 70.

buffalo emerged from a ravine and went cantering over the plain with the guide after him. This being early just at the dawn of day, presented an exciting spectacle. McMurray fired one shot, but the buffalo escaped. Coming to the brink of the precipice, we could look down upon the bare cliffs and crags below, but saw no place to descend. About 7 or 8 miles to the west we could see the water of Powder River glistening in the rising sun & a wide valley with trees and grass spread out in the distance before us, but no way to get to this inviting place. Finally a place was discovered that was barely practicable and the Pioneers set to work making a road down the steep ascent and by 7 o'clock [P.M.] the command was in the valley winding its way among the cliffs towards the river. Frequent repairs had to be made in the road, ravines filled in & which delays the column, but by ten o'clock all but the commissary train was in camp. The poor mules could not bring it along and it was left about four miles from the river. We found a fine stream of flowing water, but little muddier with fine groves of cottonwood on the banks and plenty of grass. The valley was from one mile to four miles wide and was really an enchanting place when compared to the country passed over by us for hundreds of miles. The camp was in a fine shady grove and was really pleasant. But our poor stock looked really pitiable. Some had had no feed or water for 32 hours, the weather being intensely hot which used many of them up so that the road was strewn with gaunt horses and mules. Marched 11 miles.[15]

The area that Bennett described is the rough, broken country at the divide in the northwest corner of Beaver Flats that leads down to the drainage of Alkali Creek, which in turn, after several miles, runs into Powder River. A very primitive Jeep trail in this area may be the original road cut by Cole's pioneers.[16]

Springer went ahead of the wagon train on horseback. "We again came to the valley and a descend was tried. We led our horses down, the Cavalry came down safely. But several of the wagons upset, but nobody was hurt. On we marched for the cottonwood we had seen yesterday. As we arrived there, not a drop of water to be found, things began to look awful serious, our animals began to give out more than 20 horses and the same number of mules fell down dead, on we marched." Around noon Powder River was sighted about four miles farther, and Springer

---

[15]Bennett diary, 29 August 1865 entry.

[16]The author viewed this rough trail on a field trip with Ekalaka residents Helen Stevens and Greg and Susan Tooke on 2 September 2007.

arrived there about two P.M. "After arrival in camp, I went with Bugler Vetter to the river and took a glorious wash."[17]

Jay wrote:

> From the Little Missouri River we marched across to Powder River, with little water and scarcely any grass for our animals. For the forty-eight hours before reaching the river they had none of either, and suffered most severely. Many dropped dead in the harness from exhaustion. The country for the last ten miles was rough chopped beyond description, and it required two days to get the train through.
>
> Coal veins from six inches to six feet thick, lying in horizontal state, outcropped from every hill and hollow. Gulches and canons hundreds of feet deep cut and cross each other, so that without the expenditure of an immense amount of labor in digging down banks and cutting shelving benches along the hill sides, a wagon could not be got through.[18]

The command went into camp at the mouth of Alkali Creek, on Powder River, with plenty of grass, water, and wood—quite a change from the suffering of the past few days.

✳   ✳   ✳

Walker's column finally reached the valley: "in two (2) days reached Powder River in twenty two (22) miles found some grass in the timber[.]"[19]

WEDNESDAY, 30 AUGUST 1865

A few years previous, in 1859, Capt. William F. Raynolds of the United States Corps of Engineers had been assigned to head a party to explore and map the Missouri and Yellowstone rivers and their tributaries. His party passed through the northern Black Hills and on west to Powder River. During his two-year expedition, Powder River and other steams in the region were extensively explored and mapped. However, this information and the maps that resulted were not avail-

---

[17]Springer, *Soldiering in Sioux Country*, 42–43.

[18]Hafen and Hafen, *Powder River Campaigns*, 359.

[19]Walker's official report of 25 September 1865, ibid., 94. Walker stated in his report for the next day that his command traveled twelve miles north to camp three miles below (north of) Cole's command, which would place his campsite on 29 August approximately eight miles north of today's Powderville, Montana.

able to Connor or Cole in 1865, as Raynolds did not submit his report to the secretary of war until 1866. The first printing of the map that resulted from that report was in 1868. An excerpt from Raynolds's report describing Powder River, six years before Cole's command arrived, is as follows: "The bed of the river is mainly a treacherous quicksand, and great care is necessary in selecting fords. The depth of the water is not, such as to offer any obstruction, except during freshets. The bluffs bordering the valley are throughout the much-dreaded and barren 'bad lands,' and this stream must ever remain of little or no value to the country."[20]

Nelson Cole's expedition would become very familiar with Powder River over the next twenty-three days. The river is formed in central Wyoming a few miles east of the present-day town of Kaycee. Three steams come together within a few miles: the North Fork, the Middle Fork and the South Fork, all originating in the Big Horn Mountains to the west. From its very point of origination, Powder River winds back and forth across a wide, shallow river bottom that can be either sandy or muddy. Probably not a mile-long stretch of the river over its entire length could be described as straight. The water is generally shallow and muddy. Much of the riverbank is lined with trees, mostly cottonwood. Because of the shallow, sandy-muddy bottom, the river is prone to cut new channels during spring runoff high-water periods. The river eventually empties into the Yellowstone River just west of today's Terry, Montana. From its headwaters to the mouth, in a straight line, is about 210 miles, but because of the winding nature of the river, the actual distance traveled by Powder River is many times more.

Colonel Cole, fully aware of his dwindling supplies, decided to rest in camp to recuperate the men and stock and sent a scouting party to ascertain the whereabouts of Connor's column: "My rations at this time were nearly exhausted, and it was necessary to communicate with General Connor as soon as possible to procure more. To expedite this I sent Lieutenant Hoagland, Second Missouri Light Artillery, with Raymond, my most reliable guide, and a detachment of twenty men, to scout across the Tongue River to ascertain the best route by which

---

[20] *Report of Captain W. F. Raynolds' Expedition to Explore the Headwaters of the Missouri & Yellowstone Rivers*, delivered to Secretary of War Edwin M. Stanton, 13 February 1866.

to move the column; also to find, if possible, at what point General Connor was lying with his command."[21]

Bennett, getting a chance to catch up on his mapping responsibility, described the day:

> A party was sent to the west to explore the route to Tongue River and the Panther Mountains which is supposed to be from 25 to 50 miles away. At the latter point our place of rendezvous with General Conner is designated.
>
> As we are to remain in camp several days to recover stock, I embrace the opportunity to bring up my plats. I also designated a place to ford the river and strolled over the country a mile or two. After leaving the immediate bank of the river the country is barren and desolate like the whole region around. This whole region is filled with the finest veins of coal sometimes eight and ten feet thick and exposed in every hillside. I never saw it so plenty and so easy of access. It is mostly bituminous, but some few specimens of anthracitic was also found. The eddies in the river is filled with coal dunes carried there by the waters. Our stock is luxuriating upon the rich grass of the valley. It does me good to see them enjoy it.[22]

Springer commented on the scouting party, and then headed off for a social evening with old friends: "A scouting party was sent out with 3 days rations to hunt up Connor's command which is supposed to be down the river somewhere. The 16th Kansas Cav. came marching down the north side of the river and encamped 2 miles below us." Springer was visited by two officers that he knew from the Sixteenth Kansas. "They made a raise of 2 canteens full of whiskey; I went with them to their camp and remained all night."[23]

Lt. William T. Shaver of the Twelfth Missouri Cavalry commented on the rations situation: "We left Omaha with 60 days rations so that on the day of our arrival on Powder River, we had only 5 remaining.

---

[21]Cole's official report of 10 February 1867, Hafen and Hafen, *Powder River Campaigns,* 71–72. In this report Cole said that the scout to the Tongue River was sent on 29 August. In Cole's report of 25 September 1865 from Fort Connor, he said that the scout left his camp on 30 August, which coincides with Bennett's journal. As Cole's second report was not written until months later from his notes and memory of the campaign, the author believes that Cole is confused about this date, and so stays with Bennett's timeline. Most of Cole's other dates in both of his reports coincide with Bennett. If the entire day of the twenty-ninth until dark was spent getting the command down to the valley floor, it is doubtful that Cole would send off a scout detachment at night.

[22]Bennett diary, 30 August 1865 entry.

[23]Springer, *Soldiering in Sioux Country,* 43–44.

But we expected to meet Gen. Connor on this stream and consequently felt no uneasiness."[24]

⁜   ⁜   ⁜

Walker decided to rendezvous with Cole at his campsite at the mouth of Alkali Creek. "In the morning heard Col Cole had struck the river twelve miles (12) below   went down and camped three (3) miles below him   he informed me he had sent a scout over to Tongue River to try to find Genl. Connor   I concluded to await their return and recruit up my stock as they had become very weak   many of my men were on foot as the horses had so weakened for want of grass and having no corn they could scarcely be drove along[.]"[25] Walker decided to await the return of Cole's scouting party. Clearly unsure of their next move, both commands expected relief from their dwindling rations and starving horses and mules by locating Connor's column.

THURSDAY, 31 AUGUST 1865

Bennett described a day in camp: "I have done but little today but plat and am making considerable progress with my maps. Several of the 16th Kansas came to see us. That regiment is encamped two miles below us. Both commands are waiting the return of our scout from Tongue River, before making any further movements. Hunting parties are patrolling the country for many miles and find an abundance of Buffalo. Their meat is a delicacy for us. Weather clear and pleasant. The nights are however quite cool and need all my blankets to keep comfortable."[26]

Springer, perhaps a result of his night of socializing, wrote, "Towards morning I took sick and when I returned to camp I had to lay down. I had a severe attack of the flux, but got better in the evening."[27]

Cole and his men were probably waiting optimistically for the return of Lieutenant Hoagland's scouting party and word from Connor. It would have been easy for them to think that the worst of their odyssey was now behind them.

---

[24]W. T. Shaver, "Reminiscences," Shaver papers.

[25]Walker's official report of 25 September 1865, Hafen and Hafen, *Powder River Campaigns*, 95.

[26]Bennett diary, 31 August 1865 entry.

[27]Springer, *Soldiering in Sioux Country 1865*, 44. Springer recorded 1 September twice here and is now back in sync with Bennett's journal.

CHAPTER TWELVE

1–4 September

DESPERATION AND INDECISION

T he western column of the expedition, led by Brigadier General Connor, marched north on Tongue River, probably in the vicinity of present-day Birney, Montana.[1] Cole's scouting party, led by Lieutenant Hoagland, arrived on Tongue River somewhere north of today's Ashland, Montana, about fifty miles north of the Connor column. Connor's command had been busy. On 15 August the fort to be built had been staked out on the west side of Powder River, about fifteen miles east of present-day Kaycee, Wyoming. The Sixth Michigan Cavalry, left to build the fort, named the new structure Fort Connor, later to be renamed Fort Reno.[2] On 28 August, while camped on Tongue River, Captain North's Pawnee scouts brought word of an Indian village twelve miles to the west of their previous night's campsite. Connor started out after dark with all available troops, except those assigned to guard his wagons, making a night march for the village. At about 7:30 the following morning Connor's force attacked the village with 125 soldiers and an auxiliary force of 90 Pawnee and

---

[1]Anonymous diarist with Connor, Lyman Bennett Collection, entries from 27 August 1865 to 31 August 1865. Connor's command was camped a few miles north of the Montana border on Tongue River on 28 August 1865. On 29 August a strike force went west and attacked an Arapaho village near present Ranchester, Wyoming. They returned on 30 August and the command moved eight miles downriver. On 31 August they moved fifteen miles downriver, which would place them near Birney. The unknown diarist may have been Miller, Bennett's friend, who did not show up to accompany him as an assistant on Cole's expedition, and went with Connor's column instead, or a staff officer who was close to Connor.

[2]Capt. H. E. Palmer's account of the Connor expedition, Hafen and Hafen, *Powder River Campaigns*, 117–19.

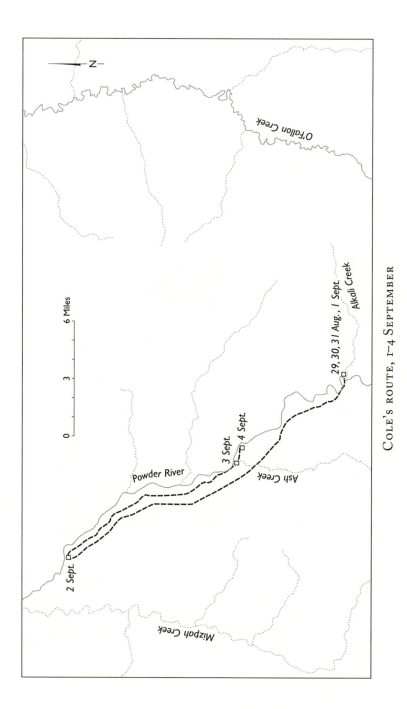

Mizpah Creek

2 Sept.

Powder River

3 Sept.

4 Sept.

Ash Creek

29, 30, 31 Aug., 1 Sept.

Alkali Creek

O'Fallon Creek

—N—

6 Miles

3

0

COLE'S ROUTE, 1–4 SEPTEMBER

Omaha scouts. The Arapaho village under headman Black Bear turned out to have an estimated population of 500, including warriors and non-combatants. After a brief fight the warriors were routed, the village and supplies burned, and the pony herd captured. Connor's command only suffered one death—an Omaha scout—and five wounded. Arapaho losses were estimated at sixty-three killed and seventeen captives taken, all women and children.[3] This fight took place on Tongue River near present-day Ranchester, Wyoming. Colonel Cole, in his camp on Powder River, knew nothing of these events.

FRIDAY, 1 SEPTEMBER 1865

Cole reported the return of Lieutenant Hoagland's detachment: "The scouting party left camp on the afternoon of August 29 [30], and returned on September 1 about 3 P.M., having stopped to rest but a few hours of time absent. They had governed themselves in their movements strictly according to my instructions, given from information derived from a map furnished by Connor. They traveled fifty miles directly west, over a country impassable for trains." Hoagland reported sufficient water but little grass and no sign of Connor's command. "Upon the reception of this report I ordered the rations reduced to less than one half. . . . it was my best policy to move toward rations."[4] Walker, who was at Cole's headquarters at this time, wrote: "Col Cole decided to turn back and go up Powder River fifty or sixty miles then try and cross to Tongue River as it was found impossible to cross at this point[.]"[5] Bennett also described the return of the scouting party and a new development: "Worked at my plats quite steadily and I am making fair progress. Our scout returned from Tongue River and Panther Mountains and report a dreary and desolate region without water or grass. Panther Mountain is 45 miles distant and Tongue River 25 miles and a very rough country to travel over. They saw nor heard anything of Genl. Conner. It was resolved to move tomorrow down the river instead of venturing in such a desolate country. A smoke was seen to the north which is supposed to be a signal from Genl. Conner."[6]

---

[3]Gen. P. E. Connor's report on the 29 August fight written on the 30 August, ibid., 46–48, Connor report of 30 October 1865, Dodge Papers.

[4]Cole's official report of 10 February 1867, ibid., 72–73.

[5]Walker's official report of 25 September 1865, ibid., 95.   [6]Bennett diary, 1 September 1865 entry.

Cole also mentioned observing smoke, which he speculated to be either Indian signals or Connor signaling from the Yellowstone. "Either case being true, it was, in my opinion, the proper course for me to pursue to move in that direction. In addition to this I deemed it possible that on reaching the Yellowstone game would be plenty, and with sufficient buffalo I could feed my command whilst searching for General Connor along the Tongue River." Based on this logic, Cole changed his previous decision to move south and decided to head north to the Yellowstone to search for Connor's command.

At this point in the expedition, Cole must have wondered what else could go wrong. He did not have to wait long to find out: "Whilst in the act of communicating my intentions to Colonel Walker, Sixteenth Kansas, then at my headquarters, a report was brought in that the Indians had attacked the herders herding stock a mile distant from camp and had driven off some of the stock." Obviously, the goal of the expedition was to engage and punish the Indians. However, with the command in such desperate condition, men with rations almost depleted, and animals starving and dying, this was not the time to start fighting warriors. Basic survival had to be a higher priority than punishing the Indians.

Cole went immediately to the scene. "On arriving near the scene of the attack I discovered the Indians to be in force, numbering some 400 or 500, and immediately ordered out the entire command, save sufficient to guard camp, to re-enforce the small party already in pursuit. The advance engaged the Indians and succeeded in recapturing most of the captured stock." Cole reported four men killed and two mortally wounded, and the Indian losses at twenty-five killed and a large number wounded.[7]

Bennett described the 1 September action, which took place on the west side of Powder River, opposite the command's camp at the mouth of Alkali Creek:

> About 5 P.M. the camp was startled by one of the pickets rushing in and reporting Indians stampeding and driving off the stock which had been sent to graze about two mile away on the opposite side of the river. Boots

[7]Utley, The Lance and the Shield, 69.
[8]Cole's official report of 10 February 1867, Hafen and Hafen, Powder River Campaigns, 72–73.

and Saddles was sounded and a small detachment under Capt. Rowland dashed off in the direction indicated in pursuit.[8] All I could learn was that 30 or 40 Indians came dashing among the stock and tried to scare it off but it being hobbled did not break and run, so each Indian took two or three horses apiece and made off with them. The guard consisted of but four or five men, were taken by surprise and fled except one man who fired away at them five or six times and hit one Indian and thinks he wounded him fatally. The Indians being too many for him, he finally retreated. Capt. Rowland had only about a dozen men and soon overhauled the Indians but they had been reinforced and now numbered 50 or 60 & gave the Capt. and his party fight, and soon killed two and wounded two men. Other Indians were observed coming to the assistance of those with whom the Capt. was engaged and the Capt. retreated after killing two Indians. On his return, strong parties were sent out in every direction. I had previously mounted my horse and went about three miles alone to a high hill to see if any of the savages could be seen. Seeing swarms of mounted men issuing from camp, I went to the nearest party and learned the particulars of Capt. Rowland's fight. I went with them to the place and saw one man stretched upon the ground cold and still in death. Another bloody and disfigured object was observed a few hundred yards off approaching us. He had no cloths but a shirt & was taken for an Indian and a charge made upon him when the horrid object was found to be one of our own men. He had been shot several times with arrows and his head horribly gashed and stripped of his clothing and left for dead. His shirt was torn and bloody, his head and hair one mass one mass of blood and deep gashes on his face and head besides arrow wounds from which the blood was oozing made a most horrid sight. The poor man was cared for as soon as possible.

A little ways further on was another poor fellow writhing with agony, his body pierced with arrows and a bullet hole through his stomach. He had been scalped and his skull was completely bare. He likewise had been stripped and was a most pitiable object to behold. Water was given him and every thing that could be was done, but we all knew that he must die. In a ravine a few hundred yards away was another dead body making two dead and two wounded. It was soon learned that Lt. Faran [Ferran] with only six men were in pursuit of the Indians and Capt. Rowland was sent to assist and bring him back.[9] Soon two of the Lt.'s men came in and reported him falling back and the Indians after him and our men out of ammunition. Of course the Capt. hurried on as fast as he could together

---

[8]Capt. E. S. Rowland was a member of Battery K, Second Missouri Light Artillery. *Civil War Soldiers and Sailors System.*

[9]Lt. James A. Ferran was a member of Battery K, Second Missouri Light Artillery. Ibid.

with a company of the 16th Kansas. The doctors and ambulances were on the ground after sun down and carried the dead and wounded men to camp. One poor fellow died before reaching camp. It was an hour after dark when I reached camp and learned of more fighting besides Capt. Rowland. The Indians came upon a hunting party of three men dismounted and soon killed two of them. But the third knowing that it was death to run and expecting death anyway resolved to sell his life dear as possible and shot two of the Indians and drove the others away. He went and scalped one of the dead Indians and then hurried for camp. He soon met a party of men and they went to the place just in time to drive the Indians a second time who were after their dead comrades, and succeeded in capturing two of their ponies. There are various reports as to the numbers of the Indians, some estimate is as high as 300. It is known that four of the Indians were killed and is thought more. At least quite a number are wounded. Our losses as near as I can form it up is 5 men dead, one seriously wounded and three slightly wounded and from 20 to 50 horses.

In the evening two of our men were coming into camp and were fired on by the pickets and both wounded, but not very seriously. The pickets were overly watchful and fired before giving the requisite challenge. I think this day's work will make us more careful in the future. It has developed the presence of hostile Indians all around us. We had seen none before and very few old signs and the men and officers were very remiss. This is a sad lesson for us and I hope it will not be thrown away unheeded. We are now in the heart of an enemy's country 800 miles from civilization. The loss of animals and stores will be the ruin of us all. Besides we have but very little provisions left, unless we meet Genl. Conner soon we will be in a bad fix.[10]

Capt. E. S. Rowland described the action from his perspective: "I at once proceeded to repel the attack with all of the mounted men then in camp, seven in number. On arriving at the point of attack found that the Indians had succeeded in driving off a number of horses. I at once attacked them. In the skirmish I lost 3 men killed and 2 wounded. A much larger number of the Indians were killed and wounded. Lieutenant Ferran of my company followed with a small number of men and by a different route; came upon the Indians that were driving the horses and killed two and wounded several others."

---

[10]Bennett diary, 1 September 1865 entry.

The dead in this engagement from Rowland's Battery K were Sgt. L. L. Holt, Pvt. Jesse Easter, and Pvt. Abner Garrison. The wounded were Sgt. J. L. Duckett and Pvt. W. Walker.[11]

Lieutenant Springer was visiting with Major Landgraeber when the alarm was sounded that Indians were attacking the herd. He described that about fifty warriors had dashed in and gathered twenty horses and fled. The herd guards had "dropped their guns and run, only 2 or 3 showed fight." Small detachments were sent out in different directions. "[S]ome of our men were out hunting who had quite a tussle with the Indians." Springer reported, "5 of our men were killed by arrow shots from the Indians, and one of them scalped, two were wounded, one of them severe."[12]

Pvt. James H. Thomas from Company F, Twelfth Missouri Cavalry, recalled, "We had to depend upon grazing our stock and although front and side hobbled they [the warriors] would dash in at dusk or about daybreak and succeed in running off many horses and mules, our boys would pursue and overtake stock that had stampeded over 20 miles with heavy army hobbles still on their legs and the leather had ground their ankles off raw to the naked bones."[13]

Col. Oliver Wells, commander of the Twelfth Missouri Cavalry, reported a separate action that took place four miles to the east of camp, up Alkali Creek. "On the 1st of September, the command being on the east side of Powder River, a portion of one company met a party of Indians about four miles from camp on our back trail. But little firing was done. The Indians scattered and our men did not pursue, owing to the inferiority of our horses. The officer reports one Indian shot and having fallen from his horse. On the same day the Second Missouri Artillery encountered the Indians on the opposite side of the river."[14]

The warriors who attempted to run off the command's horses on 1

---

[11]Rowland official report of 2 September 1865, *The War of Rebellion.*

[12]Springer, *Soldiering in Sioux Country*, 44–45.

[13]H. J. Mills had enlisted under the assumed name of James H. Thomas. He wrote, "My father was a strong union man but was bitterly opposed to my quitting college and joining the army, hence the name of James H. Thomas." H. J. Mills, letter to Walter M. Camp, 12 April 1921, Camp Collection.

[14]Wells official report of 20 September 1865, *The War of Rebellion.*

September came from the northern coalition of Sioux that had recently been in the vicinity of Fort Rice, Dakota Territory.[15]

⁂   ⁂   ⁂

Walker discussed the scout party's return with Cole, and after receiving the bad news, made his decision to move north toward the Yellowstone. Although he was with Cole when the Indians first struck, only one company of the Sixteenth Kansas participated in the action:

> [I]n three days the Scouts returned stating they had been to Tongue River on the 31st of August   found no grass on it   had went to Raw Hide [Rosebud] where we were to join Genl Connor   found no trace of him whatever Col Cole decided to turn back and go up Powder River fifty or sixty miles then try and cross to Tongue River as it was impossible to cross at this point I determined to go down Powder River to the Yellowstone thence up the Yellowstone to Tongue River. That evening the Indians attacked Col Cole's camp   that changed his plan as he then believed the Indians had gone below   before we had Believed from all signs they were above us[.][16]

SATURDAY, 2 SEPTEMBER 1865

In the morning, Cole's and Walker's commands moved north, with the Sixteenth Kansas in the lead. Cole described a hot, dusty day on the trail:

> [T]herefore, on the morning of the 2nd of August [September], crossed to the west bank of the river and moved down, following in the trail of Colonel Walker, Sixteenth Kansas, who had decided to try the Yellowstone before turning back, although his rations were as nearly depleted as my own. After marching twenty-five miles through heat and dust, camped with nothing but bark for forage. Colonel Walker camped ahead of my command about three miles. . . . On examination it was discovered that at a distance of about eight miles farther down the stream its waters sunk into the sand and the bed was comparatively dry.[17]

Bennett described a bleak landscape and the fast deteriorating condition of their animals:

---

[15]Utley, *The Lance and the Shield,* 69.
[16]Walker's official report of 25 September 1865, Hafen and Hafen, *Powder River Campaigns,* 95.
[17]Cole's official report of 10 February 1867, ibid., 74–75.

We did not march until 8 A.M., the time being occupied in burying the
dead Indian and preparing our own dead for burial. It was thought advisable not to bury our dead at this place as the Indians might come and dis-
inter them and mutilate their bodies, so they were sewed up in blankets
and buried at camp this evening. The wounded man died shortly after
reaching camp, making six that have died and one missing, a total loss of
seven. Our loss of horses was about 20.

It was supposed that the 12th Mo. Cav. had lost 7 men, but they came
into camp today. They had been on a hunt and strayed farther than they
supposed and was out all night, being lost a part of the time.

We marched down the west side of Powder River, the 16th Kansas in
advance over a rough and sterile country. About one P.M. we came to a
deep ravine which could not be got around and a road was dug down the
bank 20 feet then up the same distance the other side. After crossing we
looked for a place to camp where grass could be obtained but every where
a perfect desert stretched around us. On the left was high bare hills nearly
perpendicular washed and furrowed by rains and winds until they were
frightfully rough & craggy. On the right was the river, fringed by a considerable growth of cottonwood timber, but not any grass. We marched
until night and finding no grass or any prospects of any, we camped on the
south bank. A few rushes was all our stock could get after a march of 24
miles over a particularly rough road. Many horses fell dead; others became
too much exhausted to go further and were abandoned. This is a terrible
gloomy and sterile region. It is impossible for man or beast to exist here.
Tis dried until nothing is left but the dry and barren hills.

The valley between the hills is filled with an alluvial deposit washed
down from the hills that is from ten to 40 feet deep. I saw cottonwood
trees that was buried in the soil nearly up to the top. Some of them die and
then take fire & burn into the ground until a hole is made like a well from
ten to 20 feet deep. Water channels have been cut by the side of others
exposing their trunks buried into the earth. A fierce wind commenced
blowing afternoon and increased after sundown and at times during the
night I thought my tent would be torn down. Great clouds of dust were
raised hiding the column from sight a few miles from where one was riding. There is not a single feature about this country that would recom-
mend it except one, universal dreariness. Marched 24 miles.[18]

Springer reported an officers' meeting in which Colonel Cole informed them of his orders for the first time. "We had arrived at the

---

[18]Bennett diary, 2 September 1865 entry.

MIZPAH CAMP

appointed place of meeting. General Connor was not there, nor on the Tongue River." Cole informed them of their low ration situation and told them they could either head for Fort Laramie (three hundred miles south) or to the mouth of the Powder to see if Connor was on the Yellowstone. He left the decision to the officers and they decided to head north for the mouth of the Powder. They took their dead with them to be buried at the evening camp. After the funeral, the command marched over their graves to prevent the Indians from digging them up.[19]

The Indians were following the command, as 1st Lt. John H. Kendall, commander of Battery L, Second Missouri, reported: "I have the honor to report the result of a skirmish with a part of my company and some Indians on the 2nd of the month: I lost two men killed. My men killed 2 Indians and captured 2 ponies with some other trophies. The men killed by the Indians had been out hunting and were returning to camp when attacked."[20]

[19]Springer, *Soldiering in Sioux Country*, 45–46.
[20]Kendall's official report of 4 September 1865, *The War of Rebellion*. This is the only mention of the hunting party's fight—neither Bennett nor Springer mention this action. It does not appear in any of the official reports other than Kendall's own. George Hyde, in his biography of George Bent, reports this incident almost word for word with Lieutenant Kendall's report. George Bent was not involved here, so it was no doubt written from this same source. Hyde, *Life of George Bent*, 236.

The 1931 photos on this and the opposite page by local rancher Dan Bowman show the general area of Cole's northernmost campsite (2 September 1865) on Powder River. (*oppsite*) "Looking down Powder River (north) [past] Scouts point. Powder River Bridge Showing in the right fore ground." *Courtesy of the Montana Historical Society, photo 950-367.* (*this page, top*) "Looking E[ast] across Powder River from the back of Col. Cole's lowest camp. Cole's Buttes in the middle background (1865)." *Courtesy of the Montana Historical Society, photo 950-371.* (*this page, bottom*) "Looking N E down river from Cole's lowest camp on P.R. [Powder River] (1865). Col. Cole's wagon trail as it appears after lapse of 66 years." *Courtesy of the Montana Historical Society, photo 950-370.*

Dan H. Bowman, a rancher near Mizpah, Montana, arrived in Powder River country in 1882.[21] An amateur historian, he had a deep interest in the Indian war period. Bowman was particularly curious about the Cole expedition as the campsites on the lower Powder were practically in his backyard.[22] He placed the 2 September campsite about three and a half miles south of the present-day Mizpah bridge on the southwest side of the river.[23] Bowman based this conclusion on abandoned equipment that he had observed in the 1880s and wagon ruts that were still visible well into the twentieth century. Bowman took a photograph of the ruts at the campsite in 1931.[24] He also took a picture of a butte that he identified as "Cole's Buttes" across Powder River from the campsite location.[25]

At the particular spot where Bowman located the campsite, the river takes a gradual bend to the west though the river flows south to north, and one normally identifies the bank as either east bank or west bank. What would normally be referred to as the west bank becomes the south bank. Bennett said in his entry for the day: "we camped on the south bank."

✳   ✳   ✳

Walker and his command moved north to the vicinity of today's Mizpah Bridge and discovered that the country grew considerably bleaker. This caused him to re-evaluate his decision to move north to the Yellowstone:

> I marched twenty seven miles down the river and from two miles below our last camp we did not find any particle of grass and but little timber

---

[21]Daniel Hutchison Bowman was born in Andrew County, Missouri, on 4 March 1863. He moved to Montana in 1882, working as a cowboy, sheepshearer, sawmill operator, and at other jobs, until he began his career as a cattleman in 1899. His ranch, the Spearhead Stock Company, grew to more than twenty thousand acres. Bowman had a deep interest in the history of the area and in the 1920s corresponded regularly with the likes of Walter Camp and Luther H. North. Following his wife Lillian's death in 1936, he retired from ranching. He died in Miles City on 17 March 1956 at ninety-three years of age, and is buried beside his wife in the Custer County Cemetery at Miles City. *Miles City Daily Star*, 19 March 1956; Bob Barthelmess, *As We Recall*, 213.

[22]Bowman to Walter M. Camp, 2 January 1920, Camp Collection.

[23]Bowman to Camp, 14 February 1921, ibid.

[24]Montana Historical Society Photo Archives, photo #950-370.

[25]Ibid., photo #950-371.

the bluffs came closer to the river and the bed of the river seemed fuller of quicksand   I was compelled to camp without any grass whatever   I went two miles further to try any find grass   could find none   found the river had become dry at this point   I got on a high bute [*sic*] and could see for ten miles down the river   It was barren as a floor   I then tried to see if I could cross towards Tongue River and even pack mules could not be taken across at that point without much digging   I came back and examined my supplies and found that I had but six days rations on hand[.][26]

Cole stated in his report that the Sixteenth Kansas had camped ahead or north of his command about three miles. This would place Walker's campsite just above or south of the bluffs overlooking today's Mizpah bridge. Their camp was probably on the location where the Balsam Ranch complex is located today. Dan Bowman took photographs from these bluffs overlooking the bridge, pointing his camera both to the north and south.[27] Bowman called these bluffs "Scouts Point," and the view is much like the one Walker described.

SUNDAY, 3 SEPTEMBER 1865

A sudden change in the weather had a deadly effect on the stock. Cole, after getting discouraging reports about the country to north, reluctantly made a decision to reverse their direction of travel and move south towards Fort Laramie:

During the night a terrible storm set in, a kind of storm that is liable to sweep over this country in any season, during which the temperature of the atmosphere suddenly changed from intense heat to extreme cold. The want of nourishing forage, the exhaustion incident to the intense heat of the days march, coupled with effects of the storm, proved fatal to a large number of horses. I now very reluctantly turned back, on the 3rd, and moved to the first point where sufficient grass could be obtained for my dying stock. During the march down the river and back to grass 225 horses and mules died from excessive heat, exhaustion, starvation, and extreme cold, and in consequence a number of wagons had to be destroyed, together with a considerable amount of no longer needed quartermaster's stores.[28]

---

[26]Walker's official report of 25 September 1865, Hafen and Hafen, *Powder River Campaigns*, 96.
[27]Montana Historical Society Photo Archives, photos #950-366, 367, 368.
[28]Cole's official report of 10 February 1867, Hafen and Hafen, *Powder River Campaigns*, 75–76.

Bennett described the reaction of the men to Colonel Cole's decision to move south:

> In the morning we learned that the whole region before us was one scene
> of desolation, even on the Yellowstone. It has been impossible to commu-
> nicate with Genl. Conner and our stock dying and provisions running out,
> it was resolved to turn back and make Fort Laramie as soon as possible.
> This determination was received with cheers by the men as we turned our
> faces southward. Shortly after leaving camp the horses began to give out
> and drop down by the way and in the course of the day we lost about 150
> mules and horses. This shows how low our stock is reduced. We camped
> about 11 A.M. where we found considerable grass and our stock was turned
> to it after being without 30 hours. Much property is being abandoned and
> destroyed; saddles, harnesses and other property. Marched 17 miles.[29]

Springer also described the men's reaction, with a brief commentary
on the weather: "Sept. 3rd we were surprised by receiving orders to
retrace our way and start for Ft. Laramie, a loud hurrah: hurrah:
showed how gladly it was accepted. O, God, what weather. It was cold
as in mid winter."[30]

The 3 September campsite was located at the mouth of Ash Creek
on the west side of Powder River. Rancher Dan Bowman recalled seeing in the 1880s the remains of abandoned wagons and equipment.
"About 6 or 7 miles below the mouth of Alkali Creek on the west side
of Powder River I saw the remains of 8 or more wagons, the wood
work of which was burned."[31] The mouth of Ash Creek is approximately seven miles below or north of the mouth of Alkali Creek.

       ❋   ❋   ❋

Walker, discouraged by the country ahead of them to the north, called
his officers together, explained the dire situation, and let them vote on
which direction he should take his command:

> I called my officers together on the morning of the 3rd Sept   shewed [*sic*]
> them my orders told them what Col Cole's scout had said my signals had
> not been answered   stated that General Connor should have been at

[29]Bennett diary, 3 September 1865 entry.
[30]Springer, *Soldiering in Sioux Country*, 46.
[31]Bowman to Walter M. Camp, 2 January 1920, Camp Collection.

Panther Mountain ten (10) days ago if nothing had happened   that the
want of grass would not stop him as he had corn   that we were now
within twenty (20) miles of the Yellowstone   from that to Tongue River
it was about sixty (60) miles   that our stock could not go two (2) days
longer without grass   that I would leave it to them if we should risk all
and go on or return up Powder River where we should at least get water
and cottonwood that would keep the stock from starving and try to cross
the country where I thought the country was not so broken   with one
accord they voted to return   I now put my men on half rations dismounted all those whose horses had given out and started up river on
reaching Col Cole's camp I found he had turned back too[.][32]

MONDAY, 4 SEPTEMBER 1865

The command moved only a short distance to better grass. Cole, not
wanting to leave anything of value for the Indians, sent back a detachment to destroy any equipment left behind. "On the day following I
moved camp about a mile and a half for grass, into the edge of a strip
of timber which skirted the river. During the afternoon a detachment
of the Twelfth Missouri Cavalry, who were sent to the camp of the previous day to destroy the abandoned property, were attacked by a force
of about seventy-five Indians, who were repulsed, with the loss of one
warrior killed. Upon being pursued they retreated down the river."[33]

Bennett described another lively encounter with the Indians:

> We broke up camp at 7 A.M., the 16th Kansas passing us and taking the
> advance. Supposing that Col. Cole's command would follow closely after,
> I joined the column of the 16th and had gone perhaps 7 miles when I found
> that our column was not following after. I turned back and rode 5 miles
> and found the command only 2 miles from the camp of yesterday. The rea-
> son of so short a march was finding a fine plat of grass and our worn and
> jaded horses needing recruiting, it was determined to stop and feed.
>
> On getting to camp I went to work on my maps and while very busy a
> whirl wind came along & carried off my tent in an instant and is casting my
> papers over the ground. The tent was put up again more substantial and I
> was not interrupted in my work until about 5 P.M. when a rapid firing a half

---

[32]Walker's official report of 25 September 1865, Hafen and Hafen, *Powder River Campaigns*, 96.
[33]Cole's official report of 10 February 1867, ibid., 75–76.

mile from camp attracted my attention and the alarm of Indians was given. Going out of the tent I perceived 15 or 20 of our men on the hills hotly engaging with about 50 Indians who were flying swiftly around on their ponies and using their bows and arrows at the men, but their own carbines kept them at a respectful distance. It seemed to be the aim of the Indians to draw the men out and get them scattered and then attack in detail. The camp was aroused. The stock quickly gathered in and all were ready for an attack. Small squads, some on foot and others on horse back dashed out to where the fight was going on. My horse was quickly saddled and when just about to mount, the Col. asked for him as his had not been brought up and mounting my horse away he dashed. Now the Col.'s mule was saddled and I dashed out in the same direction. The Indians, seeing so many men come at them retreated and are after them pell mell. Our poor jaded horses were no match for their fresh ponies and they could outstrip us. The chase was an exciting one at times, those on the fastest horses would get ahead of the party and in their eagerness, they would get separated. The Indians noticing this would turn and then there was an exciting chase. The party behind pressing forward to rescue those ahead and the Indians dashing like the wind to cut them off before help came up. Once they got nearly upon one of our men. His cloths [sic] was cut with an arrow and they dismounted him and took his mule. He made a very narrow escape. We kept up the chase until dark and then groped our way over the hills and in darkness to camp. We saw a large body of Indians about 4 miles above on the river, but it was so dusky being after sun down that we could not tell their numbers. It was thought that one Indian was killed as he was seen to fall and was taken up by the others and carried away. Every precaution was taken to prevent an attack during the night. The guards were doubled and we all slept with our arms in order and near at hand and with an eye partly open. No alarm however. Marched 2 miles.[34]

Springer also described the destruction of equipment: "[W]e burned 12 wagons before we started out, also burnt a lot of quartermaster and camp and garrison equipage, also any amount of ordinance stores; for instance saddles, curry combs, brushes, &c. We marched only 3 miles and again encamped. The weather is very nice but very windy."

A party was sent back to the last campsite to destroy everything that could be used by the Indians. About 4 P.M. Springer heard firing from downriver. He participated in the chase to drive off the Indians. He

---

[34]Bennett diary, 4 September 1865 entry.

describes how one warrior was cut off and his companions came to his rescue. "A squad of about 30 warriors came helter skelter across the prairies to assist and rescue their warrior; as I saw this I shouted to Capt. [Sydney] Bennett to bring up all the men he could gather up." Springer said two Indians "bit the dust," and the soldiers suffered no casualties.[35]

Lt. William Thompson Shaver of the Twelfth Missouri Cavalry reported on the day's action: "On the morning of the 4th finding it impossible to get along with our large and cumbersome train, it was deemed expedient to reduce it as much as possible. Several wagons were destroyed; a party of men sent to destroy them (after going into camp) were attacked by Indians and driven into camp. The Indians were driven off, and did not again make their appearance until the morning of the 5th."[36]

Col. Oliver Wells reported, "On the 4th of September the Indians attacked a lieutenant and fourteen men, who had been sent to the camp of the previous day on Powder River, and followed him to the command. My whole regiment was engaged in skirmishing this day, in front, in rear, and on our flank, yet I would not judge there were over 150 Indians at this time in the whole party, their manner of fighting and irregular movements make it very difficult to judge."[37]

Rancher Dan Bowman, who had observed in the 1880s the wagons and equipment left behind, recalled, "Second engagement occurred at the mouth of Ash Creek on the west side of Powder River. This was Sept. 4th."[38] Bowman is, of course, referring to the campsite of 3 September, and the skirmish that occurred when a party was sent back to burn the equipment on the next day. The warriors encountered on this day were from the northern Sioux coalition that included such notables as Sitting Bull, Gall, and White Bull.

On this day Capt. Samuel Flagg reported another scurvy casualty: "September 4, Private H. Grote died of scurvy. In the evening of the same day were attacked by some 700 or 800 Indians."[39]

---

[35]Springer, *Soldiering in Sioux Country*, 46–47.
[36]Shaver, "Reminiscences," Shaver papers.
[37]Wells's official report of 20 September 1865, *The War of Rebellion*.
[38]Bowman letter to W. C. Brown, 6 February 1930, Daniel H. Bowman Research Collection.
[39]Flagg's official report of 20 September 1865, *The War of Rebellion*.

✳   ✳   ✳

Walker and the Sixteenth Kansas continued their trek south and camped about ten miles south of Cole's command. Because of the limited grass and starving animals, it made good sense to camp apart and to spread the grazing animals over a larger area. Walker wrote, "I was compelled to march twelve miles further to get grass   the Indians were now all around us on the hills[.]"[40]

✳   ✳   ✳

The men of both commands probably slept uneasily, if at all, with their weapons close at hand. They undoubtedly expected to see a return of the same warriors in the morning.

---

[40]Walker's official report of 25 September 1865, Hafen and Hafen, *Powder River Campaigns,* 96–97.

CHAPTER THIRTEEN

5–7 September

DAWN ATTACK

TUESDAY, 5 SEPTEMBER 1865

The warriors returned early the next morning in greater numbers and were engaged with the troopers before the command got under way. Cole described what took place: "On the following morning, when the command was preparing and almost ready to move, Indians were discovered in large numbers in the hills to the west, moving through the gulches to the southward. It soon became evident that they were endeavoring to cut off some of my teamsters who were gathering up straggling mules. A well directed volley from the train emptied some few saddles and caused the balance to make a retrograde movement as soon as they could secure their fallen braves."[1]

Bennett also described the early morning action:

> Before sunrise, a volley from the pickets on the north side of camp aroused us all and we were soon ready for anything that might turn up. We learned that the pickets had discovered a few Indians in the early dawn prowling and about three quarters of a mile away and had fired at them, but of course without any other effect than to warn the Indians that they were discovered. Had the pickets kept cool a short time it is very likely they would have come within range and some of them been picked off.

---

[1] Cole's official report of 10 February 1867, Hafen and Hafen, *Powder River Campaigns*, 76–78. According to Dan Bowman, the "Battle of the 5th was fought in the timber about 2 miles or so above the mouth of Ash Creek & was fought on both sides of the river." Bowman letter to W. C. Brown, 6 February 1930, Bowman Collection.

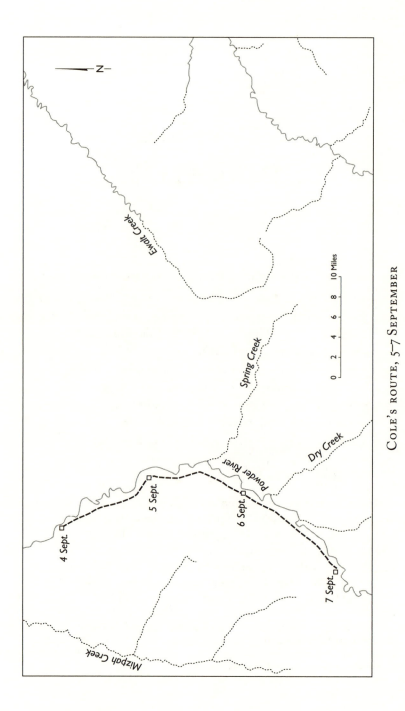

Cole's route, 5–7 September

As daylight came on, above every hill and rock surrounding camp appeared to be covered with Indians. Their heads could just be seen projected above the bluffs and peering out from behind rocks and ravines. Between the hills large numbers were mounted on ponies which were skipping about from point to point with the greatest of ease and speed. They generally kept from 3/4 mile to 2 miles away and out of range of our carbines. Still the men would occasionally fire as they saw one emerge from behind some rock or hiding place. At length a body of about 20 came dashing out of a ravine towards the wagon train which was parked just south of camp. The teamsters had been armed the night before and while some few ran into camp, others stood their ground and poured an irregular fire among the yelling Indians. Some soldiers coming up to the help of the teamsters, the Indians dashed out of range, but one of their number was seen to fall from his horse and was picked up by his comrades and carried off apparently dead. This body went across the valley and over on the opposite side of the river.[2]

Cole also told of the warrior movements in the vicinity of the camp: "Whilst in person on the west side of camp I discovered that large bodies were moving up the valley toward the south, and also there was a considerable force on the east bank of the river." A defensive perimeter was set up, and the Indians attempted to draw out small parties using their decoy strategy. This continued for three hours, until a detachment from the Twelfth Missouri Cavalry crossed the river, without orders, in pursuit of a decoy party and promptly was confronted by a larger group of warriors. The warrior's ponies were in superior condition to the worn-down cavalry mounts, and the detachment was quickly overtaken. Cole described the action with emphasis on the effectiveness of the weaponry of the two sides in close quarters:

The carbine is an unwieldy arm to handle when on horseback, and cannot at close quarters compete with a well-handled pistol, but against bows and arrows in the hands of men who can use them with the most surprising rapidity they are entirely useless. The detachment was driven into the river, with the loss of two men killed and two wounded. They only escaped annihilation by the prompt action of Captain Boardman, who moved a portion of his company to their support, and by well directed volleys drove the Indians back with heavy loss.[3]

---

[2]Bennett diary, 5 September 1865 entry.
[3]Cole's official report of 10 February 1867, Hafen and Hafen, *Powder River Campaigns*, 76–78.

Bennett, once again near the center of the action, gave a detailed description as the fight progressed:

By this time all were under arms and a number of men mounted and a charge was made from camp in two directions, but the Indians would not stand, but ran before our men and their fresh ponies could keep out of our reach. Some of the men, as on the night before, dashed ahead of the detachment and became separated, when as if by magic, Indians would rise up from ravines and from behind rocks and hills and endeavor to cut them off and many made a very narrow escape indeed. One poor fellow went a little too far, his horse was killed and he was immediately surrounded with Indians who hacked him almost to pieces and his body was pierced with arrows, one going through his body. He killed one, but was so terribly mutilated that he gave up, but was rescued from the Indians and brought into camp more dead than alive. Finding that it was of no use to pursue them as their horses were fleeter than ours, our mounted parties returned and were stationed on the picket lines on the outskirts of camp. The Indians used every artifice to draw us out in order to get a chance to pick off some straggler or reckless dare devil that alone, or feeble supported advance within their reach. Our stock were nearly drilled to death, in fact numbers were dying constantly as it would not do to give chase when it was known that their horses were much the best. As we were in our advance parties, the Indians closed around us and were all around camp and on the hill tops, but also a safe distance from danger. Lt. Smiley was on the bank of the river in rear of camp to prevent the Indians making an attack in that direction.[4] Seeing a few Indians on the opposite side, he crossed over with about a dozen men. He scarcely gained the opposite bank when about a hundred Indians arose from a grove of young Cottonwood and brush that had concealed them and charged furiously on to the Lt. and his party. His men fought bravely and emptied several saddles but coming up among his hand full of men, they proved too numerous and the Lt. had to retreat leaving one man dead and two wounded. Capt. Boardman coming up with his Co. and a number of stragglers from camp poured in so close and hot a fire upon the Indians that they in turn fell back and Lt. Smiley recrossed the river and brought over his wounded men. They were terrible cut up about the head with tomahawks and arrows had passed completely through their bodies. The loss of these men were wholly owing to reckless carelessness and going in [with] so few numbers, out of reach of support and among a swarm of Indians.[5]

---

[4]Lt. Phillip Smiley was a member of Battery H, Second Missouri Light Artillery. *Civil War Soldiers and Sailors System.*
[5]Bennett diary, 5 September 1865 entry.

Springer had just finished breakfast when the alarm "Indians!" was raised. Colonel Wells ordered Springer and ten men to the northwest side of the camp, where Dr. Corey and his wife had their tent. He observed Lieutenant Smiley's small party of six men, from the Second Missouri, on the east bank and went to their assistance. Pvt. John Shook, one of Springer's squad, recalled that the ten men from Company B, Twelfth Missouri, crossed to the east bank without orders, then charged the Indians, but had to fall back when confronted by "about 100 Indians."[6] Springer and his men had a running fight with the warriors. Pvt. George McCully of Company B was killed during the fight back to the lines. Pvt. James D. Morris, also of B Company, died later that night of an arrow wound to the abdomen. Springer's horse had a bullet wound and an arrow wound.[7]

An Indian command post was spotted. Cole reported, "I opened with shell upon this particular spot, and although not doing any serious damage caused the evacuation of this and all points within the range of my guns and a cessation of attack on the part of the Indians. . . . Finding myself unable with my exhausted and broken down stock to gain any adequate advantage by remaining longer in this position, I moved up the river to the first spot at which I could find grass, a distance of twelve miles."[8]

Springer described the order of the command as it moved out after the artillery had cleared the hills: "About 9 o'clock we left camp, divided into three battalions, the first battalion in front, the second in the center for the protection of the wagons, the third under Major Landgraeber protected the rear. They killed 7 Indians after we left camp, there couldn't have been no less than 20 Indians killed."[9]

Bennett also wrote of the Indian command post and the effect of the artillery on it:

The chiefs could be seen upon hill tops with looking glasses reflecting the rays of the sun in such a manner so to direct any party of Indians for two or three miles. Finding that a fair fight could not be had, the trains and column commenced the march about nine o'clock after a fight of three or four

[6]Shook's letter to H. J. Mills, 4 April 1921, Camp Collection.
[7]Springer, *Soldiering in Sioux Country*, 47–50.
[8]Cole's official report of 10 February 1867, Hafen and Hafen, *Powder River Campaigns*, 76–78.
[9]Springer, *Soldiering in Sioux Country*, 47–50.

hours. The artillery was brought to bear upon them and cleared the hills of Indians and only now and then could one be seen darting behind some bluff and hiding place. The columns and trains were in motion and the rear guard had not yet got out of the camp when from every direction hundreds of yelling savages came rushing into camp and charging towards the guard. They reserved their fire until the Indians were within 150 yards and then found [fired?] a volley among them that killed seven, wounded many and killed 10 ponies. The Indians retreated in as great a hurry as they had come into camp. It was supposed that one of the chiefs was killed as one large Indian, very gaudily dressed was seen to fall when the whole band rushed to him and carried him away and collecting about him they paid no attention to any of the other dead. Not a man of ours was hurt except Lt. Kelley who was struck with a spent ball, but only slightly bruised. This was too much for the redskins. They did not molest us any further in the march. A few following on our flanks one or two miles away, their object appearing to watch us, not to fight. We met the 16th Kansas coming to our assistance. They had heard our firing and did not know but they would be needed.

The results of the mornings fighting was from 12 to 15 Indians killed, 12 ponies killed, and their wounded unknown. Our loss was one killed and three wounded, all of them dangerously so that their lives are despaired of.

Major Landgraeber became a little separated from his men when the rear guard was attacked and two three Indians made for him. His carbine became out of order and he could not use it and was too much excited to think of his pistol until an Indian was nearly on him and had shot several arrows, barely missing him. At length, thinking of his revolver, he drew it and shot the Indian dead.

We marched 13 miles, camping on the west side of the river. Indians were seen prowling about, but in no strong numbers. A herd of Buffalo came to the river near the camp of the 16th and ten were killed. All slept in readiness in expectation of more fighting in the morning.[10]

As he commanded the rear guard against an attack as the command moved out, Major Landgraeber, one of the heroes of the day, described the action:

[O]n the morning of the 5th, we were again attacked by the Indians and fought them for three hours, at which time the command was ordered to march. My battalion, being detailed as rear guard, succeeded in protecting the train, and fighting the entire force of Indians for four hours, killing

---

[10]Bennett diary, 5 September 1865 entry.

many and wounding many more, who succeeded in making their escape. Among the killed was one Indian Chief. As soon as he was killed the fighting ceased on the part of the Indians. Lieut. H. L. Kelley, of Battery B, being wounded during the engagement was the only casualty on our side.[11]

Col. Oliver Wells reported his view of the fight:

On the following morning the Indians appeared on the bluffs in front and rear, and in the valley on both flanks of the camp. An irregular skirmishing was kept up for two or three hours before the command moved out, and the artillery was brought to bear upon some points occupied by the enemy. Their number at this time was variously estimated at from 500 to 2000 men. We lost 2 men killed and had 1 man severely wounded. I have no satisfactory evidence that over 4 or 5 Indians were killed by my command. Major Landgraeber, Second Missouri Artillery, in command of the rear guard, had a brisk engagement after the troops had vacated the camp, and I believe some 7 or 8 Indians were left dead on the ground.[12]

Lieutenant Shaver described the day's battle: "[T]he morning of the 5th about sunup, when they [the warriors] attack our camp in large numbers, but were driven off with a loss to us of two men of the 12th killed and one severely wounded."[13]

Capt. Samuel Flagg wrote, "In the morning of September 5 were attacked by about 900 Indians of different tribes, who, after some severe fighting, were repulsed. Lieut. H. L. Kelley being slightly wounded."[14]

Sgt. P. C. Stepps recalled: "The following morning just at the break of day a band of some two or three hundred warriors attacked the camp but ran into Co. C of the 12th which was mounted and moving out on picket duty. In the skirmish that followed one of C's men was wounded with a poisoned arrow and died two or three days afterward in great agony. No Indians were left on the field in this skirmish, but it was thought a number of them were wounded and some possibly killed but carried away on their ponies."[15]

---

[11]Landgraeber official report of 20 September 1865, *The War of Rebellion.*
[12]Wells's official report of 20 September 1865, ibid.
[13]Shaver, "Reminiscences," Shaver papers.
[14]Flagg's official report of 20 September 1865, *The War of Rebellion.*
[15]P. C. Stepps, "Expedition Store Brought to Close," *Casper Tribune-Herald,* 31 August 1930. Use of poisoned arrows was not a common practice by the Plains Indians, but it could be true. Perhaps it was an infected wound, rather than a poisoned arrow.

✳   ✳   ✳

The Sixteenth Kansas were camped fifteen miles upriver when Cole's command was attacked. Lieutenant Colonel Walker reacted to the roar of the artillery downriver: "the morning of the 5th Sept after leaving camp a few miles ahead hearing cannonading in the direction of Col Cole's camp some fifteen (15) miles back corralled one train and left Major [Clarkson] Reynolds with the first Battalion to guard it as the Indians were on the bluffs around us and took the rest of my command and went to Col Cole's assistance but found he had driven the Indians off   was compelled to go into camp with but little grass[.]"[16]

WEDNESDAY, 6 SEPTEMBER 1865

The command continued to move south, keeping a watchful eye toward the warriors while looking for suitable grass for their starving stock. Bennett described the march and precautions taken in camp against a surprise attack:

> Several parties of Indians were lurking around camp yesterday evening until dark, but the camp was not disturbed by them in the night, and about 7 A.M. the march was resumed. Our column on the west bank of the river and the 16th Kansas on the east. The 16th had better roads than we and went about 16 miles, camping 6 miles above us. We had several deep ravines to cross and dig roads down and up their banks so that at 3 P.M. we had made but ten miles and went into camp where there was an abundance of buffalo and other grass.
>
> A single party of two men were sent across the river a mile from camp to a high bluff to see if Indians could be seen. On ascending the bluff, a party of about a dozen Indians were seen a mile in their rear and the men commenced signaling to that effect, but before his dispatch was completed the Indians made for the bluff and the boys came into camp in a hurry. Col. Cole sent me out with 20 men to protect the station and we went to the hill, but no Indians were to be seen. I dispatched down to camp the words "nary Red" and remained upon the hill until nearly sundown without observing any signs of Indians. Those the party first saw went into the timber 2 miles below camp and could not be seen.

---

[16]Walker's official report of 25 September 1865, Hafen and Hafen, *Powder River Campaigns*, 97.

The country gets better as we go up stream being less rugged and more grass, but even here is as near the abominating desolation as can be. Marched 10 miles.[17]

Cole also wrote about the incident: "[A] signal station was established on a high bluff near camp overlooking the surrounding country, and from it I was in constant receipt of information of the movements of a small band, probably twenty five in all, who were following in my trail. They made no attempt at approaching nearer than a mile and a half and warily avoided attack by small detachments sent after them."[18]

Springer reported that they buried their dead from the day before "on the bank of the confounded and damned Powder river. . . . A little hunting party reported another encampment up the river above the 16th Kansas, whether redskins or whites, they could not tell. . . . My wardrobe needs a new supply, my boots, my shirts, my pants and my stockings hat and everything is fearfully dilapidated; I am not the only one in such a condition but the whole command is in the same plight."[19]

✳   ✳   ✳

Walker and the Sixteenth Kansas moved out and camped six miles south of Cole's campsite. He reported, "[N]ext day marched twenty four (24) miles and found better grass here   struck a large Indian trail of ponies judged to be at least several thousand evidently the party that had fought Col Cole they had come to the river from the Southeast and went up the river they had no lodges with them"[20]

THURSDAY, 7 SEPTEMBER 1865

Cole's command had been trailing the Sixteenth Kansas Cavalry by several miles for the last few days. So far Cole had borne the brunt of

[17]Bennett diary, 6 September 1865 entry.
[18]Cole's official report of 10 February 1867, Hafen and Hafen, *Powder River Campaigns*, 78.
[19]Springer, *Soldiering in Sioux Country*, 50.
[20]Hafen and Hafen, *Powder River Campaigns*, 97. Walker omits any mention of 7 September, while Bennett covers their movements for both days. Like the other date discrepancies, the author trusts Bennett's timeline and assumes that Walker was confused with his notes and combined the movements of 6 and 7 September into one day.

the Indian fighting, as Walker's column was a few miles away on each occasion. The two commands would camp in close proximity on this day, as Bennett described the march:

> Started at 6 A.M. and finding a level valley and smooth roads we made good progress and after about six miles struck the trail of the 16th Kans. who had crossed to the other side [of] the river owing to rough roads. The 16th had a poor camp with but little grass and after marching five and one half miles finding excellent grass in a large grove of cottonwoods went into camp. Our column came up shortly after and camped in their immediate neighborhood, making about 11 miles.
>
> A party of five men were from the 12th Missouri straggled from the column in search of game and were on the opposite side of the river and a mile from the command. Even this small party had separated, two being 1/4 mile from the others. Suddenly 18 Indians dashed out of a ravine upon the two men who attempted to flee, but their mules upon which they were mounted were no match for the Indian ponies, and one fellow was overtaken and shot with three arrows which killed him, but he wounded one of his pursuers so that he had to be carried away by the other Indians. The other man was thrown from his mule just as 15 Indians were nearly upon him. He fell in a small hollow where he was tolerably well sheltered and rising on his knees shot the foremost Indian dead just as he was pulling his bow to send an arrow into the soldier. This stopped the Indians a short time but soon they came on with a yell and the soldier poured in a few more shots, killing another Indian and a pony and making them run. But they soon came on again and our man killed a third of their number and wounded two or three more and they beat a hasty retreat.
>
> Three of the Indians attempted to scalp the man that was killed, but the three men of the hunting party who were in advance, hearing the firing behind them, came up and fired upon them, and they left without getting the scalp. Thus the courage and coolness of one man killed three Indians and wounded at least three more besides killing a pony. They evidently got the worst of it on this little encounter. It is surprising how well the Indians recluse themselves, not a trace will be seen of them, but as sure as one man or a small number stray from the lines, suddenly from some ravine, from behind some hill, or hole in the ground a party of Indians will dash and the party is gone up. We have now lost nine men from the command and three or four wounded and in every instance it has been from their own independence in dashing ahead without being supported or from straggling away from the command. I should think such sad and serious

lessons would be a warning to the men to stick close to the command and mind their business. Marched 11 miles.[21]

Springer identified the casualty from the hunting party: "[O]ur hunting party had been attacked and Private Bradshaw of Comp. A 12th Mo. Cav. was killed. Our men killed three Indians and one splendid pony."[22] Colonel Wells of the Twelfth Missouri also commented on the hunting party: "On the 7th of September a party of our hunters met about thirty or forty Indians. One of our men was killed and two Indians left dead on the ground in the hands of our men, and another, believed to be mortally wounded, was carried off by his party."[23]

The campsite of 7 September was five or six miles south of today's Powderville on the west side of Powder River.

---

[21]Bennett diary, 7 September 1865 entry.
[22]Springer, *Soldiering in Sioux Country*, 50–51.
[23]Wells's official report of 20 September 1865, *The War of Rebellion*.

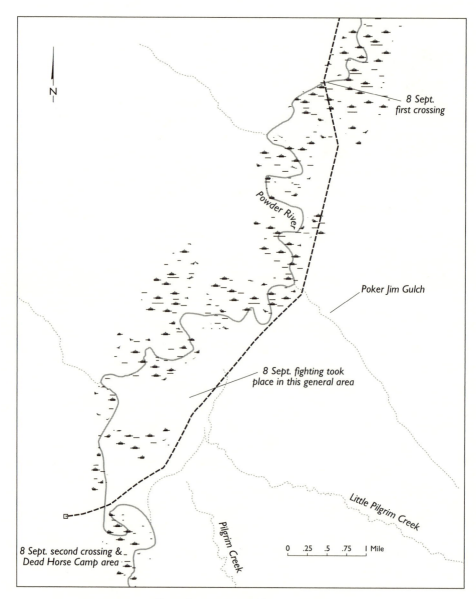

Poker Jim Gulch

Powder River

8 Sept.
first crossing

8 Sept. fighting took
place in this general area

Little Pilgrim Creek

Pilgrim Creek

0   .25   .5   .75   1 Mile

8 Sept. second crossing &
Dead Horse Camp area

COLE'S ROUTE, 8 SEPTEMBER

CHAPTER FOURTEEN

8 September

THICKER THAN FIDDLERS IN HELL

Located several miles above the mouth of the Little Powder River, a second group of Indians camped on the east side of Powder River. They were the mixed village of Northern and Southern Cheyenne, Ogallala and Brule Sioux, and Arapaho. Cole's expedition left their 7 September campsite and marched toward this large encampment, approximately twenty miles to the south, on the morning of 8 September.

The two commands moved out, following the winding course of Powder River on the west side, with Walker's Sixteenth Kansas in the lead, followed by Cole's column. Lyman Bennett described the morning travel:

> It was a cold damp morning. The clouds hung low and the mist was nearly as penetrating and chilly as rain. The 16th Kansas took the lead, but Capt. Boardman with his engineers was in advance with the Pioneers of the 16th. We had gone almost five miles when the flankers of the 16th came in and reported seeing five Indians and the tracks of a large number besides. This put us a little on the alert, but no more were seen except the head of one peering over a bluff 2 miles to the left. Said head quickly disappeared and showed itself once more at another point, but little attention was paid to this, as they were supposed to be the small party that had been dogging us for two or three days past. We had a long stretch of beautiful road along a wide level valley and then came to a bend in the river which skirted high precipitous bluffs for a mile. To move the command over these bluffs was

impossible and we proposed a road across the river which was found without any difficulty. While Capt. Boardman with his pioneers was preparing the road, the 16th moved on in advance and were perhaps 2 miles ahead.[1]

Colonel Cole reported the action that followed: "Colonel Walker, who was in my advance about three or four miles, sent back a courier, informing me that he was attacked by between 3000 and 4000 Indians, who were driving him back." Cole's train was crossing the river at this time, and he ordered it "out of the timber and corralled." The Twelfth Missouri was sent "to skirmish through the woods along the river bank to drive out a body of Indians who were posted in the woods."[2] Lt. Charles Springer said this took place about 1 P.M. Springer, who was with the Twelfth Missouri clearing out the woods, described the scene in front of the command: "The whole bottom and hills in advance were covered full of Indians, or to use a soldier's expression, they were thicker than fiddlers in hell."[3] Cole moved his artillery to the front and "opened upon on a large force in a ravine, who were apparently preparing to take in flank a skirmish line of the Sixteenth Kansas." He then went forward with one battalion of the Second Missouri, "leaving the balance to guard the train."[4] Out in front, Lieutenant Colonel Walker, with his Sixteenth Kansas Cavalry, reported the first contact with the attacking warriors: "[T]he next morning (Sept 8th) we came to a tremendous gulch in our front reaching from the bluffs which were here very high all broken with deep ravines to the river   while we were making a way to get round the gulch a report came back that the advance guard under Lieut. Balance was surrounded with Indians   advancing to the top of a bute [*sic*] I saw the whole valley in front of me covered with Indians and the guard dismounted holding their ground nobly [*sic*][.]"[5]

The "tremendous gulch" that Walker described was probably Poker Jim Gulch, located about two miles north of Little Pilgrim Creek and about two and one-half miles south from the probable site of the

[1]Bennett diary, 8 September 1865 entry.
[2]Cole's official report of 10 February 1867, Hafen and Hafen, *Powder River Campaigns*, 78–80.
[3]Springer, *Soldiering in Sioux Country*, 51–53.
[4]Cole's official report of 10 February 1867, Hafen and Hafen, *Powder River Campaigns*, 78–80.
[5]Walker's official report of 25 September 1865, ibid., 97–98. Second Lt. Charles Balance was a member of Company F, Sixteenth Kansas Cavalry. *Civil War Soldiers and Sailors System.*

crossing of the wagon train. Bennett reacted immediately and rode forward to assist Walker:

> We had just completed the road and the head of Col. Cole's column had crossed the river when a firing was heard with the 16th and looking that way, we saw Indians swarming out from the woods and ravines and blackening the hills and valley. The advance guard of the 16th were near a mile ahead of the column, beyond easy supporting distance and numbers about 25 men. These were quickly surrounded by hundreds of the savages who came charging and yelling like devils. The officer, believing himself too weak to hold out against such numbers, fell back rapidly ¼ of a mile to the river bank which was high and afforded good cover for them. One soldier, however who was poorly mounted was overtaken and killed, the savage monsters in scalping him took all the skin from head, face and ears, besides cutting off one of his arms.
>
> Coming to the river bank, it was too high and steep to get the horses down and they were abandoned and the party sought cover under the bank where the Indians were held at bay. Another soldier was nearly too late, the Indians riding up to him and knocking him off his horse with a war club, but his comrades under the river bank, by a timely volley, drove the Indians away and saved his life. His head was badly bruised however.
>
> I saw this attack of the Indians, though two miles away, and put spurs to my horse and galloped to the scene of action as fast as my horse could carry me. Arriving there Col. Walker had come up with support and I assisted in placing the men in position. But the Indians were more wary than before and would not come up within range, but would gallop to and fro along our front but just beyond the range of the guns. A few ponies were however hit and either killed or wounded too severely for the Indians to take off the field. One Indian was gyrating around and making gestures for us to come on when a volley was fired at him and his horse [was] brought down, throwing the Indian completely, but he was quickly up and off as fast as his legs would carry him.[6]

Bennett continued:

> Capt. Boardman finally came up on the right with his company and [I] went and joined him. He dismounted his men, every fourth one holding

---

[6]Bennett diary, 8 September 1865 entry. This could be the portion of the fight that George Bent recalled as the "bravery runs" made up and down in front of the soldiers' line by the famous Cheyenne warrior Roman Nose. The warrior whose horse was shot very well could have been Roman Nose. Bent's biographer, George Hyde, says that this episode took place on 5 September, but this description of action comes closest to it from the soldiers' side. Hyde, *Life of George Bent*, 239–40.

the horses and then advanced on foot. We went far in advance of any of the others, but the Indians being mounted, kept out of our way, but dare not charge us. While pushing the Indians before us, we suddenly saw a squad of about a dozen dismounted men in the very midst of the Indians and fighting them valiantly. Who they were we could not tell, but hastening forward we found it was Mr. Gay and a party of hunters who had left camp in the morning to get some game. The party had descended from the bluffs into a basin near the river bottom and began to think about getting some deer when they found themselves surrounded by hundreds of Indians. They proceeded to a thick cluster of trees, tied their horses each took a tree and every time an Indian came near, a ball was sent at him. In this way they had fought about an hour, when the sound of the howitzers and the fight going on to the left apprized them of a general engagement. Many of the boys lost their prudence and wished to leave their position, though knowing it was death when away from the protection of the trees. Finding the banks too steep to take their horses, they left them tied to the trees and struck out in the direction the fighting was going on and though surrounded by hundreds of Indians, not one was harmed. Luckily Capt. Boardman was near and they were rescued from their truly critical position. We went back for their horses but the Indians had gobbled them.

We pushed ahead towards the Indians a mile ahead of the main line, the Indians keeping out of our way, not daring to stand to fight us and was usually from 200 to 300 yards in advance, popping at them at every opportunity and one at least [was] made [to] bite the dust. Finally becoming pretty well tired out with tramping on foot, I returned and mounted my horse. Col. Cole coming up about that time, I went with him at the head of the main column into the woods.[7]

Walker reported the action from the perspective of the Sixteenth Kansas:

I ordered Major Reynolds forward with his battalion to their support until we could get our wagons, packs, and howitzers over the gulch   he was at once surrounded by at least one thousand Indians but dismounting he soon drew them out of range of the carbines   we were now attacked from all sides, front, rear, and flanks   but the Indians seemed to have but few fire arms   it was impossible to charge them over such ground on horseback   we could drive them easily in any direction but they would follow our men back   they could go with their ponies where it was difficult for our men to go on foot   We had driven them thus for some miles when

[7]Bennett diary, 8 September 1865 entry.

Col Cole came up with part of his command   he being the ranking officer I turned the command over to him[.][8]

Cole then took over direction of the fight. Skirmishers were sent out
and with their Spencer carbines were able to drive the warriors back.
"Driving the Indians from a well selected position for attack, I found
them exerting but little of the energy they had displayed on the 5th
instant, as they gave way before every attack made on them boldly by
parties of even half a dozen men." He then sent a detachment to drive
the Indians off of the bluffs overlooking the valley. "They were successful in scattering this large force without the loss of a man. A number of
Indians were seen to fall." Cole again brought up his artillery and cleared
the woods of a large body of Indians.[9] At some point during this action
he had ordered the wagon train to proceed south again. Bennett, who
was involved in this action, describes the last of the fighting on this day:

> A line of skirmishers was deployed to clear the timber & I pushed on
> with them. The Indians would not stand in the timber, but from a range
> of higher bluffs beyond they appeared in considerable number and once in
> a while would fire a shot at us and though at long range, some of their
> shots came among us. One struck the ground under my horse. It was evi-
> dently aimed at me as I was mounted and a conspicuous mark for them.
> Mr. Raymond, as usual, was in advance and came near being struck sev-
> eral times, but made a narrow escape.
>
> Finally I determined to clear the hill of them. I ordered the men forward
> at a double quick right up the steep face of the hill until about half way up
> when the balls and arrows came whizzing rather uncomfortably near. One
> man was struck on the foot, but luckily but a little hurt. Several came in
> rather close proximity to my head and I sought shelter with the men under
> a sheltering ledge about 200 yards from below the top of the hill. Then
> ordering the men to lay low and cover the hill with their carbines and pick
> off every one that showed himself, I went back to direct another party to
> flank the hill on the right, which was done and the Indians left in a hurry.
> I was the first on the top of the hill & I had the satisfaction of seeing num-
> bers of the red devils scampering away. The men held the hill until the col-
> umn passed.[10]

---

[8]Walker's official report of 25 September 1865, Hafen and Hafen, *Powder River Campaigns,* 97–98.
Maj. Clarkson Reynolds was a member of Companies F and S, Sixteenth Kansas Cavalry. *Civil
War Soldiers and Sailors System.*
[9]Cole's official report of 10 February 1867, Hafen and Hafen, *Powder River Campaigns,* 78–80.
[10]Bennett diary, 8 September 1865 entry.

Maj. Clemenz Landgraeber describes the action: "On the 8th September we were again engaged five hours by a superior force, supposed to have been near 3,000 or 4,000; we were again victorious and went into camp near the battle-field."[11] Capt. Samuel Flagg was brief in his description of the action: "On the 8th, in bend of Powder River, were attacked by a band of 2,000 to 3,000 Indians, who were repulsed."[12]

The fighting of 8 September took place on the broad plain on the east side of Powder River in the vicinity of the mouth of Pilgrim Creek. High bluffs rise to the south of the Pilgrim Creek drainage, and it was on these hills that Bennett described driving the warriors from the heights. The river bends toward the bluffs on the east at this point, making a crossing necessary for the command to continue south. Bennett continued his description of the day's events: "Col. Cole determined to cross the river at this point, though I informed him that there was no grass there. A strong north wind was blowing and there were indications of rain, notwithstanding which we camped on the bare plain, where the winds had full sweep and there was no grass for the stock. We had just left a most beautiful camp with an abundance of grass and shelter from the winds. Men and stock were all shaking with cold and it was all I could do to keep warm in bed. We marched and fought over 15 miles today."[13]

At Cole's direction, the command crossed over Powder River to the west bank—a treeless prairie—which provided no shelter from the rapidly worsening weather. Springer described a north wind blowing "as cold as if it came direct from the north pole, and the icebergs of Greenland." He wrote of a brutally cold night for the men and stock.[14] Walker said of the storm, "Night coming on and the rain pouring down in torrents and our horses tired out we were compelled to camp without shelter or grass of any consequence   about dusk it turned piercing cold."[15]

Cole recalled the deteriorating situation: "After getting into camp a storm blew up, which grew worse as night came on and finally becoming terrific in its fury. From rain it turned to hail, then rained again,

---

[11]Landgraeber official report of 20 September 1865, *The War of Rebellion*.
[12]Flagg's official report of 20 September 1865, ibid.
[13]Bennett diary, 8 September 1865 entry.
[14]Springer, *Soldiering in Sioux Country*, 51–53.
[15]Walker's official report of 25 September 1865, Hafen and Hafen, *Powder River Campaigns*, 97–98.

8 SEPTEMBER TERRAIN, LOOKING NORTHWEST
ACROSS POWDER RIVER FROM THE BLUFFS ON THE EAST SIDE
These are the bluffs, to the south of Pilgrim Creek, that Bennett and
others drove the warriors off at the end of the action on 8 September
1865. The wooded area to the right is the area where much of the
action took place at the end of the day. The treeless plain in the upper
left center of the picture is the general location of the "Dead Horse
Camp" of the night of 8 September. *Author's photo.*

then in succession snowed and sleeted, yet freezing all night long. My picket officers were forced to march their men in circles at the reserve posts to prevent freezing, as fires were not admissible. Nothing could be done to protect the stock from the peltings of this terrible storm, and numbers of them died during the night."[16]

Cole's choice of a campsite that night would draw severe criticism and would be one of many controversies in the aftermath of the expedition.

⁕   ⁕   ⁕

Born 7 July 1843, George Bent was the son of William Bent, who with his brother Charles owned the fort and trading post in southeast Colorado known as Bent's Fort. George's mother—William Bent's wife—was a Southern Cheyenne named Owl Woman, daughter of White Thunder, an influential spiritual leader of the tribe.

William Bent sent young George to school in Missouri. When the Civil War broke out, George joined the Confederate Army. He fought at the Battle of Pea Ridge in March 1862 (Lyman Bennett also fought in that battle, on the Union side). In August 1862 Bent, captured in Mississippi as a prisoner of war or a deserter, spent a short time in a federal prison in St. Louis. He subsequently signed a loyalty oath to the United States and then gained parole in the custody of his brother Bob. He promptly returned to his home in Colorado. Because of the local strong Union sentiment, George's father advised him to live with his mother's people, the Southern Cheyenne, for his safety.

On 29 November 1864 Col. John Chivington's Colorado Volunteers attacked the Cheyenne village on Sand Creek in southeastern Colorado. George Bent, in the village that morning, fought on the side of the Cheyenne warriors and suffered a wound. In the aftermath of what became known as the Sand Creek massacre, he rode and fought with the Cheyenne warriors in the raids early in 1865 along the Platte River. He was with the Cheyenne in the Powder River country when Nelson Cole's Powder River Expedition arrived in the late summer of 1865.[17]

---

[16]Cole's official report of 10 February 1867, ibid., 78–80.
[17]Hyde, *Life of George Bent*, 83–163; Halaas and Masich, *Halfbreed*, 39–153.

GEORGE BENT AND
HIS WIFE, MAGPIE, IN 1867
Bent fought with the
Cheyenne warriors on
8 September 1865 in the
fight at the mouth of
Pilgrim Creek. *Courtesy of
the Denver Public Library,
Western History Collection,
photographer unknown, Z8878.*

Historian George Hyde corresponded with Bent from 1905 until Bent's death in 1918. He put together a manuscript on Bent's life story as told through Bent's own words from Hyde's collection of letters.[18] Through Hyde, Bent gave a participant's account of the action of early September 1865 on Powder River. Bent fought with Cheyenne and Sioux warriors in one of the battles in early September, and wrote a detailed account of the action on that day.

In his classic book *The Fighting Cheyennes*, George Bird Grinnell also covered this event in very close detail and sequence to the Bent/Hyde account.[19] Bent was often employed as an interpreter by Grinnell when he was gathering material in Oklahoma from

[18]Hyde, *Life of George Bent*, xii–xvi.
[19]George Bird Grinnell, *The Fighting Cheyennes*, 183–84.

Cheyenne and Arapaho, and according to Hyde, Grinnell had "a high opinion of Bent." Grinnell, in the preface to *The Fighting Cheyennes*, acknowledges Hyde with the following: "Mr. George E. Hyde has verified most of the references and has given me the benefit of his careful study of the history of early travel on the plains."[20] So it is no surprise that the Hyde and Grinnell accounts of the action on Powder River are virtually identical.

Bent's account of what Hyde identified as the 5 September fight is as follows:

> In the morning a large body left camp about dawn and rode down the river. Woman's Heart was with this party and tells me that they had only got a short distance from the village when they met the war party, which had been watching the soldier's camps all night. These Indians reported that the soldiers were just beyond the next bend in the river and were coming in great force toward the village. This news was sent back to camp, and now a second large party of warriors mounted and started down the river. This was the party I accompanied, and the sun was already up when we moved. Other bands set off after us, and the whole valley on both sides of the river was full of warriors, all going down to meet the troops.
>
> In this vicinity the river flowed in great bends between its two enclosing lines of high bluffs. The country was very rough and difficult to traverse, and if you attempted to ride along the valley you had to cross the river every little while; at almost every bend the steep bluffs came down to the river's brink, forcing you to cross the stream, and in these bends were dense tangles of bushes and trees through which you had to force your way. Presently we heard firing off ahead, and hurrying forward we rode up on a hill and came in sight of the troops in one of these thicketed bends, engaged in fighting the advance party of warriors. Both the Indians and soldiers were shooting and yelling and the troops were firing howitzers at the Indians who had gathered on the hills. The wagons had already been corralled and the troopers had formed a hollow square. . . .
>
> Our party was on the east side of the river, and just as we rode up on this hill and came in sight of the troops we saw two companies of cavalry come out of the timber on our side of the stream and make for a high hill. Our men set up a yell and started for the soldiers, who turned around at once and went back into the timber at a gallop. We were right behind them when they reached the trees and bushes. At this point the river bank was

---

[20]Ibid., x.

very high and steep; it was impossible to get the horses down the bank without losing considerable time, and the soldiers had no time to waste. When they came out on the open bank they saw a swarm of warriors riding down from the hills on the other side of the river, and seeing that they would be cut off from the rest of the troops in a few minutes more, the men now abandoned their horses and, jumping down the bank, waded across to the other side. When our party charged into the timber, we found eighty cavalry horses tied to the bushes, with their saddles and all equipment still on them. The saddle pockets were full of cartridges, and the blanket rolls were tied back of the saddles. These horses were so lean and broken down that the warriors did not even quarrel over the division of them, although they had a fierce wrangle over the saddles and other equipments. When we came to the open river bank we saw troops on the other side, drawn up in lines around their camp and the corralled wagons, and a great body of Indians charging up and down along the lines.

We crossed over, and now Roman Nose rode up on his fine white pony, wearing his famous war bonnet that nearly touched the ground even when he was mounted, and with his face painted in a peculiar way, to protect him from bullets. As soon as he came up he called out to the warriors to form a line and get ready for a charge, as he was going to empty the soldiers guns. The Indians formed a long line from the river to the bluffs and sat on their ponies facing the troops. Roman Nose then put his pony into a run and rode straight out toward one end of the line of troops. When he was quite close he turned and rode at top speed straight along the front, from the river clear to the bluffs, the troops firing at him at close range all the way. Reaching the bluffs, he turned and rode back along the line again. In this way he made three, or perhaps four, rushes from one end of the line to the other; and then his pony was shot and fell under him. On seeing this, the warriors set up a yell and charged. They attacked the troops all along the line, but could not break through anywhere. The trouble was that the Indians had very few guns, and armed only with bows, lances and clubs they could not stand up to the well-armed troops for any length of time. The troops now opened up with their howitzers, and the Indians, who did not like the big guns, began to retire to the hills. They collected on the hilltops in great numbers and the troops attempted to drive them away by shelling the hills; but most of the shells went too high, and the only Indian hit was a very old man named Black Whetstone, who was smoking his pipe away off behind the hills when a shell came over and killed him.[21]

---

[21]Hyde, *Life of George Bent*, 237–40.

Bent's account does not fit the battle descriptions of 5 September, but it does work with the September 8 fight. Both Hyde's and Grinnell's accounts were written well before the Springer and Bennett diaries were available; they had only the military reports and Bent's account to recreate what happened. As to Bent's knowledge of dates, Hyde wrote, "Out of touch with white civilization, he did not even know the months in which events occurred; but the years he remembered, and by using the Indian reckoning by moons, he had a good idea as to dates. I have found the true dates in official records and inserted them."[22]

The author believes that Hyde made a mistake on assigning 5 September 1865 to this action. The action described by Bent should have been dated 8 September. The Lyman Bennett diary is the key here, because it provides detailed eyewitness testimony that was not available to Hyde or Grinnell.

First, Bent said that "the soldiers were just beyond the next bend in the river and were coming in great force, toward the village." On 5 September the command camped over fifty miles to the north of the approximate location of the village, by Bennett's daily mileage totals. They were not on the move south toward the village, as Bent described, but still in camp early in the morning when the Indians attacked them. They didn't get to the abandoned village site until 10 September. On 8 September they were less than ten miles from the village site and on the march, which fits Bent's description.[23]

Second, Bent described two companies abandoning their horses and retreating behind a high bank on the river. The Indians then helped themselves to "eighty cavalry horses" that were fully equipped and left tied to the bushes. There is nothing remotely resembling this sequence of events on 5 September—nothing in any of the officer's reports or in the diaries, and it does not fit in with the flow of events as the battle unfolded. Two such incidents occurred on 8 September, either of which may have been what Bent was describing.

The Lyman Bennett diary describes the advance party of the Sixteenth Kansas of about twenty-five men who, when surrounded,

---

[22]Ibid., vii.
[23]Bennett diary, 5–8 September 1865 entries.

abandoned their horses and took cover under the high riverbank. No mention is made of recovering the horses, so it could be assumed that the Indians had captured them.

Another similar incident could be Mr. Gay's hunting party, which was surrounded. Bennett's diary described how the party of about a dozen men retreated to a thick cluster of trees, tied their horses, and exchanged shots with the Indians. They then retreated down a steep riverbank, leaving their horses in the trees, and escaped. Bennett "went back for their horses but the Indians had gobbled them up."[24] Springer mentions both incidents in his diary, stating that both parties lost their horses.

There is no way to justify or rationalize Bent's claim of eighty horses lost. Such a significant loss would have surely been reported in one of the officer's reports or by one of the diarists. The reader must remember that the Bent/Hyde correspondence started in 1905, forty years after the actual event in 1865. The numbers may have increased in memory as the event faded further into the past.

Third, Bent described the fabled Roman Nose bravery ride as follows: "Reaching the bluffs, he turned and rode back along the line again. In this way he made three, or perhaps four, rushes from one end of the line to the other: and then his pony was shot and fell under him." On 8 September it appears that Bennett described the same event: "One Indian was gyrating around and making gestures for us to come on when a volley was fired at him and his horse [was] brought down, throwing the Indian completely, but he was quickly up and off as fast as his legs would carry him." It sounds like two people describing the same happening from different perspectives. Nothing remotely similar was described on 5 September.

Though Hyde and Grinnell both describe the fight on 8 September as a separate action from the one described by Bent, it is apparent that they simply took this from Nelson Cole's official report. This was Bent's only fight against Cole's expedition, as the Cheyenne packed up their camp and left. He was not an eyewitness to any subsequent events in this campaign.

---

[24]Ibid.

While most accounts written about the Powder River fights of 5 and 8 September have used the Bent/Hyde description and date, Robert M. Utley, in his biography of Sitting Bull, said that Sitting Bull fought in the 5 September battle along with the northern Sioux coalition of Hunkpapa, Blackfeet, Miniconjou, and Sans Arc warriors.[25] This is the group that was in conflict with the expedition from 1 through 5 September. The probable location of the village of these warriors was on the Little Missouri River.[26]

The warriors who fought on 8 September came from the village of Cheyenne and Sioux of Little Wolf and Red Cloud, located near the mouth of the Little Powder River. That would be the village that George Bent and Roman Nose came out of on that day.[27]

---

[25]Utley, *The Lance and the Shield*, 69.

[26]Micheal Clodfelter, *The Dakota War: The United States Army versus the Sioux, 1862–1865*, 212.

[27]Utley, *The Lance and the Shield*, 69.

CHAPTER FIFTEEN

9–10 September

DEAD HORSE CAMP

SATURDAY, 9 SEPTEMBER 1865

A scene of desolation presented itself at dawn, as many of the starving animals in the command's herd did not survive the night. Of those still alive, many would not survive the morning. Cole described the disaster:

> When daylight dawned it [the storm] had not abated in the least, and owing to the unsheltered position of my camp was especially severe on the men as well as the stock, so much so that I determined to move to some point within a few miles where I could secure shelter in heavy timber to save the remnant of my rapidly failing animals. I moved two miles and a half, marking my trail with dead and dying horses and mules. . . . During the thirty six hours the storm prevailed 414 of my animals perished at the picket rope or along the road between the camps. This loss necessitated the destruction of wagons, cavalry equipments, harness, and all tools and implements not absolutely essential to the command, and which could be taken no further.[1]

Bennett put the blame for this disaster on Cole's decision to camp in the open. This is the only time in the entire expedition that Bennett second-guessed the colonel. He wrote of the aftermath of the terrible night:

> It was a cold and stormy night. I thought several times the tent would blow over, but it remained standing while many others were blown down. The camp had been tramped until it was one batch of mud. Many horses

---

[1]Cole's official report of 10 February 1867, Hafen and Hafen, *Powder River Campaigns*, 80–81.

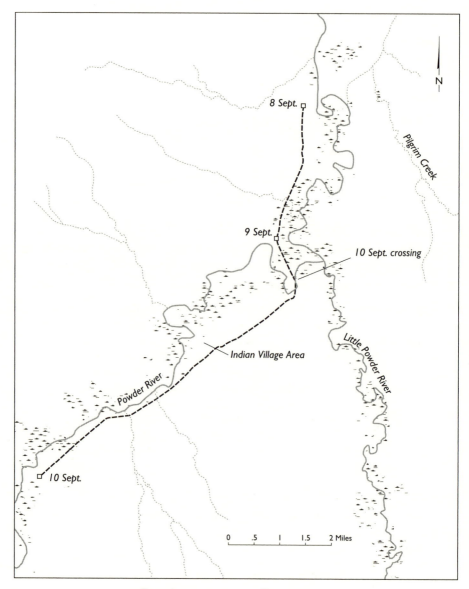

COLE'S ROUTE, 9–10 SEPTEMBER

were found dead at the picket rope and many others were so cold and hungry that they were in a dying condition and could neither stand or walk. All that could not be moved were shot to prevent their being appropriated by the Indians. In this way there were about 100 dead horses left in camp and at every rod of the way horses and mules fell down and died or were shot. We marched about 3½ miles and in that distance over 200 animals were left dead. We have now 300 or 400 dismounted men and scarcely mules enough to haul what wagons there is, and all for not camping where we ought to have camped in the timber. The fight with the Indians was rather severe on some of the animals. Nothing to eat was worse and to cap the climax a cold north wind and driving rain storm has put us horse decombat [*sic*] about 300 animals. The road was level but very muddy and 4 miles was all we could march without finishing the remainder of our stock.

We found a very good camp on the bank of the river in a cottonwood grove where [there] was an abundance of grass. The ground was covered with the trunks of fallen timber that had been cut by the Indians in winter to feed their stock upon. We collected the logs together and built rousing fires keeping warm in spite of the wind and rain. The river is raising rapidly. The water is perfectly thick with mud. In the evening Col. Cole informed us that so much of his stock had died and more in a dying condition, that much of our personal baggage must be burned. Officers went to work assorting their baggage and reducing it down to the proper proportion. Now an old hat was thrown into the fire, an old shirt, a pair of pants, a looking glass or a box of medicines until baggage was generally reduced half. In my valise was nothing I could throw away. My blankets were also needed. I threw about half my specimens away, those that were the most bulky and rolled the remainder up and arranged with Capt. Boardman to carry them. Tents, saddles wagons, harnesses, etc., etc. were abandoned and burned. We must have burned in all near a hundred wagons. Marched about 2½ miles.[2]

Sgt. P. C. Stepps recalled how he kept his horse alive: "I stayed with my horse all night and moved him around to keep him alive. When morning broke he could stand up but could move his feet but a few inches at a time. It was several days before it was safe to ride him."[3]

Springer reflected on a very somber mood in the command: "Next morning as daylight dawned, a horrid sight presented itself to our eyes. There no less than 250 animals on the ground either dead or they had to be shot. . . . We marched out of 'Dead Horse Camp.' . . . We trav-

---

[2]Bennett diary, 9 September 1865 entry.
[3]Stepps, "Expedition Store Brought to Close," *Casper Tribune-Herald*, 31 August 1930.

eled about 5 miles and encamped in a patch of cottonwood. We have lost no less than 350 heads of animals since last night. . . . There is no fun amongst the boys, they all look away down in the mouth no joking, no laughing, going on, everybody is busy with his own thoughts."[4]

Capt. Samuel Flagg reported, "On the 9th were obliged to burn tents, men's clothing, officers' transportation, papers, desk, & c., and ordinance stores, for want of transportation."[5]

Lieutenant Colonel Walker, in one of the few nights that the two commands camped together, described the desperation of his command as the situation unfolded in the morning:

> God forbid I shall ever have to pass such another night   the rain penetrated through everything to our very bones   no fires could be built as the rain at once put them out   about midnight our horses began to drop dead and by morning I had lost at least one hundred either dead or so far gone that they could not get up and I had them shot to put them out of their misery   as soon as it was light we started to get some shelter & grass   I brought up the rear   then a scene of horror took place   no sooner had the command started than horses that appeared to be pretty strong would drop down and in two minutes be stiff and dead   if they happened to be in good flesh 20 men would pounce on them and in less time than I can tell it his bones would be stripped and devoured raw   order them not to do it and you would get a vacant stare with Colonel I cannot help it I am starving[.][6]

Sunday, 10 September 1865

After the day in camp, the march resumed towards the south. Cole described the action: "On the 10th, the storm having cleared, my first move was to cross the river, which was necessary, as the impending bluffs immediately above formed the river bank. This move I was compelled to make under cover of my artillery, owing to the fact that the Indians had, vulture like, hovered around my exhausted and starving command."

The Indians harassed the rear of the column as it was moving out of camp, "but having no taste for the shells that were generously thrown

[4]Springer, *Soldiering in Sioux Country*, 53–54.
[5]Flagg's official report of 20 September 1865, *The War of Rebellion*.
[6]Walker's official report of 25 September 1865, Hafen and Hafen, *Powder River Campaigns*, 98–99.

amongst them, soon retired to their of late respectful distance beyond range. I crossed over above the mouth of the Little Powder River and moved up the east bank, passing over the ground from which a large Indian village of from 1500 to 2000 lodges had recently moved. My guides pronounced them to have been Sioux, Cheyennes, and Arapahoes."[7]

Bennett also described the Indian village site:

After completing the destruction of our train except a few wagons we wished to carry along with us, we commenced the march and coming to the river, found it swollen so that it could not easily be crossed. Indians also menaced the head of the column and their heads could be seen in the hundreds projecting above the tops of the hills. We finally found another ford a mile above and crossed the command loosing [sic] only one wagon though many men and horses were thrown in the water. A few Indians hovered around our advance for a few miles and then hauled off and we saw no more of them. We passed where had been camped a day or two ago, an Indian village of at least 1000 lodges with indications that they had left in [a] rush, as many articles were left behind. They probably left during the last battle and was upon dry fork, where at one time we proposed to go and where I advised the Col. to go, as I believe the distance is at least 50 miles nearer to Ft. Laramie. During the night the pickets saw many wolves and bears about the lines and trying to get into camp and many shots were fired at them. Marched 6¾ miles.[8]

The Twelfth Missouri guarded the rear of the column, and Springer and his men had to burn the wagons and supplies. The Indians hovered around and shots were exchanged. As they left their old camp, the warriors "came charging down from the hills, but a volley from Comp. A and C sent them back amongst the hills." The Indians continued to bother the rear as they forded the Powder and moved on up river.[9] Springer's regimental commander, Colonel Wells, reported, "On the 10th the Indians nearly enveloped the camp as the command moved out, and followed on our flank and rear until about noon. But little was accomplished, however, and much useless firing was done. The Indians had this day four or five good muskets. One of our men

---

[7]Cole's official report of 10 February 1867, ibid., 81.

[8]Bennett diary, 10 September 1865 entry.

[9]Springer, *Soldiering in Sioux Country*, 54.

was slightly wounded and three Indians were shot, but carried off by their comrades."[10]

Walker wrote, "On the 10th Sept we found where their villages had been apparently abandoned in great haste the day they fought us they had left their council house standing which Col Cole ordered to be destroyed   they had went over towards the Little Missouri   Our horses were too feeble and one third of our men were barefooted and starving   no game to be had in that part of the country   it was decidedly impossible for us to follow them[.]"[11]

Although none of the chroniclers mention it in journals or reports, probably more supplies or wagons were abandoned or burned at the 10 September campsite. In a paper written in 1953 local rancher Henry Stuver described an abundance of military artifacts found on his property at the 10 September location.[12] This is not surprising, considering the condition of the horses and mules. Stuver's ranch was located two and one-half miles south of today's Highway 212 on the east side of Powder River.

✳   ✳   ✳

Late in the afternoon of 10 September, Capt. Frank North and fifty of his Pawnee scouts came upon the scene of Cole's Dead Horse Camp, just abandoned that morning. North had been assigned by Connor to search for the missing commands of Cole and Walker on Powder River. Seeing the bodies of the hundreds of dead animals and the still-smoldering wagons and equipment, he sensed that a great battle had taken place and assumed there must be a large force of Indians ahead of them. Rather than follow Cole's trail to the south, the perhaps overly cautious North chose to return to Connor's column on Tongue River and report his findings. Ironically, the beleaguered commands of Cole and Walker were a mere six and three-quarters miles to the south of North at that point.[13]

---

[10]Wells's official report of 20 September 1865, *The War of Rebellion*.

[11]Walker's official report of 25 September 1865, Hafen and Hafen, *Powder River Campaigns*, 99.

[12]J. H. Stuver, "The History of the Cavalry Relics Found on our Ranch."

[13]Grinnell, *Two Great Scouts and Their Pawnee Battalion*, 117; Connor's official report of 4 October 1865, File 3, Volume 145, Dodge Collection.

CHAPTER SIXTEEN

11–14 September

DAMNED POWDER RIVER

It now became a question as to whether we would not better break up into small bands and try and save our lives by pushing forward to some base of supplies. Fort Laramie seemed to be the nearest point which must have been four five hundred miles distant. This plan was not approved by the commanding officer, as it was almost certain death for the most of us if divided into small squads, for the Indians still swarmed us so it was determined to stay together a while longer.

Sgt. P. C. Stepps[1]

MONDAY, 11 SEPTEMBER 1865

With their rations almost gone, the command continued south along Powder River. Cole reported light fighting with the warriors, while his starving men plodded on: "The command by this time was reduced to less than quarter rations, and were lowered to the necessity of eating their horses and mules to sustain life. Indians were occasionally still seen in large numbers on all sides beyond the range of our guns. They but once showed a disposition to fight, when they were repulsed, with a loss of several killed and wounded. After that last repulse they disappeared from my vicinity and were seen no more."[2]

Bennett described the day: "We had a good road up the river valley, generally in the bottom. Capt. Boardman's company being in advance to clear out any obstructions in the way. At times we passed through the woods and fallen timber had to be removed. Otherwise our road was a good one. We went into camp early and had plenty of grass. The

---

[1]Stepps, "Expedition Store Brought to Close," *Casper Tribune-Herald*, 31 August 1930.
[2]Cole's official report of 10 February 1867, Hafen and Hafen, *Powder River Campaigns*, 82–85.

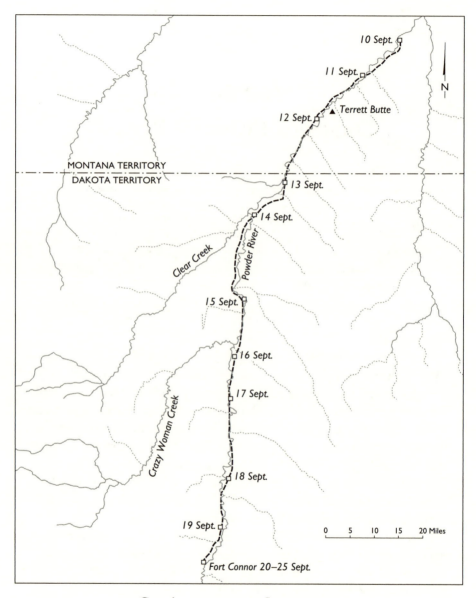

10 Sept.

11 Sept.

▲ Terrett Butte

12 Sept.

MONTANA TERRITORY

DAKOTA TERRITORY

13 Sept.

14 Sept.

Clear Creek

Powder River

15 Sept.

16 Sept.

17 Sept.

Crazy Woman Creek

18 Sept.

19 Sept.

N

0 5 10 15 20 Miles

Fort Connor 20–25 Sept.

COLE'S ROUTE, 11–25 SEPTEMBER

men are so reduced in rations that every horse or mule that gives out by the way is killed, the meat cut up and eaten by the soldiers. Marched 11½ miles."[3]

Lt. William Thompson Shaver recalled, "The men were out of rations and did not dare go out to hunt for fear of the Red Devils and resorted to mule meat as the only alternative to keep starvation off."[4] Lt. Charles Springer was not in very good spirits: "The weather was bright but cold, the Indians didn't show themselves at all. . . . We marched about 15 miles and encamped at 2 o'clock in the bottom of the damned Powder River." Springer was ordered to turn over all of his horses to the Second Battalion, and expressed his unhappiness: "The men were mad, and I think it an outrage; these men that have horses yet, are men who have taken care of them, other men who left their horses [to] suffer and not attend to them properly; still nearly 200 miles to any place of civilization, and my men will have to walk it and the most of them have no boots."[5]

TUESDAY, 12 SEPTEMBER 1865

Lyman Bennett's positive outlook was amazing at times. As the starving command struggled along, with many of the men now on foot, Bennett took time to describe the beautiful scenery: "Marched on west side of Powder River, crossing in the morning. The road was generally good, being on second bottom with high rocky mountains on either side [of] the valley, the tops of many being covered with pine. The scenery was truly romantic. The mountains being high and worn into many fantastic shapes, such as ruins, castles, etc."

Terrett Butte is a prominent landmark on the east side of the river that looks like a medieval castle built on a mountaintop. Bennett was probably describing this and other uniquely shaped mountains along this scenic stretch of the river. He continued with his record of the day's march: "There was one bear killed a deer and a number of sage hens. At supper we had some fresh meat which was called buffalo, but after we had eaten it, it leaked out that it was mule meat. I could

---

[3] Bennett diary, 11 September 1865 entry.
[4] Shaver, "Reminiscences," Shaver papers.
[5] Springer, *Soldiering in Sioux Country*, 54–56.

hardly keep it down when I found what I had eaten, though it tasted well while I was eating it. Marched 15½ miles."[6]

Springer walked with his men on foot. "On a very high and steep hill, Capt. [Sydney] Bennett of Company 'A' inscribed our names, letter of company and No. of regiment upon a huge boulder of rock." The column camped on the other side of the river, and Springer and his men had to wade to get to camp. "I hear the 16th Kansas is going to cut off from us and go ahead to Fort Laramie."[7]

WEDNESDAY, 13 SEPTEMBER 1865

Tempers in the expedition were wearing thin as Bennett described two incidents involving Lieutenant Colonel Walker of the Sixteenth Kansas Cavalry:

> The 16th Kansas took the lead today with the intention of leaving us for good. Their transportation is such that they can easily do this. I learned that some of the 16th went into the mule corral and killed 2 of the best mules and ate them, making Col. Walker decidedly wrathy. He also arrested an officer of the 2nd Mo., but let him go again when he found he would get into difficulty by it.
>
> We had a good road when not crossing the river, which we did 8 times in the course of the day. The river is very muddy and rapid. I think I never saw a more dirty stream and in many places deep & with quick sand in the bed. In many places it is quite rocky and the water runs over them with a musical tone.
>
> The bluffs narrow down the valley considerably. We have passed the highest, but still they are quite high and rugged and with the tops covered with a thin growth of pine. I ascended a high hill after supper and had a magnificent view of the rugged country around. Marched 15½ miles, good camp, grass & wood plenty.[8]

Lieutenant Springer still walked with his men. "I took the lead and marched on foot behind the train as rear guard. The command crossed the river 8 times, but we footmen kept on one side and climbed over hills and cliffs." The command camped two miles behind the Sixteenth Kansas.[9]

---

[6]Bennett diary, 12 September 1865 entry.
[7]Springer, *Soldiering in Sioux Country*, 56.
[8]Bennett diary, 13 September 1865 entry.
[9]Springer, *Soldiering in Sioux Country*, 56.

TERRETT BUTTE

On 12 September 1865 Lyman Bennett described the mountains along Powder River, as the command moved south: "many fantastic shapes, such as ruins, castles, etc." He was probably describing Terrett Butte, a prominent landmark on the east side of the river. *Author's photo.*

On this day the command marched over an area that would be the site of a future battle in the Great Sioux War of 1876. On 17 March of that year, Col. Joseph J. Reynolds with about 370 men attacked a Cheyenne village north of today's Moorhead, Montana, on the west bank of Powder River.[10]

THURSDAY, 14 SEPTEMBER 1865

Indians harassed the column today, a harsh reminder to the men to remain ever vigilant. Bennett described the march:

> The howling of wolves around camp aroused me before daylight this morning and having slept enough, I got up arranging my toilet by starlight. The column was moving at 6 A.M. up the river valley over much the same roads as yesterday, the valley, being narrow in many places and flanked by high hills, though not as high as those we were among yesterday. We had marched perhaps six miles when I heard a sharp firing ahead and galloping up, I found that a party of five Indians on the opposite side of the river had charged upon a single man who had straggled and were hot upon him. His

---

[10]J. W. Vaughn., *The Reynolds Campaign on Powder River*, 68–90; Paul L. Hedren, *Traveler's Guide to the Great Sioux War*, 44–45.

horse stuck in the quicksand and the Indians got it & his equipment. Some men on this side [of] the stream, seeing the danger in which the trooper had got himself, fired over and prevented the Indians killing him. After the Indians had fell back behind the bluff, I heard them shout and two shots fired indicating that they had come across another straggler and killed him. The men straggled over the country for miles in search of game in parties of one, two or three and it will be strange if none are reported missing. We had begun to think that the Indians had left us for good, but here they are again and we may look for more fighting. I rode on ahead and halted all the stragglers and they were made to go with the train.

Among the natural curiosities I observed today was the stump of a tree probably ten feet high and three feet in diameter that was petrified to stone. It was standing in a vertical position as it naturally grew. The roots and trunk and bark were all preserved, but turned into solid rock. I also passed a coal bed that was at least 20 feet thick of solid coal. In fact coal crops out from every hill side, but this is the finest vein I ever saw.

An antelope, several deer and sage hens were shot today. Passing by a dead horse left by the 16th Kansas, as I saw scores of men cutting the flesh from the bones for their supplies. I believe some of the men are half diminished. We crossed the muddy river nine times. I had rather drive a team one mile over a steep hill than cross this steam once. High mountains were seen about 40 miles to the west, the tops of which were covered with snow. They are Powder River Mountains, a branch of the Big Horn, but snow so early and enough to whiten them all over surprises me. We passed the mouth of Clear Creek, a fine clear stream of cold water coming down from the mountains. I regret that our course does not lead up it instead of the muddy one we are following.

The Indians have troubled the 16th a little today and tonight we camp within a mile of them. Excellent grass, the best since leaving the Loup. Marched 9½ miles.[11]

Springer saw the Big Horn Mountains for the first time. "About 10 o'clock we came in sight of some big mountains whose summits were covered with eternal snow." He went on to describe scenes of men butchering and eating horses and mules literally as they fell.[12]

Unbeknownst to these desperate men, Connor, about fifty miles to the northwest on Tongue River, had search parties in the field looking for the missing commands of Cole and Walker. These beleaguered soldiers' seemingly hopeless situation would soon take a turn for the better.

---

[11]Bennett diary, 14 September 1865 entry.
[12]Springer, *Soldiering in Sioux Country,* 56.

CHAPTER SEVENTEEN

15 September

MESSENGER FROM THE GENERAL

Prior to the events of the fifteenth, Brigadier General Connor was concerned about the two missing columns of his expedition. He had had no communications from either Cole or Walker since they left their respective starting points, and they were past due for their 1 September rendezvous with his command on Tongue River. On 6 September he speculated, "I fear that the men deserted so fast that they were compelled to turn back."[1] On Friday, 8 September, Connor sent Capt. Frank North and fifty of his Pawnee scouts toward Powder River to ascertain the location and condition of Cole's and Walker's commands. On 11 September North returned with disturbing news: he had discovered hundreds of dead cavalry horses and mules—Cole's "dead horse camp" of 8 and 9 September.[2] With this alarming news in hand, Connor penned a letter to Cole and/or Walker, and dispatched a team of messengers on 12 September.[3] He recalled the sequence of events regarding the timing of sending out the messengers:

> On the 11th September Capt North returned from Powder River and reported having seen Colonel Cole's camp of a few days before with about three hundred (300) dead horses in it, they having been shot it is presumed

---

[1]Connor to Captain Price, 6 September 1865, Vol. 145, File 3, Dodge Collection.

[2]Capt. H. E. Palmer's account of Connor's command, Hafen and Hafen, *Powder River Campaigns*, 141–42.

[3]Diary of unnamed member of Connor's staff, entries of 12, 13, and 14 September 1865, Lyman Bennett Collection.

CPL. CHARLES L. THOMAS
With two Pawnee scouts, Thomas,
Company E, Eleventh Ohio Cavalry,
reached Cole's command on
15 September 1865 with a message
from Brigadier General Connor.
He was awarded the Medal of Honor
for his ride. *Courtesy of Ron Tillotson,
Hardin, Illinois.*

by his order. The Indians were so numerous on this trail Capt North deemed it advisable to return, it being in his judgment folly to attempt to force a passage to Colonel Cole under the circumstances, with the small force at his disposal. Colonel Cole's trail was going up Powder River. I then moved up Tongue River a short distance to good grass and sent another scout 12th September which was driven in the next day. I again sent out a Scout (14th Sept) of two Ohio men and two Pawnee Indians and the same evening sent Capt Marshall 11th Ohio Cavalry with fifty men of his company and fifty Pawnee Scouts under Capt North fearful that the former Scout would not reach Colonel Cole, and knowing him to be about out of provisions, with orders to cut their way through to him at all hazards and bring him to me, and not to return without finding him.[4]

---

[4]Connor's official report, submitted on 4 October 1865 to Major Barnes, Vol. 145, File 3, Dodge Collection. Capt. Levi G. Marshall was a member of Company E, Eleventh Ohio Volunteer Cavalry. *Civil War Soldiers and Sailors System.*

When the first set of couriers returned to Connor's camp on 13 September, he asked for volunteers to find Cole's command. According to Cpl. Charles L. Thomas of Company E, Eleventh Ohio Cavalry, he was the only one who came forward to volunteer.[5] When Thomas advised Connor that his horse had been wounded in the attack on the Arapaho village, Connor told him he could have any horse in the command. Thomas told of what happened next: "I asked for Capt. Jewit's [Lt. Oscar Jewett][6] gray, he was the finest horse I ever saw. I didn't blame the Capt. for not wanting me to take him. When Jewit told the Gen. that was his private horse & that he objected to my riding him, say Connor was Irish Red Heade [*sic*] pock marked & freckle face, he put Jewit under arrest. Said the job was open to ever [*sic*] dam man in the command and that they all knew the danger of the undertaking. He said to Jewit if you say one other word I will detail you to go with the sergent [*sic*] & he will ride your gray."[7]

Thomas left Connor's camp, presumably riding Jewett's gray horse, on the morning of 14 September, accompanied by two Pawnee scouts, whose names are lost to history. They headed east, coming to Powder River north of Cole's campsites of 8 and 9 September. The next morning Thomas described the scene of Dead Horse Camp. They had several hot encounters with warriors as they followed Cole's trail south along Powder River. Thomas recalled the last fight with warriors on the ride:

> Still another Indian was struck by our bullets, and he fell off his horse in the trail. He was tied to his pony by a hair lariat and was dragged along for some distance. I separated him from his horse and took the animal to have a remount should my own horse give out or get shot, which I expected every moment.

---

[5]Connor's official report, submitted on 4 October 1865 to Major Barnes, Dodge Collection. Connor wrote that "two Ohio men and two Pawnee Indians" were sent on 14 September, so there is a question here of how many men were sent. Hull, "Soldiering on the High Plains," 37. Sgt. Lewis Bynum Hull, Connor's quartermaster sergeant, wrote in his diary on 14 September: "Two of Co. E and two Pawnee start up Powder River to hunt up lost command."

[6]Connor's official report of 4 October 1865, Dodge Collection.

[7]Thomas to Walter M. Camp, 1920, Camp Collection. Cpl. Charles Thomas finished a 1904 letter describing his ride: "P.S.—My horse had lock jaw the next morning and I shot him and finished my trip on the Indian's horse." One must wonder about Lieutenant Jewitt's reaction to that news. Strom, *Centennial Book—Dwight Kansas*, furnished by Ron Tillotson, Hardin, Illinois.

I discovered that the Indian's horse I had taken belonged to a member of the 6th Missouri Cavalry.[8] I still found his letters and pictures in the saddle-pockets. There was also in one of the pockets a tintype picture of the Indian himself and $95 in United States notes. How I longed to scalp this fellow. But my time was too precious to indulge in acts of vengeance.[9]

In addition to his daring ride through hostile country to reach Cole's command, Thomas rescued trooper J. E. Hutson of Battery L, Second Missouri Light Artillery, who had fallen behind the command and was unable to walk. Thomas brought Hutson with him to Cole's camp in the evening of the fifteenth on the spare Indian horse that he had collected en route.[10] Corporal Thomas described the rescue of Hutson in his 1894 application for the Medal of Honor:

> The sun is getting low & so is my spirit, but all at once I see something that makes my heart leap. By the side of the trail, lays a man. It is one of Cole's men. He has been dismounted for several days, is bare footed, has walked for miles through prickly pear & cactus until he could walk no more. He had thrown away his gun and accoutrements & layed down resigned to await his fate which in a short time would have been death & he would have been numbered with the unknown dead. I got him on my Indian horse & when the sun sank to [the] west that night I rode into Cole's camp & gave him Connor's dispatch.[11]

Friday, 15 September 1865

In his official report of 25 September 1865, Cole wrote to Connor, "On the 15th a messenger and three men arrived with a message from you [Connor]. They had left their camp the previous morning and had

---

[8]Thomas probably meant the Sixth Michigan Cavalry, which had four companies stationed at Fort Connor. There is no record of the Sixth Missouri operating anywhere in the area.

[9]Walter F. Beyer and Oscar F. Keydel, *Deeds of Valor*, 2:130.

[10]Thomas to Walter M. Camp, 1920, Camp Collection.

[11]Letter by C. L. Thomas to Charles Curtis, 2 July 1894, Reference Library, Fort Laramie National Historic Site. Ron Tillotson, Thomas's great-great-grandson, provided a copy of Thomas's Medal of Honor Certificate, dated 16 October 1916. Charles Thomas was awarded the Medal of Honor on 18 August 1894. The description of his act of bravery for the award reads: "For distinguished gallantry in action against hostile Indians on the Powder River Expedition, Dakota Territory, Sept. 12–17, 1865, when he volunteered to deliver a message to Col. Cole's command which was surrounded by a large number of hostile Indians, he succeeded in his undertaking and also saved the life of a comrade while performing this most gallant service."

traveled across to Powder River, and striking my trail near one of my old camping grounds, had followed it up, overtaking my command in the afternoon."[12]

Connor's message read as follows:

Headquarters
Powder River Indian Expedition
Camp No. 27, Tongue River, September 11, 1865

Colonel Cole, Second Missouri Light Artillery, or
Lieutenant-Colonel Walker, Sixteenth Kansas Cavalry:

My scouts have just returned from Powder River, and report having seen a large number of horses shot and ordinance property destroyed at a camp of one or both of your columns on Powder River, sixty miles east of here. I send three scouts to tell you of my whereabouts and guide you by the best route to me or Fort Connor, on Powder River. You can place implicit confidence in the scouts and be directed by them in the route you will take. I hope and trust your condition is not as bad as I fear it is.

Very respectfully, your obedient servant,
P. EDW. CONNOR
Brigadier General, Commanding
[endorsement on envelope]

---

[12]Cole's first report to General Connor of 25 September 1865, *The War of Rebellion*; Cole's official report of 10 February 1867, Hafen and Hafen, *Powder River Campaigns*, 85. In his second official report of 10 February 1865 Cole wrote: "On the 13th of September a courier party of two soldiers and two Pawnee Indians, sent to me with dispatches by General Conner, arrived in my camp." The date 13 September is in conflict with Bennett and Springer, as well as Cole's first report, as they all say that the messengers from Connor's camp came in on 15 September. This messenger, Cpl. Charles L. Thomas, Company E, Eleventh Ohio Cavalry, was mentioned in the journal of Capt. Henry E. Palmer, Connor's quartermaster, as departing Connor's camp on 12 September. That would coincide with Cole's second date of arrival on 13 September; Diary of unnamed member of Connor's staff, entries of 12–14 September 1865, Lyman Bennett Collection. In a journal kept by an unidentified member of Connor's staff, it states that on 12 September: "Three Guides were sent off this morning to communicate if possible with the command on Powder R." Then, on the 13th his entry reads, "Towards evening, the three Guides who went out yesterday (being Antoyne, a halfbreed and two thorough-breds by the name of Brannam & Geo. Myers (alias Pop Corn) returned." On 14 September the entry reads: "Early this morning, before we left camp, the Genl. sent off three messengers, two white soldiers & one Pawnee, who volunteered from the ranks to go to Powder R. in search of other com'd." Based on this, and on Bennett's and Springer's journals, the author feels that Cole, in his second report, and Palmer were confused on the dates, or Palmer may not have seen the first set of messengers return to Connor's camp. The campsite where Corporal Thomas delivered Connor's message to Cole was in the vicinity of present-day Arvada, Wyoming.

The scouts first sent with this were driven back by Indians and returned last evening. You should come over to this river immediately. Send word to me, at all hazards, of your condition on receipt of this. I will keep moving up this river at the rate of fifteen miles a day.

P. EDW. Connor
General, Commanding[13]

Learning of the existence of Fort Connor and the nature of the country towards the Tongue and the general's command from the messenger, Cole decided that he should continue towards Fort Connor and supplies.

Trooper Ansel Steck of Company D, Twelfth Missouri Cavalry, described Thomas's arrival: "On about the 15, Sargent [sic] C. L. Thomas of Co. E 11 O came to our command with a message from Gen Connor directing us to where we could get rations which we needed very much as a great many of the men were almost past going any farther, having been on mule meat for several days."[14]

The command traveled a good distance this day, in spite of numerous river crossings. Bennett described the view of the Big Horn Mountains, and later the arrival of the messenger:

Was up before day and ready to start with the column at 6 A.M. Our road as yesterday was up the river valley crossing it 9 times during the day. The hills are getting lower and the indications are that tomorrow we will have good roads. I climbed some high bluffs today and had good views of the surrounding dry region and of the snow capped summits of the Powder River or Big Horn Mountains. On the hills were masses of shells of different marine animals, generally in ledges of rock or in broken fragments. My transportation is so limited that I collected a few specimens and carried them in my pockets.

We passed the 16th Kansas and camped near a mile beyond them. In the evening a messenger from Genl. Connor arrived, giving joy to the camp. He reports the Genl. moving up the Tongue with his command. That owing to

---

[13]F. B. Rogers, *Soldiers of the Overland*, 234–35. The date on the first message and the endorsement on the envelope confirm the sequence of events regarding the scouts arriving at Cole's camp on 15 September. The letter is dated on 11 September. The first scouts were sent out on 12 September. They returned on 13 September, the endorsement was written on the envelope, and Corporal Thomas was sent out on 14 September, arriving at Cole's camp on 15 September.
[14]Ansel Steck's statement of 1 August 1894 supporting Cpl. C. L. Thomas's application for the Medal of Honor, Reference Library, Fort Laramie National Historic Site.

the desolate nature of the country, he did not get nearer than 70 miles of the Yellowstone. That he has had several fights with the Indians, killing 200–300, capturing 500 ponies and a few squaws and destroying a village. We move tomorrow with lighter hearts. When the news circulated among the camp, the men would raise a shout. The friends would call to each other "another dead mule dead." As if there could not be any better information for the boys than for a horse or mule to die in order for them to eat.

Marched 20 miles.[15]

Lieutenant Springer still walked with his men, marching in front of the teams. He reported that the scout from Connor arrived in camp after dinner and the location of Fort Connor was learned.[16] Lieutenant Shaver recalled, "No tidings had yet been heard of Connor nor did we learn of his whereabouts until the 16th [15th] Sept when a scout of his that had been looking for us for some time overtook us & reported that Connor was on Tongue River at least one hundred miles distant. We were also informed that Connor had established a post on the head of Powder River and they supposed we were two days march of it, but we did not reach it until the 20th Sept."[17]

✳   ✳   ✳

In an interesting sidelight to the story of Corporal Thomas's heroics, George Bird Grinnell wrote in *Two Great Scouts and Their Pawnee Battalion* that Captain North and his Pawnee scouts discovered Cole's command first and brought the message from Connor on 19 September.[18] This is contradicted by overwhelming evidence previously introduced in this chapter.

Prior to his death in 1885, Frank North had collaborated on a manuscript with newspaperman Alfred Sorenson dictating his experiences with the Pawnee scouts.[19] This was published in serial form in the *Omaha Bee* shortly after Frank's death. The Sorenson account is virtu-

---

[15]Bennett diary, 15 September 1865 entry. It is interesting that Bennett makes no mention of the close proximity to Fort Connor, as this has to be their first news of the location of this new fort much closer than Fort Laramie.

[16]Springer, *Soldiering in Sioux Country*, 57.

[17]Shaver, "Reminiscences," Shaver papers.

[18]Grinnell, *Two Great Scouts*, 118–23.

[19]Alfred Sorenson, "A Quarter of a Century on the Frontier, or the Adventures of Major Frank North, the White Chief of the Pawnees."

ally identical to Grinnell's and obviously the source for his book. North must have been unaware of Thomas's role as a messenger to Cole, as no mention of Corporal Thomas is made in Grinnell's book or Sorenson's manuscript. Frank North did arrive at Cole's camp on 18 September, with the party, led by Capt. Levi Marshall, which had left Connor on the evening of 14 September. It is very clear that Cpl. Charles L. Thomas made first contact with Cole and delivered Connor's message.

In December 1919 noted historical researcher Walter M. Camp wrote to Dan H. Bowman, the amateur historian whose ranch was on Powder River near Mizpah, Montana.[20] Camp was looking for information on the Cole expedition. The two corresponded for several years. It was apparent from their early correspondence that Camp felt that Frank North was the first to contact Cole. Bowman began a correspondence with Luther North (Frank's younger brother) in early 1920.[21] Walter Camp interviewed Charles L. Thomas in the spring of 1921 and wrote to Bowman on 31 May 1921. Excerpts of Camp's letter to Bowman are as follows:

> I have seen the Sergt. [Corporal] Thomas who went to Cole with 2 Pawnees and have had a long talk with him. He is a nice old man, 79 years old, and accurate in his habit of speech. He says he did not write the article which is in the set of books that you have, but told his story to one of the compilers, who wrote up the thing to suit himself, and diverted into romance and exaggeration. [22]
>
> Thomas has official documents which leave no doubt about what he did and the whole thing is very clear to me now. He has given me a lot of data that we can use on our search. He found Cole about 80 miles above the last big bunch of horses killed, which would put the point of meeting Cole well up toward the Wyoming line, if not quite over into Wyoming. I also have a good description as to where he and the Pawnees left the Tongue.[23]

[20]Camp letter to Bowman, 28 December 1919, sc-454, Bowman Collection.
[21]North letter to Bowman, 7 March 1920, ibid.
[22]Referring to Beyer and Keydel, *Deeds of Valor, Vol. 1 and 2.*
[23]Thomas's estimate of eighty miles from Dead Horse Camp to the location that he caught up with Cole's command just below Arvada, Wyoming, is very accurate. Using *Topo USA* topographic software to measure the distance, the mileage between the two points is very close to eighty miles.

I would advise dropping all discussion about what North did. You won't have any doubts about the matter when you hear from me the story that comes from Thomas direct, and learn what documents he has. . . .

Old Sergt Thomas is very interesting and what he does not remember he does not try to tell.[24]

A question still persists about a second soldier riding with Thomas on his mission to Cole. Thomas's descriptions of the incident were all written in 1894 or later. His meeting and correspondence with Walter Camp was fifty-six years after the event, so there is room for memory lapse or self-promotion in his recollections of the event. Connor wrote, "I again sent out a Scout (14th Sept) of two Ohio men and two Pawnee Indians."[25] If there was a second man from the Eleventh Ohio riding with Thomas, his name has disappeared into history. Cole wrote, "On the 15th a messenger and three men arrived."[26] The fourth man here could have been Trooper Hutson, whom Thomas had rescued only hours earlier. While this is still an unanswered question, Corporal Thomas's amazing ride remains an exciting adventure, which his country recognized by awarding him its highest military tribute, the Medal of Honor.

---

[24]Camp letter to Bowman, 31 May 1921, sc-454, Bowman Collection.
[25]Connor's report of 4 October 1865, Dodge Collection.
[26]Cole's official report to Connor, 25 September 1865, *The War of Rebellion.*

CHAPTER EIGHTEEN

16–19 September

MISERABLE ROAD TO TRAVEL

SATURDAY, 16 SEPTEMBER 1865

Cpl. Charles Thomas left Cole's command to return to Connor on the morning of 16 September, accompanied by a party under the command of Lt. Thomas H. Jones.[1] Capt. H. E. Palmer, of Connor's command, met the return party with Lieutenant Jones while out hunting on September 17, which would coincide with a departure from Cole on the previous day.[2]

Bennett reported a difficult day, as the remains of the train struggled up Powder River:

> We had a miserable road to travel over, the worst since the expedition left Omaha. The valley was walled in on either side by bare bluffs too steep for an animal to climb. Deep gulches have been worn down from the hills over which it is impossible to cross. In the valley the river winds from side to side and to follow that route, one must cross the river every mile and run the risk of getting mired in quicksand. Some of the animals got in the sand and mired and could not be got out and were left to die. It is a terrible country.
>
> We passed a branch coming from the mountains to the west. The water was cool and comparatively clear. We make this out to be Sandy Fork. It was curious to see the men and animals come into camp bespattered with mud and all forlorn, hungry and jaded. Marched 12 miles.[3]

---

[1]Cole's first report to General Connor of 25 September 1865, *The War of Rebellion.*
[2]Capt. H. E. Palmer's account, Hafen and Hafen, *Powder River Campaigns,* 144–45.
[3]Bennett diary, 16 September 1865 entry.

The creek that Bennett described as coming in from the west was Crazy Woman Creek. Springer went hunting without any success. He had six shots at a bear but it escaped into a thicket. Some men from Company G killed the bear later, but would not give Springer any meat. After complaining to the hunter's commander, Capt. William Kerrigan, he finally got twenty pounds of it. "I wanted a mule to kill and eat, and asked the quartermaster; he sent me a mule out of my own team, and I only had 4 left, which sent me trembling with rage."[4]

SUNDAY, 17 SEPTEMBER 1865

Cole decided to send a messenger to Fort Connor to request supplies for his starving troops: "On the 17th I sent Lieutenant Schmitten and an escort with dispatches to the commandant of the post at Fort Connor, stating the condition and locale of my command, requesting him to send rations to meet me as soon as possible."[5]

Bennett says it all in his first three words of today's entry:

Worse and worse. The road which I thought could not be worse was today decidedly worse than yesterday A.M. Though we worked hard and pushed to our utmost, we could make but 9 miles.

Mr. Gay and a party was sent forward to Fort Connor. I cannot tell how far that Post is away, but it cannot be far, perhaps 25 miles. Marched 9 miles.

We were startled about sundown by the report of a gun in camp and cries of distress and going to the spot found a soldier shot through the body and in a dying condition. A comrade was cleaning his gun when it accidentally went off, killing his messmate.[6]

Captain Flagg also reported the shooting: "On the 16th of September Private F. Hacke was accidentally shot."[7] Bennett said it happened on 17 September.

Springer went with two men in the direction of Fort Connor, but they did not sight the fort. They saw a party of Indians but had no con-

[4]Springer, *Soldiering in Sioux Country*, 57.
[5]Cole's report of 25 September 1865, *The War of Rebellion*. Lt. Fritz Schmitten was a member of Second Missouri Light Artillery. *Civil War Soldiers and Sailors System*.
[6]Bennett diary, 17 September 1865 entry.
[7]Flagg's report of 20 September 1865, *The War of Rebellion*.

tact with them. They returned to camp with the meat of a cow elk that they killed, thus saving the life of Shorty, "the best mule in my team."[8]

MONDAY, 18 SEPTEMBER 1865

With the arrival of visitors from Connor's command, Bennett learned more details of Connor's attack on the Arapaho village in August:

> Broke up camp at 6 A.M., the 16th Kansas 4 miles in advance and opening the road for us. It was slow & toilsome work to get over the bluffs, cross the valley and drag our slow length along. The roads were terrible and notwithstanding every effort we made but 18 miles. Several elk were killed during the day which with three mules which were killed by the commissary and issued to the company. We had barely got settled into camp when Capt. Marshall with 50 men rode into camp from Genl. Connor's command.
>
> They had left the same day the four men who reached us a few days ago, but marching more slowly only reached us this evening. He found us all in a deplorable condition, half starved, ragged and worn down. His men were instantly beset by ours asking for bread and tobacco. Some of the men offered five dollars apiece for hard tack, but our new friends generously gave all their rations to our men which was hardly a taste around. Tobacco commanded fabulous prices but these men would not receive a cent. From Capt. Marshall I learned additional details of Genl. Connor's expedition. But few Indians were seen and few killed, less than 100 in all. We learned that we were about 25 miles from Ft. Connor. Take it all in all; this arrival did us much good. Lt. Smitton [Schmitten], who was sent yesterday ahead to get supplies has not been heard from. We will certainly meet him tomorrow with something to eat. Marched 18 miles.[9]

Springer went hunting again without success, although others in his company shot deer and elk: "[W]e fared sumptuously and no mule meat for tomorrow either." An order was received for the dismounted men to push on ahead to Fort Connor tomorrow, while most of the mounted men would remain with the train.[10]

---

[8]Springer, *Soldiering in Sioux Country*, 58.

[9]Bennett diary, 18 September 1865 entry. The fact that the men had money to offer for food and tobacco is a good indication that the paymaster from Fort Kearny did show up on 5 July at Columbus and pay the men their back pay.

[10]Springer, *Soldiering in Sioux Country*, 60–62.

TUESDAY, 19 SEPTEMBER 1865

Cole ordered everyone ahead to the fort, except enough men to protect the slower-moving wagon train: "On the 19th I ordered Colonel Wells, 12th Missouri Cavalry, to move to Fort Connor with all dismounted men able to march and all mounted men save 150, which I retained to guard the trains. . . . During the afternoon Lieutenant Schmitten returning, met this part of the command, and after supplying their wants pushed on and reached me a few hours later."[11]

As chief engineering officer, Bennett stayed with the train to get them through this last difficult terrain. He reported:

> The roads today were perfectly execrable worse than ever, winding over the highest bluffs and in the deepest cannons [canyons]. In crossing the river at times whole teams would mire in the quicksand and be hauled out with ropes. The Col. and very many others got very soaked in water & mud by his animal falling in the river. About noon we heard Lt. Smitton was on the way with rations which put new life in the command.
>
> Col. Wells was sent ahead this morning with three fourths of the command. Col. Cole stays behind to bring up the [rest of the] command.
>
> At 4 P.M. we met Lt Smitton with 2 troops and a wagon load of bread and a sack of coffee. In a moment the wagon was swarming with hungry men trying to get something to eat. A guard had all it could do to keep them away until the bread was issued. Many of the men have not tasted bread for two weeks and only a small amount of mule or horse meat. Their hunger was almost unsupportable and they were ready to commit any excess to get bread. Marched 15 miles.[12]

Springer gave his horse to a private who was unable to walk and then traveled on foot to Fort Connor, arriving at 2 P.M. after a hike of thirty miles. He then went straight to the mess hall "and for the first time in 4 weeks, I sat down with good grace at a well supplied table." In the evening, the Pawnee scouts held a scalp dance to celebrate their success at the Tongue River fight. The officers went to the sutler around midnight, at which point "The cherry brandy and cigars commenced circulating very freely."[13]

[11]Cole's official report of 10 February 1867, Hafen and Hafen, *Powder River Campaigns*, 86.
[12]Bennett diary, 19 September 1865.
[13]Springer, *Soldiering in Sioux Country*, 62.

Capt. Frank North and his Pawnee company were with the party under Captain Marshall that had been in Cole's camp on 18 September. They no doubt rode ahead to Fort Connor the next day and celebrated with their scalp dance.[14]

[14]In addition to Grinnell's mention of Frank North reaching Cole's command erroneously on 19 September instead of 18 September, Luther North repeats this story in a letter to the editor of *U.S. Army Recruiting News,* dated 26 November 1928: "My brother, Major Frank North stated that he reached Cole's command with rations on September 19th, and tells of distributing 300 rations of hardtack to Cole's men. As there are 13 hardtack to a ration, those 3900 with bacon, coffee, sugar, etc., ought to have helped."

THE VIEW EAST FROM THE SITE OF FORT CONNOR
In the foreground is the tree line of Powder River.
On the horizon is the northernmost of the Pumpkin Buttes.
Cole's command arrived here on 20 September 1865. *Author's photo.*

CHAPTER NINETEEN

20–25 September

AT FORT CONNOR

WEDNESDAY, 20 SEPTEMBER 1865

The newly constructed Fort Connor sat on a high bench on the left bank of Powder River. Work had begun on an eight-foot-tall stockade of cottonwood logs cut from standing timber across the river, which would eventually surround the fort. Two buildings were completed by the time Cole's command arrived at the fort, with more buildings under construction. The Pumpkin Buttes dominated the horizon to the east of the fort. Fort Connor would be renamed Fort Reno in November 1865.[1]

The command finally reached Fort Connor. Bennett told of the last few miles of the arduous trek. The attitude of the command changed from the drudgery and despair of the last few weeks to one of relief and joy at getting back to the outer edge of civilization:

> The march commenced with a light hearted and full bellied command and the men, though many of them were barefooted and ragged trousers, on merrily as though the goal of their highest ambition had been reached. After three or four miles over hills and ravines as rugged as that we have passed over, we suddenly came to a fine wide valley and good roads. The transition was as sudden and unexpected as it was agreeable and we pushed briskly on five miles of the post when the command halted and went into camp. The grass had been fed off with a range of five miles of the fort [and that] was the reason for camping here. We found newspapers as late as

---

[1]Robert A. Murray, *Military Posts in the Powder River Country of Wyoming, 1865–1894*, 17–19.

August 15th and devoured news from America with eagerness. We also found plenty of rations which had been brought down from the fort. Our troubles for the present are at an end and the boys can once more raise a whistle, a song, or a laugh; a thing not known for several days past.

I have had a glorious wash and an entire change of wardrobe and written letters home. A mail starts in the morning for Ft. Laramie and letters are flowing in by the hundred. We marched about 12 miles today. The hills are low here. Big Horn Mountains are in sight to the west and Pumpkin Butte to the east. Marched 12 miles.[2]

Lieutenant Springer and those who had come in the day before now moved to the same camp location. "About 2 o'clock PM our teams came in and everything was in right shape once more."[3] Lt. W. T. Shaver described the joy of the men at finally being off the long and grueling trail. "Here the men would again enjoy in Hardtack, Bacon, & Coffee, and seemed to think them luxurious."[4] Major Landgraeber reported, "The 20th of September arrived at the fort, having lost nearly all my stock and much of my quartermaster's property and ordinance stores. The health of my command has been generally good, except suffering for the want of proper food and clothing."[5]

THURSDAY, 21 SEPTEMBER 1865

After almost three months of hardship on the trail, the command now relaxed near Fort Connor. Many busied themselves writing letters to family, as the command had been out of touch with civilization for most of this time. Bennett reflected on the day's activity and recalled the hardships on the trail:

We lay quiet in camp, nothing occurring to break the quiet except the departure of a mail for Ft. Laramie laden with messages of love to the absent and tales of suffering and hardships endured and the wonders seen upon the way. It was a busy day with the commissary who issued a full supply to the half famished command. Letter writing and tales of our own

---

[2]Bennett diary, 20 September 1865 entry.
[3]Springer, *Soldiering in Sioux Country*, 62.
[4]Shaver, "Reminiscences," Shaver papers.
[5]Landgraeber's official report of 20 September 1865, *The War of Rebellion*.

experience was the occupation of all hands. I heard of one poor fellow, who seeing a mule mired and struggling in the middle of the river, threw a pole from the bank of the stream to the mule and crawled out to him, cut pieces of meat from the living animal and devoured it after roasting but little before a fire. I heard of a party of half a dozen secretly driving an animal into the bushes out of sight of their comrades and slaughtering it and taking what meat they wanted before being found out and the crowd depriving them of a liberal allowance.[6]

Lieutenant Springer looked for social activity: "I dressed myself in my 'best,' put a paper collar on, and rode to the Fort." Once there, he socialized with several officers of the Sixteenth Kansas at the sutler store.[7]

FRIDAY, 22 SEPTEMBER 1865
Bennett wrote a description of the partially completed Fort Connor:

> Went to Ft. Connor in company with Capt. Boardman. The works consist of a small unfinished stockade and two log buildings completed and a half dozen more in process of erection. There is plenty of timber on the river for fuel & building purposes, but of a poor quality being cottonwood. The hills about the fort are low and easily passed over but the country is dry and desolate, but little growing but cactus and sage brush. The garrison consists of about 200 men all busy erecting quarters and defenses.
>
> No news from Genl. Connor. We are expecting and hoping for him all the time. Visions of home are constantly floating through my head. When shall I hear from the dear ones there.
>
> We had a cold severe wind and a little rain. The dust was whirling through the air and covered everything we had in our quarters and nearly choked and blinded the men.[8]

Charles Springer and his fellow officers of the Twelfth Missouri wanted to go home: "The 22nd Sept. our supply train was ordered to be turned over, the officers had a meeting and all agreed upon making a request through Col. Cole for the regiment to be sent to the states and mustered out. What the results will be remains to be seen."[9]

---

[6]Bennett diary, 21 September 1865 entry.
[7]Springer, *Soldiering in Sioux Country*, 62.
[8]Bennett diary, 22 September 1865 entry.
[9]Springer, *Soldiering in Sioux Country*, 62.

SATURDAY, 23 SEPTEMBER 1865

Bennett resumed work on mapping the expedition. "The grass being exhausted in camp, we moved to another two miles nearer the fort and in the thick woods sheltered from wind and cold. Here I resumed work on my plats and made some little progress. I have very much to do, not having taken anything but notes on the rout [*sic*] up the river."[10]

SUNDAY, 24 SEPTEMBER 1865

Brigadier General Connor's column arrived in the evening from Tongue River. Connor was greeted with new orders: "Upon my arrival on 24th September I found orders assigning me to Command of District of Utah announcing new organizations of Districts and muster out of troops."[11] The District of the Plains had been abolished and Connor reassigned with General Orders Number 20, issued on 22 August.[12] Connor would be replaced by Brig. Gen. Frank Wheaton, who then commanded the new District of Nebraska.[13] Any plan that Connor may have had to continue the campaign into the fall and winter was now a dead issue. He wrote, "I regret that my orders compelled me to abandon the Campaign before I had sufficiently finished the hostile Indians within my former command so as to insure good conduct from them in the future."[14]

Bennett commented on Connor's arrival as well as on mail delivery for Cole's command: "Genl. Connor arrived today from Tongue River, but as yet has given no orders. We are all impatient to be moving homeward. A large mail also came to hand but the news was old and stale and worst of all, not a word for me. But it did the men in camp good to hear again from those from whom they have for months been isolated. I have written several letters, the mail leaves in the morning for Laramie."[15]

Springer received two letters in the mail, one from "my dear Katie" and the other from his brother. "Katie wrote me that her brother

---

[10]Bennett diary entry, 23 September 1865 entry.
[11]Connor's official report, submitted on 4 October 1865 to Major Barnes, Dodge Collection.
[12]Hafen and Hafen, *Powder River Campaigns,* 48.
[13]McDermott, *Circle of Fire,* 143.
[14]Connor's official report, submitted on 4 October 1865 to Major Barnes, Dodge Collection.
[15]Bennett diary, 24 September 1865 entry.

George belonged to the 2nd California Cav. Company L." Springer ascertained that Company L was in Connor's column.[16]

MONDAY, 25 SEPTEMBER 1865

Bennett met with the engineer of Connor's column and was ordered to move out for Fort Laramie with the general and his staff:

> Was waited on by Capt. [Sam] Robins [Robbins], Engineer for Genl. Connor and insists that I should proceed with him to Ft. Laramie to assist in making of a map of the Indian Operations on Powder & Tongue River. Col. Cole remonstrated and even protested against this by the Capt. and even Genl. Connor was inexorable, and I had to succumb. We start tomorrow morning. The command also starts for Laramie, but we will be before them three or four days.
>
> I went to the Fort and took dinner with the Capt. Saw Miller and had a good time. Learned that he had been most shabbily treated by Stonebruner. He expressed many regrets that he did not go with me.[17]

Springer visited Connor's camp. He was disappointed to find out that Company L of the Second California, with Katie's brother George, was escorting the Sawyers party.[18] Returning to his own camp, he learned that orders were issued for the regiment to march for Fort Laramie in the morning.[19]

Cole wrote his official report of the expedition to Connor on this day.[20] He also commented, "On the 25th I received orders to move on the following morning to Laramie."[21]

---

[16]Springer, *Soldiering in Sioux Country*, 62–63.

[17]Bennett diary, 25 September 1865 entry. The Miller that Bennett mentioned is no doubt the same Miller that Bennett was expecting to join the expedition, mentioning this on 3 July and again on 6 July, as his assistant. Why he didn't show and how he ended up with Connor's column is unknown. Miller could be the author of the diary quoted in Chapter 19, which was written by an unknown civilian employee or staff officer. If he was to be Bennett's assistant, he probably had a similar engineering background. The diary is written in much the same style as Bennett's and was with Bennett's papers when he died. Further investigation is needed to determine who Miller was. The Stonebruner mentioned here is also unidentified.

[18]Hafen and Hafen, *Powder River Campaigns*, 225–85. The Sawyers Expedition was in Powder River country in August and September 1865 exploring a proposed route from Sioux City, Iowa, to the Montana goldfields. Led by James A. Sawyers, they had several confrontations with the Indians in the region, and General Connor had to divert some of his troops to protect their train.

[19]Springer, *Soldiering in Sioux Country*, 63.

[20]Cole's first report to General Connor of 25 September 1865, *The War of Rebellion*.

[21]Cole's official report of 10 February 1867, Hafen and Hafen, *Powder River Campaigns*, 88.

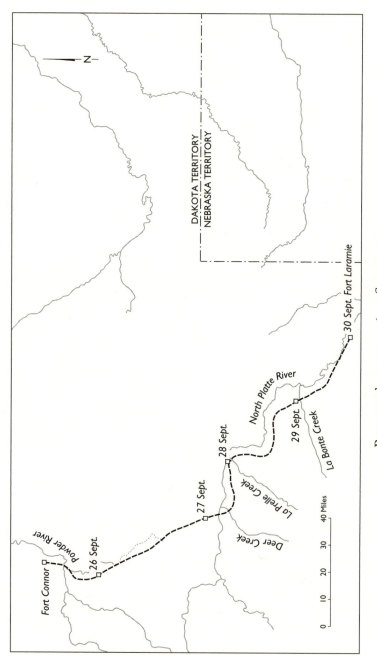

BENNETT'S ROUTE, 26–30 SEPTEMBER

CHAPTER TWENTY

26–29 September

ON TO FORT LARAMIE

T he first news of the campaign hit the outside world on the day after Cole had submitted his official report to Brigadier General Connor. This exaggerated news flash probably came from a message carried to Fort Laramie by the mail detail that left Fort Connor on 21 September.

Glorious Indian News
General Connor Defeats Them!
Great Slaughter of the Indians!
Three Battles Fought and our
Forces Still in Pursuit

Just as we go to press we learn that Gen. Connor is after the Indians, having fought three engagements and defeating them with great slaughter. Our losses in all three battles is twenty-five killed. We will give the particulars tomorrow.

P.S. Since the above was in type we have received the following additional particulars:

The center column of Gen. Connor's command under Col. Cole had three engagements with Sioux, Cheyennes, and Arapahoes on the first, second, third, and eighth and ninth of September, routing them each time with great loss, variously estimated at from two to six hundred Indians killed, with loss of horses, camp equipage, etc. Our loss, twenty-five killed and three wounded.[1]

---

[1] *The Daily Rocky Mountain News*, 26 September 1865.

Tuesday, 26 September 1865

Bennett, now separated from Cole's command, traveled with Connor and his staff. He wrote:

> Was up long before day, ate but little and proceeded on horse back to Genl. Connor's camp, and waited at least two hours before they were ready to start. There were three ambulances and fifteen men of us. The 2nd & 12th were on the road and we passed their long column, mostly on foot, and many without shoes, and other clothing scarce. Genl. Connor threw out an old pair of boots to one of the men, who was loud in his protestation of gratitude. We followed for 17 miles up the bed of a creek. At places water could be found by digging. Then we proceeded 25 miles until dark, when we came to a small puddle of water and camped. It was lucky we camped as we did, or we would [have] not got any [water], as a large ox train camped nearby & did not get enough water for half the cattle. Sage brush was our fuel. We made out poorly indeed but none grumbled. A mail party going along with us found 18 or 20 mules and horses, evidently strayed from the Indians. Some were government stock and others belonged to the stage co. We drove it in & thereby facilitated our movements as some of the mules gave out and we replaced from the herd. Wolves howled in close proximity to our herds during the night. Pumpkin Butte is but a few miles distant and shows quite prominent, also the Big Horn Mountains. The land is dry and barren in most places, but buffalo grass grows on many of the hills.[2]

Springer marched with his company towards Fort Laramie. He observed the same incident previously described by Bennett: "Sept. the 26th we started out at 6 o'clock AM. General Connor who was going to Fort Laramie in an ambulance passed us on the road, and as he saw some of our footmen barefooted he gave the boots from his own feet to our men. We encamped on Buffalo Creek 13 miles from Fort Connor."[3]

Cole moved his worn-out command towards Fort Laramie: "The first day out I marched but ten miles, when I encamped to await for a train of forty wagons which General Connor had ordered to report to me to transport my foot-sore men, of which I had some 400 or more."[4]

---

[2]Bennett diary, 26 September 1865 entry.
[3]Springer, *Soldiering in Sioux Country*, 63.
[4]Cole's official report of 10 February 1867, Hafen and Hafen, *Powder River Campaigns*, 88.

WEDNESDAY, 27 SEPTEMBER 1865

Connor's group continued traveling toward Fort Laramie, as Bennett described the day: "Traveled over an undulating country with good roads, well worn by trains carrying stores to Ft. Connor. Passed over several dry beds of creeks being the head waters of the Cheyenne. Where we camped was plenty of good spring water & rushes for the mules. Sage brush, cactus and in places buffalo grass grows on the prairie. But little rough road and we made 45 miles. Capt. Robbins, Lt. Jewett and one of the signal officers are the cooks, while the rest of us haul sage brush and hunt Buffalo chips for fuel. Wolves howl us to sleep."[5]

Springer still traveled with Cole's command. "Marched 28 miles and camped on the North Fork of the Cheyenne River with plenty of good water."[6]

THURSDAY, 28 SEPTEMBER 1865

Connor's party reached the North Platte River, as Bennett observed:

We found the country more uneven and as we descended into the valley of the Platte, it was quite rough, so much so that at one place we were all obliged to get out and fasten ropes to our vehicle to prevent its tipping over. The Platte was clear with a fine pebble bottom and looked fine to me after being away and seeing more but sluggish muddy & brackish streams & puddles. We struck North Platte and telegraph road at Deer Creek station, a small post with a rough log block house and quarters. The Black Hills were a few miles south and altogether is a romantic spot.[7] We went 20 miles down the Platt & camped on La Prele Creek, a fine stream of cold water.[8]

Springer reflected on the unpredictability of Wyoming weather: "Marched through a dust storm, turned to snow, then to rain." The sun then came out and they camped on the south fork of the Cheyenne River.[9]

---

[5]Bennett diary, 27 September 1865 entry.

[6]Springer, *Soldiering in Sioux Country,* 63.

[7]Not to be confused with the Black Hills of South Dakota, the Laramie Mountains of south central Wyoming were commonly referred to as the Black Hills during this period.

[8]Bennett diary, 28 September 1865 entry.

[9]Springer, *Soldiering in Sioux Country,* 63–64.

FRIDAY, 29 SEPTEMBER 1865

Connor's group continued its path along the Platte, making good time, as Bennett reported on the day:

> Left the La Prele and at 10 A.M. reached La Bonte, a military station on the telegraph road for the protection of the line. Before reaching La Bonte, found large beds of gypsum and procured a few specimens. The Black Hills approach very near on the south and look fine. Mr. Miller drew a sketch of the post. Resuming our trip over a rough and dusty road we reached Horse Shoe Station and camped 2 miles below where good water & grass was plenty. Wolves and owls kept us awake much of the night. Observed a few variety of oak and other timber new to me, also much vine & with currant bushes in abundance. Toured 45 miles.[10]

Springer wrote, "The command marched 30 miles to the Platte with a stop for dinner at Sage Creek." He set an example for his men by walking with them.[11]

---

[10]Bennett diary, 28 September 1865 entry.
[11]Springer, *Soldiering in Sioux Country*, 64.

CHAPTER TWENTY-ONE

30 September–4 October

THE EXPEDITION ENDS

SATURDAY, 30 SEPTEMBER 1865

Fort Laramie, at the confluence of the Laramie River and the North Platte River, was first established in 1834 by William Sublette. Named Fort William, it became an important fur-trade center. The post was rebuilt in 1841 and named Fort John, but was usually called Fort Laramie. The fort became an important stop for emigrants on the Oregon Trail in the 1840s. In 1849 the army bought Fort Laramie and made it an outpost along the overland road, with the purpose of protecting travelers on the trail. The army rebuilt the old fort, and it served as a vital transportation and communications link during the Civil War.[1]

Finally, after three months in the wilderness and under the worst of conditions, Bennett arrived at Fort Laramie:

> Left camp at day light, passed for 10 miles over a smooth but dusty road and then over some high spurs of the Black Hills and had very bad roads. Stopped for lunch at Maggie's Springs 15 miles from Ft. Laramie. There are good springs of pure water that furnish a copious supply. Were named after a prostitute named Maggie. Near the springs, found fine crystal formations in the lime stone rock.
>
> Reached Laramie at 1 P.M. The Genl. went to Mr. Bullock's first to see his wife & children. We were heartily welcomed by the officers of the post who thronged around us to learn of the Powder & Tongue expedition. The band serenaded and a fine dinner was provided for us weary and dirty sons

---

[1]LeRoy Hafen and Francis Marion Young, *Fort Laramie and the Pageant of the West*, 17–38, 137.

of guns, Soap, water, and towels were the next resort and in a short time our dusty habiliments gave place to clean blue broadcloth and gilt buttons.

Wrote letter & had a good time generally, but found none for me. It is cruel not to hear from home for weeks & months.[2]

Springer and the rest of Cole's command were still four days away from Fort Laramie. He strained himself hauling firewood and had to ride in a wagon. Springer had his back rubbed with chloroform liniment while sitting by the fire that evening and went to bed.[3]

SUNDAY, 1 OCTOBER 1865

Bennett relaxed on his first full day at Fort Laramie: "Wrote letters all day, read a little and rested as best I could. Weather is warm, clear and pleasant. But the country very dry and dusty."[4]

Springer, as always, recovered quickly from his ailment and participated enthusiastically in the events of the day. "Next morning I got up, all the pain was gone and I felt as good as ever. After a good hearty meal, I mounted my horse and off we started on our homeward bound journey." He was able to make contact that evening with Katie's brother, George: "Now I can tell Katie I have seen her brother George personally."[5]

MONDAY, 2 OCTOBER 1865

Bennett resumed work and expressed a desire to head east as quickly as possible: "Commenced work on plats of our road. Will urge the matter forward as fast as possible, in order to leave for Leavenworth as fast as possible. Found some familiar faces and acquaintances. There was an Indian scare today but amounted to nothing. Met Mr. Bard of Leavenworth on his way to Salt Lake City with his goods. He's met with some losses."[6]

---

[2]Bennett diary, 30 September 1865 entry.

[3]Springer, *Soldiering in Sioux Country,* 64–65.

[4]Bennett diary, 1 October 1865 entry.

[5]Springer, *Soldiering in Sioux Country,* 65. Pvt. George W. Robertson was a member of Company L, Second California Cavalry. *American Civil War Research Database.*

[6]Bennett diary, 2 October 1865 entry.

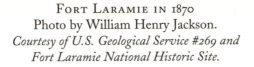

FORT LARAMIE IN 1870
Photo by William Henry Jackson.
Courtesy of U.S. Geological Service #269 and
Fort Laramie National Historic Site.

Springer wrote, "We marched past the first sign of civilization, a lit-tle Fort or telegraph station, called Horse Shoe." They camped about 6 miles below the station.[7]

TUESDAY, 3 OCTOBER 1865

Bennett recorded a very light entry: "Col. Cole in today, but the com-mand camped 9 miles out & the Col. returned. Had a pleasant time coming from Powder River. Nothing known as to future [page torn]."[8]

Springer still marched with his company. The command marched past La Bonte and went into camp nine miles from Fort Laramie. "The evening was very warm and I took a glorious bath in Platte River."[9]

[7]Springer, *Soldiering in Sioux Country,* 65–66.
[8]Bennett diary, 3 October 1865 entry.
[9]Springer, *Soldiering in Sioux Country,* 66.

WEDNESDAY, 4 OCTOBER 1865

Bennett met the legendary mountain man Jim Bridger, one of the guides in Connor's column:

> Many military changes occur; soon Genl Connor goes to Salt Lake. Col Cole & his regt. to St. Louis. The 12th remain[s] here. Capt Robbins & engineers go to Leavenworth. The Signal Corp. goes home. Progress finally with the map. Was introduced to Maj Bridger, the old mountaineer I have always heard of from my boyhood. He has a son in the 2nd Mo.[10] And they met at Ft. Connor. The old man was displeased to see his son in the ranks a common soldier. Everybody is busy here. The changes render it necessary for all to stir around. Went to the camp of the 2nd and had a short visit with old messmates after dark. Got some fine specimens today.[11]

Springer reported that the next morning the command marched to within one mile of Fort Laramie and went into camp. He expressed a very negative opinion of the Second Missouri Light Artillery:

> The 2nd Mo. Art proceeded 2 miles below the Fort and went into camp and so I hope that we will never see the regiment again, for it is the confoundedest [sic] crowd I have ever been with. While all had full rations their men went to the butcher and took the pouches of the killed cattle and eat them. It is the hungriest set I ever saw. But they never heard a shot fired from the enemy during the 4 year war, they have been laying around St. Louis, and never went out of the state of Missouri.[12]
>
> I had forgotten to mention that on the evening of the 2nd of October our gallant Col. Wells was whaked [sic] under arrest by Col. Cole for reasons not known.[13]

Bennett's last journal entry was recorded on 4 October. Springer continued his journal until 21 November, although nothing of note took

---

[10]Pvt. Felix F. Bridger was in the Second Missouri Light Artillery. *Civil War Soldiers and Sailors System.*

[11]Bennett diary, 4 October 1865 entry.

[12]Springer, *Soldiering in Sioux Country*, 66–67. Springer had been consistently negative about Colonel Cole and the Second Missouri Light Artillery throughout the expedition. As stated earlier, this was a possible reaction based on Springer's resentment that resulted from the Twelfth Missouri Cavalry being placed under the command of an artillery officer, with their colonel being subordinate to Cole.

[13]Ibid., 67. In a note covering this incident, B. F. Cooling III said, "Wells later explained his arrest as coming from failure to submit an after-action report with alacrity expected by Cole." Ibid., 81.

place in his remaining days at Fort Laramie. All three men and the command had arrived at Fort Laramie, and the expedition was completed. One of the great adventures of the early West ended anticlimactically as the various elements of the far-flung expedition went quietly to their next destinations, whether home or the next assignments.

⁜   ⁜   ⁜

The view of the army, anxious for success and to justify their costly, near disastrous campaign, can be seen in Dodge's report to Pope:

Central City, September 27, 1865
Maj. Gen. JOHN POPE
Saint Louis, and
Maj. J. W. BARNES,
Fort Leavenworth:

On August 28 General Connor surprised Medicine Man's band of Indians on Tongue River; killed 50, captured village, all winter provisions, and 600 horses—all the stock they had. On the 1st of September the right column under Colonel Cole, had a fight with the Sioux, Cheyennes, and Arapahoes on Powder River, and whipped them. On the evening of the 3rd of September attacked them again, driving them down Powder River ten miles. Next morning at daylight attacked again, fight lasting until 10 A. M., when Indians were defeated with loss of 200 killed. They fled in every direction, losing large numbers of horses, camp equipage, provisions, &c. On 8th instant Colonel Walker, commanding center column, who was in advance of Colonel Cole, met Indians in large force. Colonel Cole came up and, after a short but spirited engagement, they totally routed Indians, driving them in every direction with great loss, several of principal chiefs being killed in this fight. On the night of 9th of September a severe snow-storm raged, in which 400 of Colonel Cole's horses perished. I was in that storm on Powder River. It was very severe, and I lost several animals. Our total loss in all the engagements less than 50 killed and wounded, including 1 officer. Colonel Cole or Colonel Walker had not communicated with General Connor and were on Powder River, but by this time they have communicated, as they had ascertained where General Connor's column was.

G. M. DODGE
Major-General[14]

---

[14]Dodge's report to Pope of 27 September 1865, *The War of Rebellion*.

However, the glowing reports of the campaign's success were met with skepticism by the editor of Omaha's newspaper, the *Nebraska Republican*:

INDIAN FIGHT—We published in another column a dispatch from Fort Laramie reporting several engagements with the combined forces of the Cheyennes, Sioux and Arapahoes on Powder River. As usual the Indians are said to have been defeated with "great slaughter. They fled in every direction." But it seems that the Indians are every time the attacking party; and after being "totally routed and beautifully cleaned out," they come to time as fresh as ever the next day. The forces engaged in these battles are under command of Col. Cole—the right wing of Gen. Connor's command. The report is not official and probably comes from some unauthorized and frightened runner. Our losses are not heavy and while we have no doubt that there has been an engagement, we must take this report with many grains of allowance. It is improbable upon its face. From 200 to 600 Indians killed and wounded is too large a margin and the statement that two hundred horses and mules froze to death in August is preposterous. All kinds of stock live far north of Ft. Connor the year round without feed. This portion of the report is a genuine roorback.[15]

_____

[15]*Nebraska Republican*, 29 September 1865. Both the *Nebraska Republican* (Omaha, issue of 29 September 1865) and the *Montana Post* (Virginia City, issue of 7 October 1865) printed the same word-for-word report of Cole's fights on Powder River:

Fort Laramie, Sept. 26th.

Information has been received to-day from General Connor's right column, under command of Colonel Cole, to the 21st inst. It has been encamped near Fort Connor since the 20th inst. He has lost 600 horses and mules, two hundred of which were frozen to death in one night. On the first of September he was attacked by a war party of Sioux, Cheyenne, and Arapahoes on Powder River. They were repulsed with heavy loss, our loss being only four killed and two wounded. On the 3rd the Indians appeared again in force and were driven ten miles. The next day the engagement was renewed and lasted until noon, the Indians being again defeated with great slaughter, their loss being from 300 to 600 killed and wounded.   The Indians fled in every direction, but our troops were unable to pursue them, on account of the poor condition of their stock. Our loss was one killed, and one officer and two men wounded. The Indians lost a large number of horses.

The Indians again attacked our troops on the 8th, but after a short and spirited engagement they were totally routed and beautifully cleaned out. They lost many of their principal chiefs. Our reported loss in the three engagements, is seven killed and one officer and two men wounded. Another battle was expected on Powder River, but the Indians suddenly disappeared. Colonel Cole will camp at Fort Connor, or wait till information is received from Gen. Connor.

CHAPTER TWENTY-TWO

AFTERMATH

Col. Nelson Cole received orders at Fort Laramie to proceed with his command to Fort Leavenworth on 7 October to be mustered out of the service.[1] He left the army on 18 November 1865.[2] Over the next month the various batteries of his regiment were mustered out, and the Second Missouri Light Artillery disappeared into history.[3]

Cole then returned to St. Louis and resumed his career in the lumber business. In 1868, with his partner Stephen Glass, they formed the Cole and Glass Manufacturing Company. The company function was that of a decorative molding, turning, and planing mill. The average workforce numbered around one hundred.[4] Some of his old employees who had volunteered with him at the start of the war came back and remained working there for many years. He served on the St. Louis City Council for six years, building a reputation as an opponent of all schemes intended to defraud the public. Cole also served as a commissioner for Lafayette Park.[5]

President William McKinley commissioned Nelson Cole as brigadier general of the Volunteer Army in May 1898, the month that war was declared with Spain. He applied for active service in either Cuba or the Philippines, but his tour was limited to stateside duty.

---

[1]G. M. Bailey orders to Cole of 27 October 1865, *The War of Rebellion.*
[2]"In Memoriam. Nelson Cole, Brigadier General U.S.V."
[3]History of the Second Missouri Light Artillery, *The War of the Rebellion.*
[4]Leonard, *Industries of St. Louis,* 112–13.
[5]"In Memoriam. Nelson Cole, Brigadier General U.S.V."

During the winter of 1898–99, while in command of his brigade at Columbia, South Carolina, he contracted a serious cold. He mustered out of the service in March 1899 and returned to St. Louis. He died from complications of his illness on 31 July 1899 and is buried in Belle-fontaine Cemetery in north St. Louis.[6]

❋   ❋   ❋

Lyman G. Bennett left the army's employment in March 1866 and returned to Kendall County, Illinois.[7] Colonel Cole, in his 1867 official report recognized Bennett thusly: "To the untiring energy and devotion to his profession of Mr. L. G. Bennett, my engineer officer, is due the accurate record of the valuable information of the region passed over. Constantly moving, he by observation made himself thoroughly familiar with the topography of the country, and gleaned much in relation to the mineralogy along the route."[8]

Bennett returned to Oswego and reclaimed the position of county surveyor from 1869 to 1871 and also served as deputy circuit clerk. He then served as circuit clerk of Kendall County from 1872 to 1880.[9]

In December 1880 Bennett moved to Greene County, Missouri, and purchased a farm on the west edge of Springfield. He continued to work as an engineer and surveyor, which included platting additions to the City of Springfield and surveying railroad lines in Missouri and Oklahoma. In 1890 and 1891 he surveyed in Indian Territory under the direction of Interior Secretary John W. Noble. He died in Springfield, Missouri, on 24 February 1904 and is buried at Hazelwood Cemetery in Springfield.[10]

❋   ❋   ❋

Charles H. Springer continued on frontier duty until April 1866 and then mustered out of the service at Fort Leavenworth, Kansas. He

---

[6]Nelson Cole's obituary, *Necrology Scrapbook, Volume 2C,* 68.
[7]*Pictorial and Genealogical Record of Greene County, Missouri,* 201–205.
[8]Cole's official report of 10 February 1865, Hafen and Hafen, *Powder River Campaigns,* 91.
[9]Records of Kendall County, Yorkville, Illinois.
[10]Bradbury, "Biographical Sketch of L. G. Bennett."

returned to St. Joseph, Missouri, and claimed a postwar pension for a hip injury sustained while on a reconnaissance mission in Mississippi in 1864. He worked as a route agent for the U.S. Mail Service and as a U.S. government storekeeper at the Kansas City Distillery in the 1880s. Springer married Katherine Stelzer on 23 March 1867.

Springer died on 25 November 1886 in Kansas City, Missouri, "of a gunshot wound through the brain." Perhaps it was a suicide; if so, one can only speculate as to the motive.[11]

-----

[11]Springer, *Soldiering in Sioux Country*, 3–4.

CHAPTER TWENTY-THREE

IN RETROSPECT

The Eastern Division of the Powder River Indian Expedition is often referred to as "the Cole and Walker Expedition," as if their meeting were planned. However, Lieutenant Colonel Walker's center column from Fort Laramie was not expected to operate with Colonel Cole's eastern column from Omaha. Brigadier General Connor's orders called for each column to operate independently with an eventual rendezvous at Panther Mountain, meeting Connor's western column there.

Walker's route seemed to be too far to the east, as Connor's orders directed him "across the headwaters of the Little Missouri, in a north-westerly direction to Powder River."[1] The route that Connor described would have taken Walker west of Devils Tower, in the vicinity of the Three Peaks or Little Missouri Buttes area, near the headwaters of the Little Missouri River. Walker joined Cole at a campsite approximately forty miles east of the proposed route, a meeting that happened strictly by chance. The correspondent known only as Jay wrote in his 30 August report, "We knew nothing of each others whereabouts until they rode into camp; for a start six hundred miles apart, over different portions of country; it was a rather close hit."[2]

After their chance meeting on Pine Draw Creek in northeast Wyoming, the two commands continued to operate independently, camping separately yet staying in fairly close proximity. It made sense to keep the two commands separate because of the limited feed and

---

[1] Connor's orders to Walker, 28 July 1865, Hafen and Hafen, *Powder River Campaigns*, 42.
[2] Jay's report, 18 August 1865, ibid., 357, 358.

water on much of the terrain that they traversed and the rapidly deteriorating condition of their stock. Cole's column bore the brunt of the
Indian fighting, with the exception of the battle on 8 September.
Cole's command literally "marched and fought," as Bennett described,
from 1 to 8 September, while Walker's command was always just a few
miles away from the fighting.

Fr. Peter John Powell, in his history of the Northern Cheyenne chiefs
and warrior societies, wrote that Cole and Walker did not get along.
"Ever since they met they had been quarreling over who was in command, for both were colonels. Now, faced with the problem of deciding the next move, the split between them widened even further."[3] This
author found no evidence of a rift between the two officers, and Father
Powell did not list a source for this statement. The only written account
of this "quarreling" found was in George Bird Grinnell's *The Fighting
Cheyennes*, so that is probably where the claim originated.[4] Grinnell got
much of his information from George Bent, who would have had no
reliable input on the relationship between the two commanders. Nelson
Cole, as a full colonel, outranked Samuel Walker as a lieutenant
colonel, so there was no question as to who had the superior rank. On
8 September, with the Sixteenth Kansas under attack, Walker reported
turning over the direction of the battle to Cole as soon as he came up
because Cole outranked him. None of the reports or journals even hints
at any problems between the two commanders.

Brig. Gen. Patrick E. Connor submitted his official report of the
campaign to Major General Dodge's headquarters on 4 October 1865,
along with those of his column commanders, Colonel Cole and Lieutenant Colonel Walker. In his report, Connor criticized Cole's effort
to meet at the planned rendezvous: "I cannot regard these Column
Commanders as having obeyed my instructions. Colonel Cole only
sent out one Scout of one officer and fourteen men to ascertain my
whereabouts, did not appear to make any effort to join me or reach the
designated place of rendezvous."[5]

[3]Powell, *People of the Sacred Mountain*, 2:382.
[4]Grinnell, *The Fighting Cheyennes*, 183.
[5]Connor's official report, submitted on 4 October 1865 to Major Barnes, Dodge Collection.

As for Walker, Connor had basically the same thing to say: "Lt Colonel Walker made no effort to ascertain where I was or to reach the designated rendezvous, but satisfied himself with the single scout made by Colonel Cole."[6]

Walker, who traveled without the encumbrance of the wagon train, should have moved his more mobile command toward Connor on the Tongue. In the author's opinion, Walker generally showed a lack of initiative throughout the campaign and chose to stay close to Cole's command as it marched up and down Powder River. One can understand Connor's frustration, as it must have seemed so simple to him for them to just continue across country, even though the terrain proved to be very demanding. The reader will recall that Cole changed his mind and the direction of his command three times in a very short time frame: First, when the scouting party returned, he decided to head south, looking for a passable route to Connor on Tongue River. Then, after their initial encounter with the Indians on 1 September, he decided to head north for the Yellowstone River. After the first stock-killing storm on the night of 2 September, he decided to head south to Fort Laramie on 3 September. Clearly, he seemed confused and unsure of what to do next.

Hindsight is always clearer, but it would seem logical to have sent additional scouting parties to search for Connor's command. Cole had the manpower to send a large enough party to be able to defend itself, with enough remaining troops to adequately defend the train. Well armed with their Spencer carbines, Cole's command had plenty of ammunition. In spite of the condition of the horses, one would think that they could have come up with fifty or one hundred serviceable mounts. Connor's criticism of the two column commanders here is probably deserved.

However, in his written order to Cole, Connor was not specific about a time frame for their meeting at Panther Mountain. He had ordered Cole to carry sixty days' worth of supplies, so one must assume that he intended to have the supply base established by 1 September. Because of his delays in waiting for a supply train at Fort Connor and his attack

---

[6]Ibid.

on the Arapaho village, he was at least fifty miles south of Cole's scouting party of 31 August. Connor must shoulder some of the blame for not setting a date for the rendezvous of the columns to re-supply.

Nelson Cole is sometimes described as "incompetent" when this campaign is discussed.[7] "Unprepared" would be a better assessment. Cole had a solid Civil War record, having served in positions of responsibility both on the department level and the regimental level. Nothing in his background prepared him for the Powder River Indian Expedition—he had never operated on the plains and had no experience with Indian warfare or in managing a command of this size. He had received sketchy initial verbal orders when organizing the campaign, and it wasn't until he had been on the march ten days that he received his written orders from Connor as to the expedition's full purpose and destination. He had only ten days to hurriedly put the expedition together and get it on the road.

The supply issue has been previously discussed in Chapter Three, but when assessing what went wrong, one has to start with the preparation. Cole was delayed in Omaha waiting for supplies. Both Dodge and Connor expressed impatience about the delays in getting started. Dodge's expectations seemed to be that the expedition should have immediately moved from the riverboats that brought them to Omaha to the trail. It was not to be, as Connor in his official report wrote: "I deem it proper for me to state that the Expedition was organized and placed in the field without having received any of the supplies intended for it."[8] They finally got on the road only after Connor instructed Cole to purchase locally in Omaha, whatever he needed.

Colonel Cole did get the expedition moving out on 1 July, but it suffered from the lack of capable or experienced guides. The wrong turn at Cedar Creek on 8 July is a good example of this. According to Cole and Bennett, the guides openly admitted they knew nothing of the country. Colonel Cole, Bennett, and other officers often did the scouting work that should have been done by the guides.

---

[7]"[B]oth Cole and Walker both showed themselves incompetent." Grinnell, *The Fighting Cheyennes*, 183.

[8]Connor's official report, submitted on 4 October 1865 to Major Barnes, Dodge Collection.

In addition to the quality of the guides, inaccurate maps posed a problem. Connor's orders to Cole did include a map, a copy of which, unfortunately, is not available. It was probably the 1857 G. K. Warren map, the most current map of the area at that time, which proved to be very sketchy and lacked detail of the terrain traveled. The map of rivers and streams in the Black Hills area proved to be inaccurate and incomplete. The Powder River country of eastern Montana was marked in bold letters: "Unexplored."[9] Supposedly Connor's maps had the proposed routes drawn on them and the location of the supply depot at Panther Mountain marked. The Warren map shows the Panther Mountains stretching between Rosebud Creek and Tongue River. Later maps do not show the Panther Mountains, as the name has disappeared into history.[10] Cole's orders, not specific as to which stream the supply depot would be on, only referred to "the north base of Panther Mountain, where you will find a supply depot." Connor's command traveled up the Tongue toward their expected rendezvous with the other two columns, so it must be assumed his instruction meant that river, not the Rosebud. However, in Walker's orders Connor specified a "general rendezvous of the four columns of the expedition on Rosebud River."[11] So there is confusion here.

Cole has also been criticized for his lack of aggressive action against the Powder River tribes.[12] While it is true that the command only reacted to Indian attacks, it was probably unrealistic to expect this worn-out command to make bold, aggressive moves. With Cole's command on half rations or less, with men dying from scurvy and many of the troops barefoot, and with their horses and mules dropping dead by the hundreds, it wasn't a time to mount offensive actions. Basic survival would have been a higher priority.

---

[9]G. K. Warren map, Wyoming State Archives.

[10]Current maps refer to mountains in this general area as the Wolf Mountains.

[11]Connor's orders to Walker, 28 July 1865, Hafen and Hafen, *Powder River Campaigns*, 41–43. The fourth column, referred to in Connor's orders to Walker, was two companies of the Second California Cavalry, from Connor's column and a company of Omaha scouts. They were split off from the main column and took a more southwesterly route, skirting the western edge of the Big Horn Mountains.

[12]Hyde, *Red Cloud's Folk*, 130, says, "With 2000 troops under their orders, Cole and Walker made no attempt to do anything further than to defend their camps."

Cole reported in his 25 September 1865 official report casualties for the entire expedition as follows: "Twelfth Missouri Cavalry, 3 killed, 1 missing; Second Missouri Light Artillery, 5 killed, one officer slightly wounded, 4 men wounded (3 since died), 1 missing."[13] These numbers are very close to the numbers taken from the various reports and diaries, with the variable being the wounded that died later.[14] Considering the ordeal that the command had been through for the past ninety days, with eight days of fighting with the warriors of Powder River, their battle-related deaths were less than one percent of the total command. The non-battle related deaths, including three scurvy deaths, totaled six, which when combined with the battle deaths is only slightly over one percent of the fourteen hundred men on the expedition.[15] Lieutenant Colonel Walker's Sixteenth Kansas Cavalry had one battle-related death, and four wounded on 8 September.[16] Walker also reported on 10 August regarding the brackish water of the Cheyenne River: "Several men died from the effects of it."[17]

Cole kept casualties in battle to a minimum through sound defensive tactics and effective use of artillery. The majority of the killed and wounded came from stragglers, small groups out hunting, and the disobeying of orders. Fortunately the expedition had an experienced artillery officer, Cole, in command, and his use of artillery proved very effective at keeping the warriors at bay in all of the engagements.[18]

Serious shortages of food for the soldiers and forage for the stock caused major problems. However, ammunition never seemed to be in short supply, for either their Spencer repeating carbines or for the

---

[13]Cole's official report of 25 September 1865, *The War of Rebellion*.

[14]See Appendix B for a casualty list.

[15]Father Powell wrote of the casualties for Cole's command: "Thirty-five had already died from hunger and exposure, and the survivors had little hope of escaping the same fate." Powell, *People of the Sacred Mountain*, 2:386. Although not supported by a note, this misstatement of the casualties obviously came from George Bird Grinnell's *Two Great Scouts and their Pawnee Battalion*, which in turn came from newspaperman Alfred Sorenson's interviews with Frank North in the early 1880s. Grinnell, *Two Great Scouts*, 119; Sorenson, "A Quarter of a Century," 109.

[16]Walker's official report of 25 September 1865, Hafen and Hafen, *Powder River Campaigns*, 98.

[17]Ibid., *Powder River Campaigns*, 92–93

[18]"The most effective weapons of all during the fighting in 1865 were the portable cannons. . . . Cole and Walker probably owed their survival to the guns they had with them." McDermott, *Circle of Fire*, 164.

artillery. The diaries and reports do not mention having to ration it in any of the fights. Low casualties resulted from this big advantage of the military over the warriors. Out-gunned, the Indians tended to stay out of range. All of the reports and diaries, when mentioning the Indians' armament, talk about them being primarily armed with the primitive bow and arrow and war clubs. When discussing Indian firearms, Lieutenant Colonel Walker said in his official report, "the Indians seemed to have but few fire arms."[19] Colonel Wells of the Twelfth Missouri, in describing the action on 10 September, wrote, "The Indians had this day four or five good muskets."[20]

The Indians employed the tactic of using small parties as decoys. They attempted to lure the soldiers out of their lines in small groups, in order to lead them into the ambush of a larger warrior force. This worked on the 1 September fight, with Captain Rowland taking the bait and pursuing with seven men. He was then surprised by a large hidden group of warriors and lost three men killed and two wounded. On 5 September Lieutenant Smiley charged a few Indians with twelve men, without orders. Suddenly confronted with one hundred Indians, rescue of his small detachment occurred only by quick supporting action from Captain Boardman. The casualties in this action were one killed and four wounded. Aside from these two incidents, the command learned about the decoy strategy quickly and generally displayed control and caution after first seeing it used.

The subject of Indian battle casualties is far more subjective. Cole claimed, "I estimate the loss of the Indians at from 200 to 500 killed and wounded."[21] This appears to be a gross exaggeration, perhaps an attempt to find something positive to report on the expedition. The reports and diaries vary considerably, which is understandable because the warriors carried most of their downed fighters off the battlefield, making verification impossible. Bennett, who observed much of the fighting, listed less than twenty-five Indian deaths over all of the fights. Springer wrote about forty-five to fifty Indian deaths. Colonel Wells counted less than twenty. Other officers, such as Landgraeber,

[19]Walker's official report, 25 September 1865, Hafen and Hafen, *Powder River Campaigns,* 97.
[20]Wells's official report of 20 September 1865, *The War of Rebellion.*
[21]Cole's 10 February 1867 report, Hafen and Hafen, *Powder River Campaigns,* 89.

Kendall, and Rowland only list a few deaths for action that they were directly involved in. George Bent said nothing about Indian casualties in any of the fights except the one that he participated in on 8 September. On that day, he said only one Indian died, an old man killed by artillery fire.[22] Lieutenant Colonel Walker, who saw action only on 8 September, said, "I cannot say as we killed one. I saw a number fall but they were at once carried off."[23] The author's best guess after studying all of the data would be that twenty-five to fifty Indians were killed between 1 and 8 September.

Nelson Cole, in his second official report of 10 February 1867, added an impassioned paragraph that summed up his feelings about why so many things concerning this expedition went wrong:

> Fatigue and starvation had done its work on both men and animals, in so much they were unfit to pursue with vigor the savage foe that circled around their starving way through this desert whose oases were but inviting delusions, for however pleasing to the wearied eye were the green dresses of the prickly pear and the sage brush, they were bitter mockery to the other senses, for they contained no life giving essence for man or beast. Certain starving soldiers might well wonder why there was no provisions made for such contingencies; why old Indian fighters had not, with their knowledge, planned a more consistent campaign; created depots here and hunted Indians there; not had a command starving here, unfit to cope with the Indians everywhere around them, and the supplies they needed so much away no one knew where, at least where neither Indians come nor they could compass.[24]

In his reference to "old Indian fighters," Cole took a direct shot at Connor and the other planners of the campaign. And they deserve to be criticized for their shoddy planning in putting this hastily organized expedition in the field without clear goals or contingencies. It did not take a mathematics professor to determine that their 140 wagons lacked the capacity to carry anywhere near the amount of grain their animals needed for even thirty days, let alone sixty.

One must also question Omaha as the starting point. Fort Pierre, in

---

[22]Hyde, *Life of George Bent,* 240.
[23]Walker's official report of 25 September 1865, Hafen and Hafen, *Powder River Campaigns,* 100.
[24]Cole's 10 February 1867 report, ibid.

the original plans before sending Sully north, was a mere 152 miles from Bear Butte, which would have shortened the distance traveled to the campaign area considerably. Cole's route from Omaha to Bear Butte was over 500 miles. Consider that it took the expedition thirty-one days to get to the Niobrara River, and they were still 140 miles from Bear Butte. Fort Pierre—upriver from Omaha on the Missouri River—could have been reached by the same steamers that had delivered the men and supplies to Omaha. The availability of mules and wagons in Omaha may have been the reason for choosing it as the jumping-off point, but that extra month's travel truly doomed this expedition from any chance of a successful mission. If they had left Fort Pierre—near today's Pierre, South Dakota—on 1 August they would have been at Bear Butte by 10 August (at fifteen miles per day) with fresh animals.

Was Cole incompetent? The author doesn't think so. The expedition's plan, concocted by generals hundreds of miles away and on short notice, was founded on vague intelligence and traveled into virtually unexplored territory. As late as 23 February 1865 General Dodge asked, "Where is Powder River, and how far from Julesburg?" in a letter to one of his subordinates.[25] Cole managed the campaign reasonably well under extremely trying circumstances. One certainly can question his decision-making process on 1 to 3 September, when he changed the direction of the command three times, as previously discussed. One can also question his judgment, as Lyman Bennett did, on the choice of the campsite on the night of 8 September. It was a decision that cost the command several hundred horses that night, but how many of those horses would have survived to the expedition's completion in their then-present condition? That was the only instance of Bennett questioning or criticizing Cole over the entire three-month period, and one could perceive him as an astute and objective observer. That Cole kept the loss of life at such a low figure under the worst of circumstance said something for his management of the expedition.

❊   ❊   ❊

---

[25]Dodge message to Mitchell of 23 February 1865, *The War of Rebellion.*

Brig. Gen. Alfred Sully, included in original plans for the Powder River Indian Expedition, was perhaps the army's most experienced Indian fighter in 1865. He had fought in the Seminole War in Florida in the 1840s, and prior to the Civil War he served on frontier duty and had operated against the Cheyenne.[26] He also fought the Sioux in Dakota Territory in 1863 and 1864 in the aftermath of the Minnesota uprising of 1862.[27] After his successful summer campaign of 1864, which included a major victory over the northern Sioux at Killdeer Mountain, Sully wrote an off-the-record letter to Maj. Gen. John Pope about campaigning against the Indians on the northern plains.[28] Excerpts from his candid 18 August 1864 letter follow:

> All of the country in the vicinity of the Little Missouri is very much broken. I might say tumbled to pieces. It affords an excellent protection in every part of for twenty-five miles for a small body of Indians to torment, worry out, and exterminate an unprotected emigrant train. At the same time the Indians have every opportunity to escape from any force at their pleasure. There will certainly be no safety in traveling there till the Indians are exterminated. Peace might be made with them, yet there would always be plenty that head of the bands could not control, who would do mischief. The country is as bad, if not worse, than Florida, to hunt the Indians in, and one year's campaign won't finish the war. It is late in the season before troops can reach this country, then when you march through the country the Indians on top of the hills can see you for miles. I am sure I would not have overtaken them had they not felt sure they could whip me. By the time you overtake them your animals are reduced for want of forage, your rations are run out, and you have to fall back. The only way to finish up these Indians is to establish depots of provisions at points in their country, and keep after them till you run them down.
>
> Although I may not have been successful in carrying out all the expectations of the government in building posts and entirely finishing the war—that is bringing the Indians to their knees to beg for peace—yet we have done everything that was in the power of man to do with the obstacles before us—want of water, want of grass, and want of everything to eat.[29]

---

[26]Langdon Sully, *No Tears for the General*, 127.
[27]Clodfelter, *The Dakota War*, 118–66; James Wright, *No More Gallant a Deed*, 116–17, 242.
[28]Utley, *Frontiersmen in Blue*, 277–78.
[29]Sully's letter to Pope of 18 August 1864, *The War of Rebellion*.

Sully wrote this prophetic letter to Pope almost a year before Cole left Omaha on his ill-fated expedition. Sully accurately described the difficulties that would be encountered by the 1865 expedition, and he wrote to the man who would have a major role in planning and overseeing the 1865 campaign. The only part of Sully's advice that Pope or Dodge seem to have heeded or passed on was the need to establish a fort or supply depot in the heart of Indian country. Fort Connor was established on Powder River, too late to be of any use to the campaign, and at a location questionable as to its value. All summer Pope and Dodge corresponded back and forth about Connor's supply-requisitioning tactics, the costs of the expedition, and reduction of manpower, rather than showing concern about supporting or extending the campaign until a definitive resolution could be reached, as Sully suggested.[30] Pope even suggested relieving Connor for "acting with a high hand, & in violation of Law and Regulations."[31] Dodge responded, "I do not see how I can relieve him, as he is now far north of Laramie, and I know of no one I could put in command."[32] Connor, in his official report at the conclusion of the campaign, advocated that in addition to Fort Connor, permanent military posts be established at the confluence of the Bighorn River and the Little Bighorn River (Fort Custer was built there in 1877), and a post on the Little Missouri River. He recommended year-round campaigning until the Indians' good behavior could be expected. Connor stated his belief that "any peace with these hostile Indians which is not first preceded by severe chastisement, such as will make them fear the power of the government, will only result in a renewal of hostilities."[33]

Just eleven years later, a general whom the army considered perhaps its top Indian fighter found himself in a similar situation in the same country, and at about the same time of year. The circumstances of Gen. George Crook's "Horse Meat March" through western Dakota

---

[30]Pope's message to Dodge of 11 August 1865, Dodge letter to Price of 15 August 1865, Hafen and Hafen, *Powder River Campaigns*, 44–45.

[31]Pope to Dodge, 12 August 1865, Dodge Collection.

[32]Dodge to Pope, 11 August 1865, *South Dakota Department of History Report and Historical Collections*, Volume 31, 549.

[33]Connor's official report, submitted on 4 October 1865 to Major Barnes, Dodge Collection.

Territory in August and September 1876 were strikingly similar—the command was about the same size, men and animals alike starving, and the country virtually identical to Cole's route (about fifty miles east of Cole's trail on the Little Missouri).[34] This has to make one wonder if any lesson was learned from Cole's debacle. Crook was by far the most experienced Indian fighter in the army at that time, and was considered the master of preparation of an expedition and the pack train. Yet the condition of his command when it finally reached succor at the Black Hills mining towns was similar to Cole's command. Many adjectives are used to describe the controversial Crook, but seldom, if ever, is "incompetent" used.

❊   ❊   ❊

Now the bigger question—did the Powder River Indian Expedition have any positive impact on a solution to American-Indian differences in the West, or did it just inflame an already volatile situation?

To answer this question properly, one has to take into consideration all three columns of the expedition. Of course, Connor's western command was only mentioned minimally here, but one can judge the overall effectiveness in the big picture of things.

In the short term, the answer is that the expedition probably had the same effect as poking a hornet's nest with a stick. The Red Cloud War occupied the army along the Bozeman Trail route on the eastern slopes of the Bighorn Mountains for the next three years, against the same Indians whom Cole's expedition encountered.[35] George Bent recalled that the warriors had a newfound confidence after their battles with Cole's worn-out troops on Powder River.[36] Connor's attack on the Arapaho village on the Tongue River would qualify as punishing the Indians. Cole's battles would be better described as fights for survival.

However, in the long term the biggest positive aspect for the army was that the Indian tribes of Powder River for the first time saw invading armies come into their heretofore unchallenged wilderness stronghold. Prior to 1865, in a paradise into which the military had not yet set

---

[34]C. M. Robinson III, *General Crook and the Western Frontier*, 192–98.
[35]Brown, *Fort Phil Kearny: An American Saga*, 177–83.
[36]Hyde, *Life of George Bent*, 240–42.

foot, the Indians reigned supreme. Never again would the Indians feel as secure in their country. It would only be twelve years before the Powder River tribes had surrendered and converted their lifestyle to the reservation. With game plentiful in 1865, the nomadic Indians followed the vast buffalo herds of the area. With the buffalo almost gone by the late 1870s, the tribes were reduced to living off of government rations.

The army also had to learn a lesson on supplying and sustaining large bodies of troops in this vast semi-arid wilderness. It learned that large armies cannot literally live off of the land in this wild country, nor can they be realistically supplied for a long campaign. Plenty of evidence shows that the army was slow to apply the lessons of 1865.

Seasoned veterans such as Gen. Alfred Sully, Brig. Gen. Patrick E. Connor, and Lt. Col. William O. Collins knew what needed to be done to be successful in campaigning against the Indians in this country, and they advised their superiors.[37] In his official report of a clash with warriors on 4 to 6 February 1865 at Mud Springs in southwestern Nebraska, Collins wrote:[38] "I beg to repeat the suggestions which I have heretofore made, that the permanent cure for the hostiles of the northern Indians is to go into the heart of their buffalo country and build and hold forts till the trouble is over. A hasty expedition, however successful, is only a temporary lesson, whereas the presence of troops in force in the country where the Indians are compelled to live and subsist would soon oblige them to sue for peace and accept terms as the Government may think proper to impose."[39]

In 1866 the army on the plains changed drastically, transitioning from the huge volunteer army of the Civil War to a greatly reduced post–Civil War regular army. It would not be until eleven years later that campaigns the size and scope of the Powder River Indian Expedition of 1865 would be attempted again. The government sought alternative peaceful solutions to the Indian problem in the West, rather than relying solely on a military solution.[40]

---

[37]Fort Collins, Colorado, is named after Indian fighting veteran William O. Collins of the Eleventh Ohio Cavalry. His son, Lt. Caspar Collins, was killed during a fight with Sioux and Cheyenne warriors at the Platte Bridge on 26 July 1865. Casper, Wyoming, is named in his honor, though it is a misspelling of his name.

[38]Michno, *Encyclopedia of Indian Wars*, 165–66.

[39]Collins's official report of the action at Mud Springs, 15 February 1865, *The War of Rebellion*.

[40]Utley, *Frontiersmen in Blue*, 341–49.

Two additional forts, Fort Phil Kearney in north central Wyoming and Fort C. F. Smith in southeast Montana, were built along the Bozeman Trail in 1866. The forts were undermanned, undersupplied, and the wrong officers were in charge, with an official policy that seemed to look the other way while Indian hostilities continued. This led to the disastrous Fetterman Fight in December 1866, where an entire command of eighty-one soldiers and civilians were killed near Fort Phil Kearny by a combined warrior force of about one thousand Sioux, Cheyenne, and Arapaho.[41] After continued hostilities throughout 1867, the forts in the Powder River country were abandoned in 1868. Once again this vast area became an Indian paradise, this time under the terms of the Treaty of 1868.[42]

Railroad surveyors pushed into the Indians' country in the early 1870s, and Custer's Seventh Cavalry had several skirmishes with the northern Sioux along the Yellowstone River in 1873.[43]

The Powder River country was then relatively quiet until the Great Sioux War of 1876. Once again the military put large armies in the field against the Powder River tribes, this time under the guise of forcing their settlement on the Great Sioux Reservation in Dakota Territory. In reality, it was to force the sale by the Sioux of the Black Hills and its associated mineral riches.[44]

The results of the Great Sioux War are well known, with the centerpiece of the war being the demise of Lt. Col. George Armstrong Custer and more than two hundred of his men at the Little Bighorn in June.[45] Reacting to a national outrage over the Custer disaster, the government moved quickly to reinforce and expand the troops in the Powder River Country.

Finally, in November 1876 the first true victory of the campaign was claimed. Col. Ranald MacKenzie led a mixed force of eleven hundred cavalrymen and Indian auxiliaries against a Cheyenne village on the Red Fork of Powder River in the Big Horn Mountains.[46]

---

[41]Utley, *Frontier Regulars*, 97–111.
[42]Ibid., 139–41.
[43]Ibid., 248–50.
[44]Ibid., 250–55.
[45]Ibid., 265–69.
[46]Jerome A. Greene, *Morning Star Dawn*, 106–40; Utley, *Frontier Regulars*, 283–84.

In the fall and winter, Col. Nelson Miles established a post at the mouth of the Tongue River at its confluence with the Yellowstone River. Originally called the Tongue River Cantonment, it was later renamed Fort Keogh. Miles waged a successful winter campaign against the Sioux and Cheyenne. By the spring of 1877, the majority of those Indians had surrendered or fled to Canada, and the Great Sioux War ended.[47] Sully, Connor, and Collins had all recommended this strategy back in 1864 and 1865. When finally done—and done right, with an aggressive commander in charge—the Indian wars on the northern plains were virtually over.

The government did establish two more forts in the heart of this country: in 1877 they built Fort Custer at the confluence of the Little Bighorn River and the Bighorn River, and in 1878, Fort Meade near Bear Butte in South Dakota.[48] These would have been effective locations for subduing the Powder River tribes had this been done years earlier, but now their purpose remained essentially to maintain the order that had been established with the conclusion of the 1876 war.

Of course, this is an over-simplification of the events that took place on the northern plains. However, between a vacillation of government policy and a tug of war between the U.S. Army and the Bureau of Indian Affairs, no continuity of policy and action existed to finalize and stabilize the Indian question. Perhaps the war for Powder River country could have been shortened by years if the lessons from campaigning on the plains from Nelson Cole's expedition had been learned and the advice of its most seasoned Indian fighters had been heeded.

In late summer of 1865, Col. Nelson Cole had led his struggling expedition into the great Sioux stronghold. Just twelve years later, Gen. William T. Sherman, while visiting the site of Fort Custer, said, "The Sioux Indians can never regain this country."[49]

---

[47]Greene, *Yellowstone Command*, 92–182.
[48]Utley, *Frontier Regulars*, 289–90, 299.
[49]Ibid., 289–90.

FINDING THE RIVER,
THE CANNON, AND THE WHEEL

THE RIVER

The Powder is called a "treacherous" river by the oldtimers; it is one of those "here today and gone tomorrow" rivers, that change their course with each big freshet, or so it seems; several acres or more of one man's choice land will wash off and pile up on his neighbor's farther down, who probably is not wanting land in that particular place.

John Broaddus, 9 April 1940[1]

owder River presents a unique challenge when attempting to recreate the events of 8 through 10 September 1865. To say that its path has been unstable is an understatement of classic proportions. When I first heard about the variable nature of the river's course, I did not fully appreciate how much this instability would affect the interpretation of events. After studying reports of the action and working with current topographic maps, it seemed a simple matter to lay out the sequence of events and make them work with the geography.

❋   ❋   ❋

The Powder River Historical Museum in Broadus, Montana, has some artifacts that could be from Cole's expedition. Among these are cartridges and bullets found near the mouth of the Little Powder River by local rancher Ron Talcott. Museum director Lee Hubbard

---

[1]Maude L. Beach, *Faded Hoof Prints—Bygone Dreams,* 64. The spelling is correct on John Broaddus's last name, although the town's name is spelled with a single "d."

arranged for me to meet with him, and Talcott agreed to take me to the site.

We drove to a location about a mile above, or southwest, of where the Little Powder River flows into the Powder River. This is right where Cole described their crossing on 10 September. Cole, Bennett, and Springer all reported Indians attacking the front and rear of the column as it crossed the river "above the mouth of the Little Powder." The cartridges were found along a high bank on the east side of the river, which could have indicated a probable advance firing position to cover the crossing. The bullets were found about two hundred yards out to the east, where warriors harassing the front of the column may have been. Unfortunately, later investigation proved that these cartridges could not have come from Cole's command.[2] This crossing had been used for years by local ranchers, as a solid crossing on this unstable river bottom was important.

The current geography of the crossing fits together with the eyewitness accounts, except that the river channel was dry. According to Talcott, in the spring of 1978 the river cut a new channel about a mile to the west and bypassed the loop where the old crossing had been, causing the Little Powder to now be "a mile longer than it used to be." This didn't change the assumption that Cole's 1865 crossing of 10 September took place here, but it certainly raised new questions about the river's path in 1865.

The maps that I have used for this project are current Bureau of Land Management (BLM) topographical maps, Delorme Topographic Atlas and Gazetteer, and Delorme Topo USA topographic mapping software. All three sources show the dry loop as the current active channel and do not show the current channel bypassing this loop.

I then checked out aerial photography of the area and found that a 1996 United States Geological Survey (USGS) aerial view of the crossing area did clearly show a current channel bypassing the dry loop

[2]Frank C. Barnes, *Cartridges of the World*, 294. Careful inspection and measuring of these cartridges reveals the following: (1) All of the cartridges are centerfire. The only metal cartridges available to the army in 1865 were rimfire. (2) Several of the cartridges were clearly stamped with "Colt 45" on the bottom. The Colt 45 was not introduced until 1873. The other cartridges were unstamped, but appeared to be forty-four- or forty-five-caliber handgun ammunition. These shell cases could not have come from Nelson Cole's command in 1865.

[3]TerraServer.com, Inc., provided the USGS aerial photo of the crossing area.

where the crossing once was.[3] The aerial view also showed other dry channels in the area. As I scanned downriver, where the action took place on 8 September, it was apparent that there had been other significant changes in the river's course over the years.

Why is this important to a fight that took place in 1865? To interpret the movements of the commands (Cole's and Walker's, as they were both engaged that day), we have to know what the landscape looked like that day. Marching from the north, they crossed Powder River from the west to east side and engaged the Indians on the land on the east side in the vicinity of where Little Pilgrim Creek and Big Pilgrim Creek enter the Powder from the east. The command then drove the warriors from the bluffs bordering the Pilgrim Creek drainage in a southeasterly direction. At the end of the fight, they crossed the river again and went into camp on the treeless west side of Powder River, the infamous "Dead Horse Camp."

My next step was to go to the BLM office in Billings, Montana, to take a look at earlier area maps to see how the path of Powder River has varied over the course of time. Their earliest maps on record, surveyed in 1907–1908, show a much-changed path from today's river. The crossing area did appear to be the same, which is good, because that helps legitimize it as the actual crossing. Over this ninety-seven-year period, many changes to the river's flow have occurred. The current maps show a big S-shaped loop in the river near the bluffs above the mouth of Pilgrim Creek. The 1907 map has a straight section of river, bypassing this loop area. The aerial photo shows both the old channel and the newer loop. The river bypassed this loop in 1978, like the crossing loop, according to rancher Francis Edwards, and the water now flows again through the 1907 channel. This changing course adds to the confusion of the interpretation of where the command made its second crossing and where Dead Horse Camp was located.

We don't know what the river's course was in 1865, forty-two years earlier than the BLM maps, so there will be some doubt unless physical evidence can be obtained. Lyman Bennett was the expedition's engineering officer and a mapmaker by trade. He talked of working on his maps all through the journey and at Fort Laramie with Capt. S. M. Robbins, chief engineer of Connor's command. Robbins submitted his report at the conclusion of the campaign, and it probably included Bennett's maps.[4] To date I have not located Robbins's report.

In the Broadus, Montana, area it is accepted as common knowledge that the river frequently changes course. I heard the story several times of a rancher downstream a few miles from Broadus going to bed at night with the river on the east side of the house, and waking up next morning with it on the west side of the house.

Henry Stuver, a long-time rancher in the area, wrote an unpublished paper in 1953 titled "The History of Cavalry Relics Found on our Ranch." Stuver's paper was a short history of the Powder River Expedition, primarily taken from Cole's and Walker's reports combined with his knowledge of the local terrain covered during the 8 through 10 September events. He described the 9 September camp, where equipment was destroyed as follows:

> Equipment could not be moved. It was found necessary to burn it, to keep it out of Indian hands. Much of it was destroyed at this camp on what is known as John Dot's [Daut] desert claim, and some of it was destroyed on what is our ranch on Powder River.
>
> When the late J. L. Wilson settled in what is now Powder River County, in the early 1880s, and homesteaded the W Bar, in 1891, his men gathered wagon loads of metal on what is now our lands. The scrap iron supplied the W Bar blacksmith shop with repair iron for a good many years.
>
> Successive floods of Powder River obliterated the camp by depositing silt and sand. However, we have found many pieces of the equipment. Much of it became lost or misplaced during the last thirty five years, as it was not properly appreciated. What relics are left are valued highly.[5]

John Daut's desert claim was in the area on the west side of the river, opposite and above the mouth of the Little Powder, so its location fits with Bennett's description of the 9 September camp. Henry Stuver's ranch was located six and one-half to seven miles south of the probable 9 September campsite on the east side of Powder River (two and one-half miles south of Highway 212). The J. L. Wilson W Bar Ranch is located on the west side of Powder River, opposite Henry Stuver's ranch.

This raised a new question: how did the abandoned equipment get

---

[4]Connor's official report, 4 October 1865, Dodge Collection.
[5]Stuver, "The History of the Cavalry Relics Found on our Ranch."

so far up river from the 9 September campsite? The answer is simple: Bennett reported that the command moved south six and three-fourths miles on 10 September, which would locate their camp for that day on Henry Stuver's broad, flat pasture land on the east side of the river. Although none of the diaries or reports mention it, it is probable that because of the poor condition of their animals, the command had to abandon additional equipment and/or wagons at that campsite, and this is what Henry Stuver found on his land.

The Stuver ranch is now part of the Russell ranch. Henry Stuver passed away some years ago. His nephew, Joe Stuver is the current publisher/owner of the local weekly newspaper, but unfortunately he is not sure what became of Uncle Henry's relics, as his belongings were distributed among his relatives.

THE CANNON

Local lore in the Broadus, Montana, area says that the Powder River Expedition abandoned a cannon at a river crossing during or after its fight with the Indians on 10 September 1865. Virtually everyone I talked with knew of the cannon story and believes that it happened. Henry Stuver, in his 1953 paper said, "For years an abandoned cannon was seen bogged down in the sands of the river near that point. The changing course of the river has buried this cannon forever."[6] It was reportedly last seen in 1905.

On 14 September 2004 I went to the 10 September 1865 river crossing with Ron Talcott, local rancher; Bob McCurdy, retired businessman and local historian; and Charlie Emmons, local rancher. All three agreed that this was the location where the cannon was seen. They described a blacksmith shop in view of the crossing, where you could look out toward the river and see the cannon. Bob McCurdy was told that when the cannon finally disappeared into the sand and mud, the last part seen was the ball on the rear end of the barrel. When I displayed some skepticism of the cannon story, Charlie Emmons was very adamant that he had talked to people in his lifetime who had seen the cannon.

---

[6] Ibid.

Cole's command had two cannons—three-inch rifled ordinance guns—with them. Walker's Sixteenth Kansas Cavalry was marching with Cole's command on 10 September and had two 1841 mountain howitzers. Cole reported using his cannons to clear the warriors out of the way as the command moved to the crossing above the mouth of the Little Powder. No mention is made in any of the reports or diaries of abandoning a cannon. However, Lyman Bennett described a turbulent crossing: "After completing the destruction of our train except a few wagons we wished to carry along with us, we commenced the march and coming to the river, found it swollen so that it could not easily be crossed. Indians also menaced the head of the column and their heads could be seen in the hundreds projecting above the tops of the hills. We finally found another ford a mile above and crossed the command losing only one wagon though many men and horses were thrown in the water."[7]

Bennett reported the loss of a wagon but made no mention of losing a cannon. Cole reported firing the cannons at the crossing but not abandoning one. Lieutenant Colonel Walker made no mention in his report of the crossing, or using his artillery or losing a cannon at the crossing. He was traveling with Cole that day, as he described the village site, and told of observing Cole having the council lodge burned. My best guess is that if there were a cannon abandoned here, it was one of Walker's mountain howitzers. Perhaps they had to abandon a howitzer in the turbulent waters and soft bottom of the crossing. Walker's report generally lacked the detail of the other writers, and Bennett generally wrote little of the Sixteenth Kansas's activity, so it wouldn't be unusual for him not to record the loss of a cannon by that regiment.

Mizpah, Montana, rancher Dan H. Bowman recalled the following in a letter to noted historical researcher Walter M. Camp in 1921:

> I saw the remains of these horses & mules & many wagons destroyed by burning the woodwork & much supplies incl. saddles, harness & etc. *They also threw into the main river near this point two of their field guns.* I saw the remains of this outfit in 1887 & the remains were quite plain as to bones, irons, etc. This point is opposite & a little above the mouth of Little Powder River on the west side & is on Sec-19-T-4, South Range 52 E in Pow-

---

[7]Bennett diary, 10 September 1865 entry.

der River County & from here down to where they turned back, wagons & equipment were abandoned & destroyed at intervals.[8]

Bowman's statement makes a strong case that in fact a cannon (or cannons) was abandoned in the river. He is specific as to the location, and he accurately recorded the section that would contain both the 9 September campsite and the 10 September crossing.

Too many strongly believe this story not to give it credence. Maude L. Beach, an area resident in the 1930s and 1940s undertook a Works Progress Administration project in the late 1930s to record the history of the livestock industry in Powder River County. Several references to the lost cannon are in the book in a short history of the Cole expedition: "The command crossed the river above the mouth of the Little Powder, and moved up the east bank; (it is here that the long buried cannon is supposed to rest)."[9] When Beach interviewed Robert Rice in 1940, he talked about a location "just above the mouth of the Pilgrim Creek. (It was here that Colonel Cole buried the cannon and other government wagons and equipment in 1865 during the ill-fated Powder River Expedition. Oldtimers have excavated wagons and other things at this spot.)"[10] This would be a description of the Dead Horse Camp area of 8 September and the equipment-burning camp of 9 September. The cannon would be within a mile or so of the 9 September campsite at the crossing.

In 1942 Beach interviewed Merton M. Edwards, who had arrived in Powder River County in 1881. He recalled a photographer from Miles City who was around for the roundups:

> His name was Hoffman [L. A. Huffman] I think, and he was around with the roundups for years. I remember that he made a picture of that old pile of iron, cannon and such like at the mouth of Pilgrim Creek, or near there, on Big Powder. The government expedition was supposed to have left it there in 1865.
>
> He made a list of that stuff too. There was a great pile of it there at that time. I remember that after I got back from Nebraska with my wife in 1895, that I went to that old pile of iron and got some old wagon tires to make shoes for a sleigh, or pair of sleighs, to haul hay for sheep and cattle when snow was deep in winter. Hoffman made a list of that iron and stuff too.

---

[8]Emphasis by author. Bowman to Camp, 2 January 1920, Camp Collection.
[9]Beach, *Faded Hoof Prints*, 27.
[10]Ibid., 228.

I don't expect the picture and list would help much now in locating the cannon they are so anxious to find, because the background of the picture would now be different, it's likely, by the old river changing its course at different times. It might be flowing right over it by this time.[11]

L. A. Huffman has gained fame for his early pictures of Montana frontier life and Indian portraits. After searching through the two major collections of Huffman photos at the McCracken Research Library of the Buffalo Bill Historic Center and at the Montana Historical Society, I was unable to find Huffman's pictures of the scrap piles or the cannon. Perhaps they were destroyed in a fire that occurred in Huffman's Miles City studio.

In another cannon-related development, the Carter County Museum in Ekalaka, Montana, has on display two cannonballs that were found on the Little Powder River in the 1890s. These cannonballs could have come from the Powder River Expedition of 1865; this was the only army movement in this country with artillery. Because of the location near the Little Powder, these balls were probably fired during the 10 September crossing. One is a 4.62-inch-diameter shell with a threaded hole in it for the Bormann time fuse. This is the type of ball that would be fired from the mountain howitzer.[12] The other ball is a solid ball or solid shot, slightly less than three inches in diameter. The three-inch ordinance rifle would fire this ball, but I find it puzzling that they would fire solid shot in Indian warfare.[13] Solid shot would be used to batter a fortification such as a building. It would make more sense to use an exploding shell, like the mountain howitzer shell, in a combat situation. I questioned museum director Warren O. White, himself a retired army veteran and firearms expert, about this. He shrugged his shoulders and said, "Well, you know the army."

THE WHEEL

In 1983, during a near-record low water in Powder River, Bob McCurdy noticed an object protruding from the exposed river bottom, just downstream from the bridge over Powder River on Highway

[11]Beach, *Faded Hoof Prints*, 110–11.
[12]Thomas, *Cannons*, 29–32.
[13]Ibid., 39.

212. It turned out to be an old wooden wagon wheel. Bob and Cap Williams retrieved the wheel from the muddy river bottom, and it is now on display at the Powder River Historical Museum in Broadus. The wheel was originally thought to be from the missing cannon of the 1865 Powder River Expedition.

It probably isn't from the cannon lost at the crossing, simply because it was found about three and one-half miles upstream from the crossing. If it was downstream, then one could rationalize that it had floated or worked its way down stream with the current, but upstream makes no sense.

The wheel could be from the expedition, as it is definitely an old one. Its construction indicates a much earlier period. Thirteen of its fourteen wooden spokes are intact.

There are several possible sources:

1. We know that there were four cannons between Cole's and Walker's two commands.

2. Cole's regiment, the Second Missouri Light Artillery, had two three-inch ordinance rifled guns. All of the pictures of this cannon that I looked at had fourteen-spoke wheels.[14]

3. Walker's Sixteenth Kansas Cavalry had two 1841 mountain howitzers. All pictures of the mountain howitzer show a twelve-spoke wheel.[15]

4. The wheel found in Powder River has fourteen spokes, which would indicate that the wheel came from one of Cole's three-inch ordinance rifles, that is, if the wheel came from a cannon.

5. To blur the issue a bit, the standard six-mule-team army freight wagon of the Civil War era had twelve-spoke wheels in the front and fourteen-spoke wheels in the rear.[16] That means that we are right back where we started. It could be a wheel from a cannon carriage or a freight wagon.

Bennett describes losing a wagon at the 10 September crossing, but the same reasoning would apply here as with the cannon. How would the wheel get three and one-half miles upstream against the current? They may have abandoned another wagon on the trail and not reported it—another little mystery that may never be answered.

---

[14]Ibid.

[15]Ibid., 32.

[16]Steffen, *The Horse Soldier, 1776–1943,* 2: 91.

COLE EXPEDITION CASUALTIES, 1865

DATE	LOCATION	BATTLE WOUNDED
1 Sept.	Powder River at Alkali Creek	Pvt. W. Walker, Battery K, Second Missouri
1 Sept.	Powder River at Alkali Creek	Sgt. J. L. Duckett, Battery K, Second Missouri
5 Sept.	Powder River at Ash Creek	Lt. H. L. Kelly, Battery B, Second Missouri
5 Sept.	Powder River at Ash Creek	Two men wounded, Twelfth Missouri
5 Sept.	Powder River at Ash Creek	Pvt. C. Elliot, Twelfth Missouri
8 Sept.	Powder River at Pilgrim Creek	Four men from the Sixteenth Kansas
10 Sept.	Powder River at Little Missouri	One man from the Twelfth Missouri

DATE	LOCATION	BATTLE DEATHS
1 Sept.	Powder River at Alkali Creek	Two unnamed men from hunting party
1 Sept.	Powder River at Alkali Creek	Pvt. Abner Garrison, Battery K, Second Missouri
1 Sept.	Powder River at Alkali Creek	Pvt. Jesse Easter, Battery K, Second Missouri
1 Sept.	Powder River at Alkali Creek	Sgt. L. L. Holt, Battery K, Second Missouri
2 Sept.	Powder River	Two men on hunting trip, Battery L, Second Missouri
5 Sept.	Powder River at Ash Creek	Pvt. George McGully, Company B, Twelfth Missouri

5 Sept.	Powder River at Ash Creek	Pvt. James D. Morris, Company B, Twelfth Missouri
7 Sept.	Powder River	Pvt. Elijah Bradshaw, Company A, Twelfth Missouri
8 Sept.	Powder River at Pilgrim Creek	One man from the Sixteenth Kansas

DATE	LOCATION	OTHER DEATHS
10 Aug.	South Cheyenne River	Walker reported several men died from bad water
17 Aug.	Second Redwater campsite	Lt. Bennett's Negro servant, cause unknown
20 Aug.	Near Colony, Wyoming	Pvt. J. Clark, Battery B, Second Missouri, scurvy
21 Aug.	Near Colony, Wyoming	Pawnee guide Lo Willacore, apoplexy
25 Aug.	Little Missouri at Camp Crook	Pvt. C. Senft, Battery B, Second Missouri, scurvy
4 Sept.	Powder River at Ash Creek	Pvt. H. Grote, Second Missouri, scurvy
17 Sept.	Powder River	Pvt. F. Hacke, Battery B, Second Missouri, accidentally shot

BIBLIOGRAPHY

MANUSCRIPT COLLECTIONS

Almstedt, Henry. Papers. File #A007. Guide to Civil War Manuscripts in the Missouri Historical Society Archives. Missouri Historical Society, St. Louis.

Bennett, Lyman G. Diary. Collection R274. Western History Manuscript Collection. University of Missouri–Rolla.

———. File. Wyoming State Archives.

Bowman, Daniel H. Map Collection. Montana Historical Society, Helena, Montana.

———. Photo Collection. Montana Historical Society, Helena, Montana.

———. Research Collection. Montana Historical Society, Helena, Montana.

Bradbury, John F. "Biographical Sketch of L. G. Bennett." Unpublished ms. R274 Lyman Bennett Collection. Western Historical Manuscript Collection. University of Missouri–Rolla.

Camp, Walter Mason. Papers, 1905–1925. MSS 57. Nineteenth-Century Western Americana and Mormon Americana, Walter M. Camp Research Collection. L. Tom Perry Special Collections Library. Harold B. Lee Library, Brigham Young University, Provo, Utah.

Civil War Scrapbook, Volume 2. Missouri Historical Society, St. Louis.

Cole Obituary. Necrology Scrapbook. Volume 2c. Missouri Historical Society, St. Louis.

Curtis, Charles. Letter of 6 July 1894. Reference Library, Fort Laramie National Historic Site.

Dodge, Grenville M. Manuscript Collection. Iowa State Historical Society, Des Moines, Iowa.

"In Memoriam. Nelson D. Cole, Brigadier." Pamphlet. Missouri Historical Society, St. Louis.

Missouri Artillery, Second Regiment, Company B, Order Book, 1862–1869. File #C1167, Western History Manuscript Collection. University of Missouri, Columbia.

Necrology Scrapbook 11c. Missouri Historical Society, St. Louis.

North, Frank Joshua. Manuscript. RG 2321. Nebraska State Historical Society, Lincoln, Nebraska.

Northcott, Dennis. "Guide to Civil War Manuscripts in the Missouri Historical Society Archives." Missouri Historical Society, St. Louis.

Palmer, H. E. Letter of 20 July 1894. Reference Library, Fort Laramie National Historic Site.

Peck, W. H., ed. Collection of reports from Powder River Expedition furnished by Senator J. Fred Toman, February 1943. Carter County Museum, Ekalaka, Montana.

Raynolds, Capt. W. F. Map. Wyoming State Archives, Cheyenne.

"Recollections of experiences on the western plains." Microfilm reel 129. Kansas State Historical Society, Topeka.

Report of Captain W. F. Raynolds' Expedition to Explore the Headwaters of the Missouri & Yellowstone Rivers. U.S. Cong. 40th Congress, 2nd Session, Senate Executive Document 77.

Shaver, William Thompson. Papers. File #B534. Guide to Civil War Manuscripts in the Missouri Historical Society Archives. Missouri Historical Society, St. Louis.

Sorenson, Alfred. Manuscript. "A Quarter of a Century on the Frontier or The adventures of Major Frank North the White Chief of the Pawnees." Nebraska State Historical Society, Lincoln, Nebraska.

Steck, Ansel. Letter of 1 August 1894. Reference Library, Fort Laramie National Historic Site.

Stuver, J. H. Letter of 6 February 1953. Reference Library, Fort Laramie National Historic Site.

———. "The History of Cavalry Relics Found on our Ranch," 1953. Reference Library, Fort Laramie National Historic Site.

Thomas, C. L. Letter of 2 July 1894. Reference Library, Fort Laramie National Historic Site.

Tillotson, Ron. Copy of C. L. Thomas's Medal of Honor Certificate, dated 19 October 1916 and other Thomas related material.

Warren, Gouverneur Kemble. 1857 map. Lyman G. Bennett file. Wyoming State Archives, Cheyenne.

———. Papers, 1848–82. New York State Library, Albany.

SECONDARY SOURCES

Ambrose, Stephen E. *Nothing Like It in the World.* New York: Simon & Schuster, 2000.

Barnes, Frank C. *Cartridges of the World.* Iola, Wisc.: Krause Publications, 1989.

Barthelmess, Bob. *As We Recall.* Miles City, Mont.: Range Rider Museum, 1989.

Beach, Maude L. *Faded Hoof Prints—Bygone Dreams.* Edited by Robert L. Thaden, Jr. Broadus, Mont.: Powder River Historical Society, 1989.

Becher, Ronald. *Massacre along the Medicine Road.* Caldwell, Idaho: Caxton Press, 1999.

Benson, Joe. *The Travelers Guide to the Pony Express Trail.* Helena, Mont.: Falcon Press Publishing, 1995.

Bennett, Lyman G., and Wm. M. Haigh. *History of the Thirty-Sixth Regiment Illinois Volunteers during the War of Rebellion.* Aurora, Ill.: Knickerbocker and Hodder, Printers and Binders, 1876.

Beyer, Walter F., and Oscar F. Keydel. *Deeds of Valor,* Vols. 1 and 2. Detroit: Perrien-Keydel Company, 1907.

Brown, Dee. *Fort Phil Kearny: An American Saga.* Lincoln: University of Nebraska Press, 1962.

Campbell, Walter S. (Stanley Vestal). *Sitting Bull.* Norman: University of Oklahoma Press, 1957. First published by Houghton Mifflin Co., 1932. Page references are to the 1957 edition.

————. *Jim Bridger, Mountain Man.* Lincoln: University of Nebraska Press, 1970. First published by William Morrow & Company, 1946. Page references are to the 1970 edition.

Clodfelter, Micheal. *The Dakota War: The United States Army versus the Sioux, 1862–1865.* Jefferson, N.C.: McFarland & Company, Inc., Publishers, 1998.

Cooke, Philip St. Geo. *Cavalry Tactics or, Regulations for the Instruction, Formations, and Movements of the Cavalry of the Army and Volunteers of the United States.* Reprint, Union City, Tenn.: Pioneer Press, 1997. First published by J. B. Lippencott, 1861. Page references are to the 1997 edition.

Coutant, Dr. C. G. *History of Wyoming and the Far West,* Vol. 2. New York: Argonaut Press, Ltd., 1966.

Essin, Emmitt M. *Shavetails and Bell Sharps: The History of the U.S. Army Mule.* Lincoln: University of Nebraska Press, 1997.

Franzwa, Gregory M. *Maps of the Oregon Trail.* St. Louis: The Patrice Press, 1990.

Gardner, Mark L. *Wagons for the Santa Fe Trail: Wheeled Vehicles and Their Makers, 1822–1880.* Albuquerque: University of New Mexico Press, 2000.

Genoa, Nebraska, Historical Stars. Genoa, Nebr.: Genoa U.S. Indian School Foundation, Inc. 1996.

Grace, Deborah. "The Horse in the Civil War," *Rolling Thunder: Newsletter for the 10th North Carolina State Troops* 3, no. 4 (July 2000).

Greene, Jerome A. *Morning Star Dawn.* Norman: University of Oklahoma Press, 2003.

————. *Yellowstone Command.* Lincoln: University of Nebraska Press, 1991.

Grinnell, George Bird. *The Fighting Cheyennes.* Norman: University of Oklahoma Press, 1955. First published by Charles Scriber's Sons, 1915. Page references are to the 1955 edition.

———. *Two Great Scouts and Their Pawnee Battalion.* Lincoln: University of Nebraska Press, 1973. First published by Arthur H. Clark Company, 1928. Page references are to the 1973 edition.

Hafen, LeRoy R., and Ann W. Hafen. *Powder River Campaigns and Sawyers Expedition.* Glendale, Calif.: Arthur H. Clark Company, 1961.

Hafen, LeRoy R., and Francis Marion Young. *Fort Laramie and the Pageant of the West, 1834–1890.* Lincoln: University of Nebraska Press, 1984. First published by Fort Laramie Historical Association, 1938. Page references are to the 1984 edition.

Halaas, David Fridtjof, and Andrew E. Masich. *Halfbreed: The True Story of George Bent.* Cambridge, Mass.: De Capo Press, 2004.

Haslip, Joan. *The Crown of Mexico: Maximilian and his Empress Carlotta.* New York: Holt, Rinehart and Winston, 1971.

Hedren, Paul L. *Traveler's Guide to the Great Sioux War.* Helena: Montana Historical Society Press, 1996.

Hicks, Rev. E. W. *History of Kendall County.* Aurora, Ill.: Knickerbocker and Hodder, 1877.

Hull, Myra E. "Soldiering on the High Plains: The Diary of Lewis Byram Hull, 1864–1866." *Kansas Historical Quarterly* 7, no. 1 (February 1938).

Hyde, George E. *Red Cloud's Folk.* Norman: University of Oklahoma Press, 1937.

———. *Life of George Bent.* Norman: University of Oklahoma Press, 1968.

Hyde, William, and Howard L. Conrad, eds. *Encyclopedia of the History of Saint Louis.* New York: Southern Publishing Company, 1899.

Leonard, John W. *The Industries of St. Louis.* St. Louis: Elstner Publishing, 1887.

Jacobsen, Jacques Noel, Jr. *Regulations and Notes for the Uniform of the Army of the United States 1861.* Union City, Tenn.: Pioneer Press, 1990.

Johnson, Harrison. *Johnson's History of Nebraska.* Omaha: Herald Printing House, 1880.

Kautz, August V. *The 1865 Customs of Service for Non-commissioned Officers and Soldiers.* Mechanicsburg, Penn.: Stackpole Books, 2001. First published by J. B. Lippincott, 1864. Page references are to the 2001 edition.

Klock, Irma H. *All Roads Lead to Deadwood.* Aberdeen, S.D.: North Plains Press, 1979.

LeGrande, Louis. *The Military Hand-Book and Soldiers Manual of Information.* New York: Beadle and Company, 1861.

Madsen, Brigham D. *Glory Hunter.* Salt Lake City: University of Utah Press, 1990.

McDermott, John D. *Circle of Fire.* Mechanicsburg, Penn.: Stackpole Books, 2003.

Michno, Gregory F. *Encyclopedia of Indian Wars.* Helena, Mont.: Mountain Press Publishing, 2003.

Murray, Robert A. *Military Posts in the Powder River Country of Wyoming, 1865–1894.* Buffalo, Wyo.: The Office, 1990.

———. *The Army Moves West: Supplying the Western Indian Wars Campaigns.* Fort Collins, Colo.: The Old Army Press, 1981.

Oehlerking, Jerry. "The Dick Williams Story: If Bear Butte Could Speak." *South Dakota Conservation Digest* (March/April 1977).

Pictorial and Genealogical Record of Greene County, Missouri. Chicago: Goodspeed Brothers Publishers, 1893.

Powell, Peter John. *People of the Sacred Mountain*, Vol. 2. San Francisco: Harper & Row, Publishers, 1981.

Reedstrom, Ernest L. *Bugles, Banners and War Bonnets.* Caldwell, Idaho: The Caxton Printers, 1977.

Robinson, C. M. III. *General Crook and the Western Frontier.* Norman: University of Oklahoma Press, 2001.

Rogers, Fred B. *Soldiers of the Overland.* San Francisco: The Grabhorn Press, 1938.

Sandoz, Marie. *Crazy Horse: The Strange Man of the Oglalas.* Norman: University of Nebraska Press, 1961. First published by Hastings House, Inc, 1942. Page references are to 1961 edition.

Smith, Joseph E. *Small Arms of the World.* Mechanicsburg, Penn.: The Stackpole Company, 1969.

Sorenson, Alfred. *History of Omaha: From the Pioneer Days to the Present Time.* Omaha: Miller and Richardson, 1889.

South Dakota Department of History Report and Historical Collections, Volume 31. Pierre: South Dakota Historical Society, State Publishing Company, 1962.

Springer, Charles H. *Soldiering in Sioux Country, 1865.* Edited by Benjamin Franklin Cooling III. San Diego: Frontier Heritage Press, 1971.

Steffen, Randy. *The Horse Soldier, 1776–1943,* Vol. 2. Norman: University of Oklahoma Press, 1978.

Stevens, Walter B. *St. Louis: The Fourth City.* St. Louis: S. J. Clark Company, 1889.

Stout, Tom. *Montana: Its Story and Biography*, Vol. 3. Chicago and New York: The American Historical Society, 1921.

Strom, Malcolm, ed. *Centennial Book—Dwight Kansas.* Shawnee Mission, Kans.: KES Print, 1987.

Sully, Langdon. *No Tears for the General.* Palo Alto: American West Publishing Company, 1974.

Thomas, Dean S. *Cannons: An Introduction to Civil War Artillery.* Gettysburg, Penn.: Thomas Publications, 1985.

Utley, Robert M. *Frontiersmen in Blue.* Lincoln: University of Nebraska Press, 1982. First published by Macmillan, 1967. Page references are to the 1982 edition.

————. *The Lance and the Shield.* New York: Henry Holt and Co. Inc., 1993.

————. *Frontier Regulars; The United States Army and the Indian, 1866–1890.* New York: Macmillan Publishing Co., Inc., 1973.

Varley, James F. *Brigham and the Brigadier.* Tucson: Westernlore Press, 1989.

Vaughn, J. W. *The Reynolds Campaign on Powder River.* Norman: The University of Oklahoma Press, 1961.

Wheat, Carl I. *1540–1861: Mapping the Transmississippi West,* Volume 5. San Francisco: The Institute of Historical Cartography, 1963.

Wright, James. *No More Gallant a Deed.* St. Paul: Minnesota Historical Society, 2001.

Newspapers and Periodicals

Black Hills Daily Times, 14 October 1879.
The Daily Rocky Mountain News, 1865 issues.
Miles City (Montana) *Daily Star.*
The Montana Post.
Nebraska Republican.
U.S. Army Recruiting News, 26 November 1929.
Council Grove Republican.
Casper Tribune-Herald, 24 and 31 August 1930.

Internet Sources

Civil War Soldiers and Sailors System. National Park Service. http://www.civilwar.nps.gov/cwss.

Electronic Research Sources

American Civil War Research Database. CD-ROM. Historic Data Systems, Inc., 2002.

The War of Rebellion: A Compilation of the Official Records of the Union and Confederate Armies. CD-ROM. Guild Press of Indiana, 1997.

Topo USA. CD-ROM, Version 5.0. DeLorme, 2004.

INDEX

References to illustrations are italicized.